Discount Voting

Voter Registration Reforms and Their Effects

In the United States, there is wide variation from state to state in the institutional arrangements – for example, registration laws – that structure the environment in which citizens decide whether to vote and parties decide whom to mobilize. This has important consequences for who gets elected and the policies they enact. Michael J. Hanmer argues that to understand how these institutional arrangements affect outcomes, it is necessary to consider the interactions between social and political contexts and these laws. He tests this theory by examining how the factors that influence the adoption of a set of registration laws affect turnout, the composition of the electorate, and party strategies. His multi-method research design demonstrates that the effect of registration laws is not as profound as either reformers would hope or previous studies suggest, especially when reform is a response to federal legislation. He concludes by arguing for a shift in the approach to increasing turnout.

Michael J. Hanmer is an Associate Professor in the Department of Government and Politics and Research Fellow with the Center for American Politics and Citizenship at the University of Maryland at College Park. Hanmer is a co-author of *Voting Technology: The Not-So-Simple Act of Casting a Ballot* (2008). He has published articles on electoral reform, voting technology, and the overreporting of voting.

Discount Voting

Voter Registration Reforms and Their Effects

MICHAEL J. HANMER

University of Maryland, College Park

CAMBRIDGE UNIVERSITY PRESS
Cambridge, New York, Melbourne, Madrid, Cape Town,
Singapore, São Paulo, Delhi, Mexico City

Cambridge University Press
The Edinburgh Building, Cambridge CB2 8RU, UK

Published in the United States of America by Cambridge University Press, New York

www.cambridge.org
Information on this title: www.cambridgte.org/9781107406124

© Cambridge University Press 2009

First published 2009
First paperback edition 2012

A catalogue record for this publication is available from the British Library

Library of Congress Cataloging in Publication data
Hanmer, Michael J., 1972–
Discount voting : voter registration reforms and their effects /
Michael J. Hanmer.
    p. cm.
Includes bibliographical references and index.
ISBN 978-0-521-11265-9 (hardback)
1. Voter registration – United States. 2. Voting – United States. I. Title.
JK2160.H36 2009
324.640973 – dc22   2009011762

ISBN 978-0-521-11265-9 Hardback
ISBN 978-1-107-40612-4 Paperback

To the memory of my father, Frank Hanmer.

Contents

Acknowledgments   *page* ix

    Introduction   1

1. Motivation and a New Theoretical Framework   20
2. The Purposeful Adoption of Election Day Registration   55
3. Election Day Registration by Choice and by Federal
   Mandate   79
4. Motor Voter by Choice and by Federal Mandate   106
5. Registration and Voting in the Post-NVRA Era   126
6. Election Reform and the Composition of the Electorate   145
7. EDR on the Ground and Prospects for the Future   162

APPENDICES

A. Variable Coding   199
B. Census Data Related to Chapter 3   201
C. Maine and EDR   204
D. Census Data Related to Chapter 4   207
E. Models Associated with Results in Chapters 3 and 4   210
F. Bootstrapped Confidence Intervals   214
G. Testing the Probit Assumptions   216
H. State Party Leader and State Election Official Survey
   Instruments   227
References   235
Index   247

Acknowledgments

This project benefited from the support, advice, and encouragement of numerous people and organizations. I am sure that these words cannot properly articulate how deeply grateful I am – but I will do my best.

My graduate school advisors, Chris Achen and Mike Traugott, are outstanding role models and mentors. They had faith in my abilities and each, in his own way, challenged me to do things I was not sure I could do; to me, this is the most important thing teachers and advisors can do for their students. I am also deeply grateful for the opportunities they have given me to collaborate with them and for their continued advice and encouragement. Although Chris was at Princeton as I finished up at Michigan, I appreciate the fact that he always made himself available. I can never repay Chris and Mike for what they have given to me; however, I strive to be as good a mentor to my students as they have been to me. Vince Hutchings was the first person to welcome me to Michigan after I was admitted. At every step of my career he has been able to provide the wisdom of an experienced scholar with recognition of what it was like to be in my place. Vince gave generously of his time; even when he was on leave or out of town he made time for meetings, calls, and defenses. Liz Gerber pushed me to think harder and more broadly about the contributions of this project. She raised the bar and challenged me to get over it. I benefited enormously from her guidance. I admire each of my committee members, both professionally and personally. For as bright, talented, and successful as they each are, they are equally down to earth. I have thoroughly enjoyed our conversations about political science as well as those about hockey, rattlesnake races, chicken wings, and parenthood, to note a few.

Over the years I have had the good fortune to get support and advice from a number of great friends and colleagues. Matt Beckmann pushed me to think, write, and argue more clearly. His calm approach to the world also helped me keep things in perspective. When I considered cutting interviews from the research design, Corrine McConnaughy convinced me to keep what turned out to be my favorite part of the project. My frequent conversations on methodological issues with Sean Ehrlich and Won-ho Park provided sound checks on my intuition and pushed me to learn more. For reading early drafts of papers that ultimately became part of this book, engaging in helpful discussions, and/or providing advice on publishing, I thank Jaison Able, Scott Allard, Mike Bailey, Adam Berinsky, Marc Busch, Raj Desai, Brian Duff, Laura Evans, Marc Howard, Jim Janicki, Ozan Kalkan, Cindy Kam, Mike Kimaid, Brian Knight, Jon Ladd, Hans Noel, Irfan Nooruddin, Anders Olofsgard, Clint Peinhart, Tasha Philpot, Chris Seplaki, George Shambaugh, Joe Smith, Michele Swers, Ismail White, and Clyde Wilcox.

I owe special thanks to Jocelyn Mitchell, who read and commented on numerous drafts of the manuscript. The project benefited enormously from her advice. My thoughts on substantive matters crystallized due to our conversations, and my ability to communicate my ideas and findings to others has improved significantly.

Paul Herrnson and Dick Niemi played important roles in helping me transition into the profession. From our several other projects, I gained invaluable experience that improved my work. In addition to reading and commenting on drafts, they have shown unwavering support and have always been available to give advice on everything and anything.

At the University of Maryland, I have had access to resources and colleagues that helped propel this project to completion. Mark Lichbach was generous and flexible in granting me time off to prepare the book for submission, and once it was accepted to make the final revisions. I benefited tremendously from advice provided by Karen Kaufmann, Geoff Layman, and Ric Uslaner. Ric also read the entire manuscript before I sent it for review and helped me make important publishing contacts. In addition to those previously mentioned, Hannah Birnir, Jim Gimpel, Frances Lee, Wayne McIntosh, and Irwin Morris engaged in helpful discussions on the publishing process.

I would also like to thank the anonymous reviewers of the manuscript, who provided constructive criticisms that led to a number of important revisions.

I am grateful to Jon Hurwitz and Mark Peffley, editors of *Political Behavior*, Springer, and the anonymous reviewers of "An Alternative

Approach to Estimating Who Is Most Likely to Respond to Changes in Registration Laws," portions of which appear in this book.

I appreciate Katherine Haenschen's willingness to allow me to use her photo for the cover.

A variety of resources at the University of Michigan made this project possible. The support of the National Election Studies Fellows program and specifically Nancy Burns and Don Kinder, the Department of Political Science and the Gerald R. Ford Dissertation Fellowship and Research Grant, and the Institute for Social Research's Founders Fellowship provided me with the time and money to conduct my field work. I would also like to thank Jake Bowers, Mary Corcoran, Rob Franzese, Rick Hall, Greg Markus, and Cara Wong, who during my time at Michigan made a number of direct and indirect contributions to the project and my professional development.

The following individuals generously gave their time to participate in interviews: Penny Ysursa (Administrative Secretary, Idaho Elections Division); Julie Flynn (Maine Deputy Secretary of State) and Deborah Cabana (Maine Director of Elections); Michael McCarthy (Minnesota Assistant Director, Elections Division), Michele McNulty (Minnesota Election Administrator), and Lisa Kramer Rodacker (Minnesota Program Administrator); William Gardner (New Hampshire Secretary of State); Kevin J. Kennedy (Executive Director, State of Wisconsin Elections Board); Peggy Nighswonger (Wyoming Elections Director) and Lori Klassen (Wyoming Elections Officer); and representatives of the state Democratic and Republican parties in Idaho, Minnesota, New Hampshire, Wisconsin, and Wyoming and a representative of the Maine Republican party.

I would also like to extend my gratitude to two officials in Michigan. Brad Whitman in the State of Michigan elections division was instrumental in the development of the questionnaire used for the interviews with the above election officials. And without the help of Chris Thomas, the Director of Elections in Michigan, I would not have been able to schedule an important interview with one of the election officials.

The following libraries and archives and their staffs played an important part in my research: the Idaho Legislative Reference Library, Idaho State Library (which let me make copies for free), and Idaho State Law Library; the Maine Law Library; the Minnesota Legislative Reference Library and Minnesota State Archives; New Hampshire State Archives; Wisconsin Legislative Reference Bureau and Wisconsin State Law Library; and the Wyoming State Law Library and Wyoming State Archives.

Jeff Lev, Liz Nelson, and Diana Watral were each outstanding research assistants. I enjoyed our many conversations and watching them continue in their success.

I would also like to thank Eric Crahan, editor at Cambridge University Press, for his enthusiastic support for the project and hard work in getting the book to print quickly. Emily Spangler, senior editorial assistant at Cambridge University Press, and Peggy Rote, project manager at Aptara Inc., provided quick answers to my numerous questions about the production process.

Going back farther in time, among the most influential people in my academic career is David A. Martin, my undergraduate advisor at the State University of New York at Geneseo. He planted the idea of getting a Ph.D. and pursuing an academic career in my head and did not let me question my ability to follow through. Without him I surely would not have entered into a Ph.D. program. On my way, I spent time at the University of Wisconsin and then as a consultant. Jack Dennis helped foster my interest in political science and suggested that Michigan and I would be a good fit. In my view, he could not have been more right. While at Wisconsin, I had the pleasure of taking classes from Chuck Manski, who introduced me to the issues of identification that shaped my thinking about election reform. My time as a consultant at the Center for Governmental Research (now CGR) was also important for this project. The skills I developed under the direction of Kent Gardner proved invaluable generally, but especially with respect to my work involving interviews with election officials and party leaders.

Going back farther still, my parents, Doreen and Frank Hanmer, and my grandfather, Bernard Hanmer, have always supported my education and never put pressure on me. From them I learned to work hard, persevere, and recognize and focus on the things that really matter. Words cannot express how much they mean to me.

Last but certainly not least, without the love and support of my wife, Kristin, I could not have completed this project. In addition to proofreading draft after draft, listening to my ideas, and putting up with me, she taught me how to conduct the legislative analysis that forms Chapter 2 of this book. She also gave me the greatest gifts I could ever hope for, our son Connor and daughter Keira, who never cease to amaze and inspire me.

Introduction

On November 4, 2008, my drive to day care with my four-year-old son and two-year-old daughter started off as it generally does. We saw the usual set of things that capture their attention – cars, trucks, buses, and dogs being walked. These sightings sparked the typical set of questions they ask, such as: "Can I buy that car someday?" and "Can I buy a dog when I'm bigger?" But outside a Metro station,[1] while stopped at a red light just before our last turn, we witnessed something we had not seen before. Three young women were chanting and waving Obama/Biden signs. Not surprisingly, this generated a new question: "What are they doing, Daddy?" In answering, I said that it was election day and the women were expressing their support for Barack Obama. Then, as a man and a woman who were walking together approached the three Obama supporters, the man joined in. His partner jumped a few steps into the street and snapped a photo of the group. This activity inspired a fresh line of questioning, first from my son, who asked: "What is the man doing? Why did they take a picture? Is it a party?" Upon hearing the word "party," my daughter asked hopefully: "Is it my birthday party?" Some confusion from my two-year-old notwithstanding, the excitement on election day was palpable.

If turnout in the United States was ever going to reach new heights, the conventional wisdom was that 2008 was the year for it to happen. For example, Bob Herbert began his *New York Times* op-ed by asserting: "All

---

[1] Metro refers to the rapid transit system used in the Washington, DC, area. Metro stations, such as the station one block away from the day care center, are often characterized by being in heavily populated areas with a variety of businesses and entertainment venues.

the signs are pointing to an enormous turnout."[2] Regardless of the outcome, the election was set to be historic, resulting in either an African-
American president or a female vice-president. The two tickets differen-
tiated themselves on the issues and their message; they also brought with
them varying levels of experience. An unprecedented fifty-state voter registration effort on the Democratic side was also part of a campaign that
saw record levels of spending. In addition to the mobilization efforts, it
had become increasingly easy for eligible citizens to register and for those
who were registered to vote. In nine states, eligible citizens could register
to vote as late as election day (known as election day registration), up
from seven states in 2004.[3] An additional state (North Carolina) allowed
citizens to register during the early voting period (starting nineteen days
prior to election day and ending three days prior to election day) and
vote on the spot. The number of states that allow registrants to vote
early, either in person or by mail, without any excuse had also increased
from 2004. All but sixteen states and the District of Columbia allowed
some form of no-excuse early voting.

Despite the high expectations, further relaxation of election laws,
mobilization efforts, and excitement in the streets, turnout in the 2008
presidential election did not live up to the hype, inching up a mere percentage point from 2004. For proponents of participatory democracy, a
turnout rate in the neighborhood of 60 percent is not particularly impres-
sive. As we move forward, policies aimed at making it easier to vote
will surely garner attention. Evidence of this appeared as soon as one
day after the 2008 election, with calls from activists and scholars for
further changes in election laws, such as universal voter registration and
registering all high school seniors.[4]

But further reforms that make it easier to register and/or vote will
not do much to increase turnout.[5] The root of the problem runs deep;

[2] Bob Herbert, "The Known Unknowns" *New York Times*, November 1, 2008 (http://
www.nytimes.com/2008/11/01/opinion/01herbert.html). See also *Election Preview 2008:
What if We Had an Election and Everyone Came?* From the Pew Center on the States
(http://www.pewcenteronthestates.org/uploadedFiles/Election%20Preview%20FINAL
.pdf).
[3] This includes North Dakota, where registration has not been necessary since 1951.
[4] Press release entitled "A Better Election Next Time?" issued on 11/05/08 from the Institute for Public Accuracy (http://www.accuracy.org/newsrelease.php?articleId=1857), last
visited 3/19/09. An article in the *L.A. Times* from 11/10/08 reveals similar sentiments
from the Brennan Center for Justice at New York University (see http://articles.latimes
.com/2008/nov/10/nation/na-voting10, last visited 3/19/09.
[5] It is important to note that my focus here is on reforms aimed at increasing turnout. There
are a variety of electoral reforms aimed at other aspects of the voting system that have
been wildly successful. Most recently, the changes in voting technology as a result of the

increasing turnout will require a new approach and the patience to implement it.

In this book, I argue that the previous approaches to understanding the effects of electoral reform are incomplete, and I offer a new approach. The most important problem with our present understanding of the effects of structural reforms on voter turnout is that the theory purporting to explain these effects is deficient – citizens will not flood the polling places just because a state or federal law makes it easier to vote.[6] The existing theoretical approach is especially problematic with respect to the lack of consideration given to the influence of the social and political contexts that led to the adoption of the reforms and the contexts into which the reforms are put into action.[7] Put another way, I contend that in order to understand how institutional arrangements affect outcomes, one must account for the interactions between social and political contexts and these institutional arrangements. Previous research on election reform has failed to do so. Because of the limitations of the existing theoretical accounts, one finds in the field of political science assumptions that do not withstand scrutiny and statistical methods that fail to account for the fit between the policy and the environment into which it is planted. As a result, what we think we know about the effect of registration reforms is faulty in a number of regards.

I develop a theoretical framework that captures the linkages between the behavior, in varying social and political settings, of the strategic politicians who establish the institutional arrangements that govern what is required to vote and the behavior of individuals whose actions are constrained by the electoral environment. The central component of my argument is that social and political contexts are important determinants of state-level voter registration laws and that the effects of these laws, in turn, are conditioned by these contexts. I test the theory on what are, arguably, the two reforms with the greatest promise for higher turnout and a reduction of the gulf between the turnout rates of the resource rich, who vote at high rates, and the resource poor, who vote

Help America Vote Act of 2002 are a good example (see, e.g., Hanmer et al. forthcoming). And for coverage of a wide range of reforms, some of which have been a success, see the work contained in *Democracy in the States: Experiments in Election Reform*, edited by Cain, Donovan, and Tolbert (2008).

[6] I refer to reforms that are enacted through legislation, such as election day registration and motor voter, as structural reforms. This is a broader definition than used by Tolbert, Donovan, and Cain (2008).

[7] Though not given sufficient weight in the study of election reform in the United States, social and political contexts have been recognized as important for understanding political behavior (see, e.g., Key 1949; Huckfeldt and Sprague 1995; Hero 1998; Franklin 2004).

at low rates. These are election day registration (EDR), a policy that allows eligible citizens to register on the day of the election, and "motor voter" registration, a policy that allows eligible citizens to register to vote through interactions with the state department of motor vehicles, such as obtaining a driver's license. Because motor voter is already national policy, enacted through the National Voter Registration Act of 1993 (NVRA), I focus most of my attention on EDR, which has gained momentum, evidenced by its recent adoption in Montana (passed in 2005) and Iowa (passed in 2007) as well as its consideration in a number of states (see www.electionline.org).[8] Moreover, some of the foremost scholars of political behavior in the United States have also expressed support for the expansion of EDR (see Alvarez and Ansolabehere 2002; Caltech/MIT Voting Technology Project 2003; Patterson 2003; and Alvarez, Nagler, and Wilson 2004; but also see Ansolabehere and Konisky 2006).

THE PITFALLS OF STUDYING REGISTRATION
IN THE UNITED STATES

Although Raymond Wolfinger and Steven Rosenstone's (1980) seminal book, *Who Votes?*,[9] spawned the recent work on the effects of institutional factors on turnout, this research tradition can be traced as far back as 1927, and Harold Gosnell's groundbreaking work, *Getting Out the Vote: An Experiment in the Stimulation of Voting*. *The American Voter* (Campbell, Converse, Miller, and Stokes 1960), is most widely known for its contribution to the understanding of the relationships between attitudinal forces and voting, but it also discusses the effects of legal factors on turnout. In brief, the scholarship that developed out of Wolfinger and Rosenstone's (1980) classic study holds that the effects of lowering the costs of voting through relaxed registration laws are uniform across contexts and, thus, the sizable effects that researchers have estimated in the states that were first to adopt EDR can be extrapolated across contexts.

---

[8] Montana's law was effective as of July 1, 2006, and Iowa's went into effect on January 1, 2008. Unfortunately, the data necessary to evaluate properly EDR in these states will not be available for several more years. As noted earlier, North Carolina has what has been called same day registration, whereby citizens can register during the early voting period and vote at that time. Perhaps a better name for this policy is early voting same day registration.

[9] Prior to the publication of *Who Votes?*, these two authors published "The Effect of Registration Laws on Voter Turnout" in the *American Political Science Review* (see Rosenstone and Wolfinger 1978). Because this work was largely incorporated into the book, all references will be to the book rather than the article.

This leads to the conclusion that if registration laws were relaxed everywhere, turnout across the nation would rise substantially. But is the assumption of uniform effects reasonable? The following thought experiment reveals the problems that emerge when the complexities of democratic practice in the contemporary United States are overlooked.

The states are often described as laboratories of democracy. Yet scholars cannot proceed as if the same level of control that exists in a laboratory prevails in the real world of electoral politics in America. To illustrate the point, begin by imagining that we could study the effect of registration laws on turnout by running an experiment. In a simple experimental design aimed at understanding the effect of registration laws on turnout, some citizens would be randomly assigned to places where registration is easy and others to where registration is more difficult, and their electoral behavior would be observed. This would reveal how behavior differs across the context defined by legal requirements. Of course, ethical and practical considerations prevent the implementation of this sort of research design.

A thought experiment that provides a closer approximation to the realities of American politics would take the simple experimental design as a base and add to it another set of conditions based on the tradition of support for participation. We know that turning out to vote has been encouraged in some places and discouraged – and even prevented for certain segments of the citizenry – in others. For the present purposes, then, this condition could be defined by the extent to which the citizenry is supportive of electoral participation. That is, localities would be separated based on their citizens' attitudes toward electoral participation. With this additional component, individuals would be randomly assigned into at least four conditions: 1) easy registration and strong participatory tradition, 2) easy registration and weak participatory tradition, 3) difficult registration and strong participatory tradition, and 4) difficult registration and weak participatory tradition. With this design, we could discover the ways in which the legal context interacts with the participatory context.

In actuality, however, states self-select their system of registration laws; as Walter Dean Burnham (1980) put it, "registration requirements did not descend from the skies" (p. 68). Moreover, the states with already strong participatory traditions have tended toward the most lenient registration requirements. Thus, without being able to construct or even observe all four conditions just set out, assumptions have to be made about the way registration laws will work across participatory contexts. The dominant assumption in the literature is that the effects from one context can be

extrapolated straightforwardly to other contexts. This means that the
effect of EDR in, say, South Carolina (which I would place in condition
4) would match the effect of EDR in Minnesota (condition 1). Simply put,
this commonly imposed assumption is untenable. Importing a law from
Minnesota will not erase the scars of South Carolina's history, nor will it
bring South Carolinians' taste for participation in line with Minnesotans',
let alone re-create the products of Minnesota's participatory tradition.

Understanding how citizens ultimately respond to changes in election
laws requires paying attention to the intentions of the elected representatives who put the laws into place and the demand for greater participation
among the citizenry. Studies that fail to account for the strategic nature
of the selection of election laws miss a fundamental part of the process – the role of politics – and proceed as if these laws were assigned
randomly.[10] For example, in Minnesota, EDR is part of the fabric of electoral politics. Making voting as easy as possible is an important state goal;
in addition to EDR, Minnesota has allowed motor voter registration since
1987. When assessing EDR in Minnesota, an election official there told
me that "it is absolutely great . . . I'd like everybody to have the opportunity to vote if they are eligible, and election day registration permits that."
Another official summed up, saying: "Uniformly, you would find all of us
supportive of the concept [of EDR], we feel that it fulfills important needs
[for] citizen participation."[11] Officials in Wisconsin hold similar views.
Kevin Kennedy, the Executive Director of the Wisconsin State Elections
Board, presented the following argument to those interested in EDR:

As the chief election official of the state of Wisconsin, I believe we need to reduce barriers to voter participation in order to encourage voter turnout. A larger
voter participation strengthens the legitimacy of our elected representative government . . . Election day registration facilitates voter participation by making the
voting process more accessible to persons when it counts the most, on election
day. (State of Wisconsin/Elections Board, Memorandum, June 19, 1995)

EDR is also available in New Hampshire, but a different view prevails
in that state. There, Secretary of State William Gardner, a Democrat who
was elected to office by the New Hampshire General Court in 1976 and
has remained in office since, campaigned forcefully against the NVRA.
During an interview with me on January 16, 2003, he explained that
motor voter would cheapen the value of the vote and that those who

---

[10] This assumption is referred to as the exogenous selection assumption.
[11] Interview with representatives from the Minnesota Office of the Secretary of State:
Michael McCarthy, Michele McNulty, and Lisa Kramer Rodacker, 2/26/03.

are interested in voting should not pay for a system that registers people who do not care about voting. These remarks echo his earlier argument to Congress that his office felt "strongly that the rights of all eligible persons to vote should be guaranteed, [but] it also assumes that these same persons will take some responsibility as citizens" (*Congressional Record*, Senate, March 11, 1993). Although New Hampshire ultimately adopted EDR, as I show in Chapter 2, it was put into action to avoid the "unnecessary confusion and excessive expense necessitated by federal legislation" (New Hampshire Session Laws 1994, c. 154, § 1). Whereas New Hampshire implemented EDR for political expediency, Minnesota and Wisconsin implemented EDR with intentions more squarely focused on making voting easier (see Chapter 2).

I do not offer these examples to pass judgment on either of these ways of thinking; sensible people will be distributed across this spectrum. However, they demonstrate that the variations do not emerge haphazardly. The same logic applies to laws intended to prevent certain types of individuals from gaining access to the political process. One need only think of the Jim Crow South for numerous examples. As I explain in detail later, ignoring the reasons why some states are inventive and interested in encouraging participation – and others are not – has serious implications for the ability to draw conclusions regarding the effect of the policy being studied.

Another problem has plagued popular as well as scholarly attempts to estimate the effect of relaxed registration laws. A brief introduction will illuminate a common mistake that led to the belief that relaxing registration laws would lead to substantially higher rates of turnout (the details can be found in Chapter 1).

Consider Figure I.1, showing turnout in 1976 for two groups of states: those that allowed EDR (Maine, Minnesota, and Wisconsin) and all other states (excluding North Dakota).[12] The graph shows clearly that turnout in the states with EDR far surpassed turnout in the rest of the states. Under the belief that lowering the costs of voting should increase turnout, one would be tempted to attribute the 15-percentage-point gap in turnout rates to the effect of EDR. But doing so is imprudent, as it fails to account for initial conditions in the two sets of states. As noted earlier, states self-select their laws, and the states that adopted EDR for the 1976 election

---

[12] I am leading to a comparison of states before and after adoption of EDR to all other states that do not have EDR. Because North Dakota did not require registration in both of the years considered, it is eliminated from the analysis.

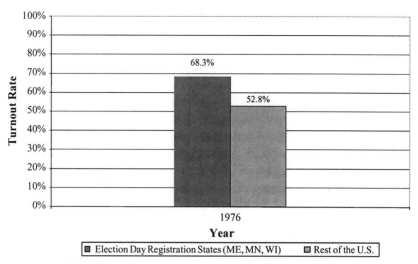

FIGURE I.I. Turnout rate in 1976 comparing states with election day registration to the rest of the United States (excluding North Dakota) (Source: FEC).

(Maine, Minnesota, and Wisconsin) were already high turnout states with histories of encouraging participation. This has consequences for the conclusions one should draw regarding the effect of EDR.

Consider now Figure I.2, which adds turnout for the two sets of comparison states in 1972, prior to the adoption of EDR in Maine, Minnesota, and Wisconsin. The bars on the left-hand side of the graph reveal that even prior to the adoption of EDR, Maine, Minnesota, and Wisconsin had an average turnout rate that was 10 percentage points higher than the rest of the states. That was a considerable advantage even *before* the cost of registering was largely eliminated. Thus, much of the 15-point gap that occurs in 1976 was already accounted for by other factors that differentiate the states that adopted EDR from the rest of the pack.

The methodological approach I use takes into account the issues just discussed. Through the use of individual-level data, careful selection of cases appropriate for comparison, and analysis of the differences in turnout before and after the change in registration laws, I provide new and improved estimates of the effects of the reforms.

What I find will be disturbing to those who are optimistic that further structural reforms will lead the United States to higher turnout and greater equality between the so-called haves and have nots. The effects of relaxed registration laws are not as high as reformers would hope or as previous studies led us to believe, especially when reform is handed down by the

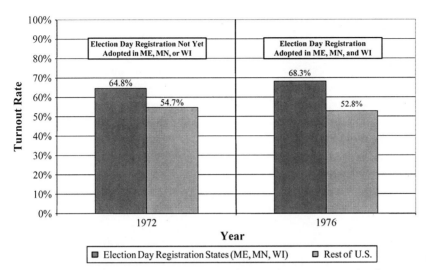

FIGURE I.2. Turnout rate in states adopting election day registration for the 1976 election (Maine, Minnesota, and Wisconsin) before and after adoption compared to the rest of the United States (excluding North Dakota) (Source: FEC).

federal government. Although the effects tend to be the largest for the least well-off, the gains barely put a dent in the wide turnout gap that exists between the best- and worst-off. Moreover, the parties have not jumped at the expanded opportunity to mobilize eligible unregistered citizens. My findings make the case for a new direction for the study of voter turnout and ways to increase it and inform debates regarding the responsibility of the citizenry, political parties, and government.

Researchers' and reformers' concentration on structural reforms has shifted the focus away from dealing with the root causes of abstention, which cannot be fixed overnight. To improve turnout in the United States, long-term strategies aimed at increasing motivation through socialization processes are necessary. It is time to face up to the fact that tinkering with registration methods, holding elections on Saturday, making election day a holiday, reducing the number of elections that are held, or other structural changes that do not inspire the desire to vote will not generate substantially higher levels of turnout.[13] Some of the more clever attempts

---

[13] The removal of the barriers erected by Jim Crow laws certainly led to substantial increases in turnout among blacks (Rosenstone and Hansen 1993). My argument applies to the post–Voting Rights Act (1965) era, when one can reasonably argue that barriers to registration exist but they pale in comparison to the restrictiveness of the Jim Crow laws. Although some of the policies listed earlier, such as changing election day to a

to raise turnout rates, such as providing heat in apartment buildings so that "people will come out and perform their civic duty,"[14] as was done for the March 2004 elections in Russia, or "branding voting" with "Democracy Is Sexy" t-shirts,[15] a tactic aimed at improving youth turnout in Canada, are not effective strategies either. Although some of these proposals – certainly not those involving the manipulation of heating and cooling systems – might be worth implementing, our expectations must be more realistic and our reasons for enacting the reforms must be altered. That is, those who argue in favor of structural reforms, rather than anticipating an immediate and significant boost in turnout, must make a normative appeal regarding the responsibility of the government to facilitate voting. The government at various levels might still play a role, perhaps by providing research and guidance on civic education plans that build attachments to democratic practices and capacity to learn about the issues, candidates, and parties. But citizens bear some responsibility too; the only way the parties will expand the scope of their efforts is if those currently on the outside demonstrate some commitment to participate. It does not take much reflection to realize the difficulty of these tasks.

HOW WE GOT HERE

Voting, at a minimum, serves as a check on the government, allowing citizens the opportunity to hire and fire their representatives. Yet many believe voting takes on a larger meaning. A variety of scholars express the view that voting is more than just a check on government, perhaps none so succinctly and powerfully as Riker (1982), who said "voting... is at the heart of both the method and the ideal of democracy" (p. 8). That

---

Saturday, have not been tested in the United States, because they fit into the larger group of policies that reduce costs but do not generate the motivation to vote, my theoretical framework (see Chapter 1) predicts that they will not boost turnout. Proportional representation systems do hold promise for modest increases in turnout (Bowler, Donovan, and Brockington 2003), but it is doubtful that there is sufficient support to implement such a fundamental change in the voting system across the country. Although there is also a growing literature on ways to increase turnout by fostering more competitive elections, McDonald and Samples (2006) conclude that these approaches have produced disappointing results.

[14] This statement was attributed to the head of the Volga Interregional Energy Management Company in Ulyanovsk. Other efforts to "assure a sufficiently high turnout" included ordering hospitals not to admit those who did not have absentee ballots and threatening the jobs of local officials (Radio Free Europe/Radio Liberty, March 8, 2004: http://www.rferl.org/content/Article/1143112.html).

[15] The National, CBC Television 5/25/04. Rush the Vote, Canada's version of Rock the Vote, was responsible for this approach.

is, many view voting as a fundamental democratic activity, a gateway to participation in a variety of other political acts, and a catalyst of citizen and societal development. Though the arguments for the importance of voting abound, in the United States there exists a gap between the lofty goals of democratic theory and reality – many citizens in the United States do not vote.

Despite some recent gains, voter turnout in the United States remains lower than rates achieved in the 1960s.[16] Moreover, turnout in the United States is low by international standards, usually ranking second last, ahead of Switzerland. Most significantly, this low turnout varies systematically with existing socioeconomic cleavages. For example, using 2000 election data from the Census Bureau's Current Population Survey, those with the highest family incomes, those earning $75,000 or more, had a turnout rate of 80 percent, whereas those with incomes less than $20,000 had a turnout rate of only 50 percent. Whereas half of those at the bottom are simply not involved in the electoral system, those at the top are overrepresented as they occupy a larger share of the voting population (29 percent) than the eligible citizen population (24 percent). This inequality in participation has real implications for the types of candidates that get elected, the policies they enact, and the health of democracy in the United States.[17] Teixeira (1992) presents this concern well, arguing that "[l]ow and declining turnout threatens [the link between policy makers and citizens] and compromises the type of democracy the United States is today and will become in the future" (p. 4).

A large and varied collection of scholars, government officials, journalists, and public interest groups views low and unequal turnout with alarm. Because socioeconomic cleavages are reflected in differential rates of voting, with important political consequences, some have gone so far as to describe the combination of low and unequal turnout as a democratic dilemma (Lijphart 1997; see also Piven and Cloward 2000).[18]

---

[16] McDonald and Popkin (2001), argue that, contrary to the conventional wisdom that prevailed from the 1970s through the 1990s, voter turnout was not in a state of decline. The improvement in the measurement of turnout provided by McDonald and Popkin (2001) is an important one; however, a decline in turnout over this period from the levels in the 1960s is apparent even with their measure, leading Patterson (2003) to argue that the "flight from electoral politics is not illusory" (p. 9) (see Wattenberg 2002, p. 7 for a similar view).

[17] For a review of the evidence on this point see Lijphart (1997). More recent evidence can be found in Griffin and Newman (2005); and for discussion of new avenues of research on this important topic see Griffin and Keane (2006).

[18] Of course, not all see low turnout as a problem (see Berelson et al. 1954, chapter 14; Caplan 2007).

Given the widespread concern that the well-being of our democratic society is at risk, over the past several decades, considerable energy has been directed toward finding a solution. With this in mind, academic researchers and reformers were drawn first to the process of voter registration. Doing so seemed quite sensible. The evidence was clear – the registration process in the United States is unique and uniquely burdensome. Unlike the situation in most Western democracies, U.S. citizens have been expected to bear the bulk of the responsibility for registering to vote. In that process they face a number of hurdles, including deadlines that require registration sometimes a month in advance of the next election.[19] Powell's (1986) observation that "registration laws make voting more difficult in the United States than in almost any other democracy" reflects the established view (p. 21). Further, the logic was easy to follow and grounded in formal theory – drawing on the influential work of Anthony Downs (1957), it was expected that reducing the costs of voting, by making registering to vote easier, would increase turnout. And last, the fixes were tangible – the changes could be enacted through legislation at the state and federal levels. As a result, a rich political science literature developed and reforms to the registration system were proposed and implemented, first by the states and then by the federal government.[20] I now turn to a description of the two laws studied here.

[19] As noted earlier, this is not the case for eligible citizens in North Dakota, which does not require voter registration. Prior to the implementation of the Help America Vote Act of 2002, this was also not the case for citizens in some small municipalities in Wisconsin, where, based on their small size, by state law they could decide not to require voter registration. The variation in registration rules across the states will also be discussed subsequently.

[20] Using a similar empirical and theoretical base, scholarship and reform efforts expanded to concerns with making voting easier for those who were already registered. A number of states permit early voting (see Richardson and Neely 1996; Stein and Garcia-Monet 1997; and Stein 1998) and/or unrestricted absentee voting (see Patterson and Caldeira 1985; Oliver 1996), and Oregon now conducts all its elections by mail (see Karp and Banducci 2000; Southwell and Burchett 2000a, 2000b; Berinsky, Burns, and Traugott 2001; and Hanmer and Traugott 2004). For a review, see Traugott (2004) and Berinsky (2005). More recently, Fortier (2006), Gronke, Galanes-Rosenbaum, and Miller (2007, 2008) have studied these so-called convenience voting policies that make voting easier for registrants; the general finding is that these laws do little to increase turnout and might even increase turnout inequality. One might argue that registration reforms also fit under the umbrella of convenience reforms. I view the line between costs and convenience as blurry and stick with the conventions that have developed in the literature; i.e., I discuss reforms aimed at nonregistrants in terms of costs and reforms aimed at registrants in terms of convenience.

BACKGROUND ON EDR AND MOTOR VOTER

There is wide variation in the institutional arrangements that help structure a citizen's decision whether or not to vote in the United States.[21] The rules that shape and govern the electoral environment vary not only from state to state, but often from county to county within a given state, and in some states, authority rests in the hands of officials at the township and city level. Among the myriad election laws and procedures, the process of voter registration in the United States has garnered significant attention. Voting in the United States is best described as a two-step process: prior to voting, eligible citizens first must register. This is true in all but one U.S. state, North Dakota, where registration has not been required since 1951. Though registration can certainly be facilitated by family members and friends, and though in some states political parties and citizen groups can hold registration drives, the decision to register or not rests in the hands of the individual – in contrast to most other Western democracies, the government does not make registration automatic nor does the government perform a canvass to seek out potential registrants. Along with the individual responsibility to register comes a deadline, known as the closing date, by which one must register in order to vote in the next election. This closing date is set at the state level, but since 1972 has been capped at thirty days.[22] Although thirty days is now the earliest closing date, a number of states allow for registration on the day of the election.

[21] In addition to variations in registration laws, and variations in the methods (early, absentee, by mail) by which one can vote, the ballots and technology used for voting also exhibit substantial variation (see, e.g., Caltech/MIT 2001; Kimball and Kropf 2005; Saltman 2006; Herrnson, Niemi, Hanmer, Bederson, Conrad, and Traugott 2008; Alvarez and Hall 2008). The inclusion of ballot initiatives, which has been shown to influence important political outcomes, also shows substantial variation (see, e.g., Tolbert, Grummel, and Smith 2001; Smith and Tolbert 2004; Tolbert and Smith 2005; Smith and Fridkin 2008); as Matsusaka (2006) and Smith (2008) discuss, ballot measures are another mechanism by which election reforms can be adopted, adding yet another layer of variability, and one that researchers should take into account when evaluating the effects of election laws.

[22] The 1970 Voting Rights Act Amendments capped the closing date for presidential elections at thirty days. The Supreme Court, in *Dunn v. Blumstein*, 405 U.S. 330 (1972) extended this cap to other elections. However, the Supreme Court made exceptions for Arizona (see *Marston v. Lewis*, 410 U.S. 679 [1973]) and Georgia (see *Burns v. Forston*, 410 U.S. 686 [1973]), ruling that the fifty-day closing dates in these states were permissible; both states later reduced their closing dates to conform to the thirty-day ceiling. The National Voter Registration Act of 1993 includes provisions that set the maximum closing date to thirty days.

In 1973, Maine and Minnesota established EDR, and Wisconsin followed in 1975.[23] Wyoming[24] adopted EDR in 1993, and Idaho and New Hampshire in 1994. As I establish in Chapter 2, EDR was adopted under two different sets of circumstances. Whereas Maine, Minnesota, and Wisconsin adopted EDR in the hopes of increasing turnout, Idaho, New Hampshire, and Wyoming adopted EDR primarily as a means to avoid the NVRA.[25]

Michigan, the state known as the pioneer of automobile manufacturing, paved the way toward a new approach to voter registration. In 1975, Michigan implemented legislation that linked driver's license transactions at motor vehicle offices to voter registration, hence the catchy tag given to this policy, "motor voter." Following Michigan's lead, other states adopted versions of motor voter legislation throughout the 1980s and into the 1990s.[26]

On May 20, 1993, President Bill Clinton signed the NVRA into law. After a lengthy and hard-fought battle, the stroke of President Clinton's pen brought with it the promise of higher and more equal turnout. This legislation ushered in a new era in the government's approach to citizens' involvement in the electoral process, shifting the burden of registration from being squarely on the shoulders of individual citizens to a shared responsibility between citizens and the government.

Beginning on January 1, 1995, motor voter was implemented across the country.[27] A clause in the NVRA permitted states with EDR at the

[23] Oregon adopted EDR in 1975, but registration was not done at the polling places. Oregon abolished EDR in 1985, due to an incident in which the registration system was exploited. In an attempt to get their candidates into office, followers of Bhagwan Shree Rajneesh bused and flew in homeless people from across the country to register in Wasco County. The plan was thwarted by state and local officials. The Rajneesees also used bioterrorism, spreading salmonella in salad bars and grocery stores, in an attempt to reduce turnout among regular residents. Rajneesh was later deported (see Carter 1990).

[24] Dating back to 1951, Wyoming has allowed EDR in primary elections.

[25] As noted earlier, Montana and Iowa adopted EDR prior to the 2008 presidential election; due to the lack of appropriate data at the time of this writing, EDR in these states is not studied here.

[26] Ohio passed motor voter legislation in the late 1970s but did not implement it. Voter registration in other governmental agencies was also built into some of the state motor voter laws. I discuss Minnesota, Nevada, and North Carolina, which also adopted and actively implemented motor voter prior to the NVRA in Chapter 4.

[27] Several states attempted to dodge the NVRA, mostly on the grounds that the NVRA was unconstitutional and an unfunded mandate. Registration in public agencies was also a particular concern in some states. In order to ensure the NVRA was fully implemented, The Voting Section of the Department of Justice filed suit against the states of California, Illinois, Pennsylvania, Michigan, Mississippi, New York, South Carolina, Vermont,

polls (Minnesota, Wisconsin, Idaho, New Hampshire, and Wyoming)[28] or no registration system at all (North Dakota) to opt out of implementing the new federal law.[29] The heart of the NVRA is its motor voter provisions, whereby eligible citizens can register to vote when obtaining or renewing their driver's licenses. It is estimated that more than 90 percent of eligible citizens have driver's licenses, thus giving motor voter the potential to bring about near-universal voter registration (Piven and Cloward 1994). Provisions to allow registration at public agencies and through the mail are also part of the NVRA. Thus, not only would most citizens go through a process whereby registration would be easy, the new law would reach out to the least advantaged in society.

Although motor voter exists now in essentially one form, both EDR and motor voter have grown out of both state-driven laws and federal mandates. Variations in the timing of adoption and the reasons for adoption present an opportunity to explore the theoretical and empirical implications of these two laws and the paths taken toward their implementation. Though few expected a jump to the top, expectations were high that registration reforms could remove the United States from its status as a bottom dweller in the international turnout rankings. However, despite the obvious suspect, plausible reasoning, and feasible remedy, reality has not been kind to those expectations. Understanding what went wrong is crucial for advancing our knowledge of voting behavior. Furthermore, without a clearer picture of how the programs work in practice,

---

and Virginia. Several of the cases were resolved when the federal courts determined that the NVRA was constitutional, and others were settled via negotiation. In the case of California, the U.S. Supreme Court refused to grant certiorari in a suit filed by the state (http://www.usdoj.gov/crt/voting/nvra/activ_nvra.htm, visited 3/10/09; see also Piven and Cloward 2000).

[28] In Maine, election day registration transactions are not always done at polling places; thus, Maine was not exempt from the NVRA.

[29] In order to resolve conflicts with Vermont's Voter Oath provision, Vermont delayed full compliance with the NVRA until July 1, 1997. As part of its Constitution, Vermont requires that first-time Vermont registrants take the Voter's Oath in person, before a person authorized to administer oaths. The voter registration form provides information regarding who can administer the Oath and notes that: "If the filing deadline is close, you can file your application without taking the oath, and take the oath on election day" (http://vermont-elections.org/elections1/2001voterapp.doc, visited 3/19/09). This allows Vermont to implement the mail registration feature of the NVRA while maintaining the Voter's Oath requirement. Text of the Vermont Voter's Oath follows: "You solemnly swear (or affirm) that whenever you give your vote or suffrage, touching any matter that concerns the State of Vermont, you will do it so as in your conscience you shall judge will most conduce to the best good of the same, as established by the Constitution, without fear or favor of any person" (Vermont Constitution, Chapter II, § 42).

in expected and unexpected ways, reformers and policy makers cannot
hope to provide better programs.

OUTLINE OF CHAPTERS

This book is structured as follows. Chapter 1 begins with a brief summary and critique of the literature, elaborating on the shortcomings of
the previous theoretical and methodological approaches that were introduced earlier. Building upon that foundation, I present a new theoretical
framework for understanding the effect of changes in registration laws
on turnout. The chapter concludes with a presentation of the research
design that develops out of the theoretical framework.

In Chapter 2, I explore the processes by which EDR was adopted
in Minnesota, Maine, and Wisconsin and then Wyoming, Idaho, and
New Hampshire. The evidence comes from the examination of legislative
records related to the adoption of EDR in these states, obtained through
archival research at the state libraries, law libraries, archives, historical societies, and legislative service bureaus. The analysis of the legislative histories demonstrates that the first wave of states to adopt EDR
(Minnesota, Maine, and Wisconsin) did so with the explicit goal of
increasing turnout whereas the latter wave of states (Wyoming, Idaho,
and New Hampshire) did so mainly out of concerns with costs and the
maintenance of state control. The case studies establish the purposeful
nature of the adoption process. This calls into question the commonly
held assumptions that influenced previous statistical analyses of the effects
of electoral reforms and serves as support for the methodology I employ.

Chapter 3 presents a new approach to assessing the effects of electoral
reform that corrects for the shortcomings associated with previous treatments of the subject. In it, I describe the methods used for my statistical
analysis and discuss the ways in which they improve upon traditional
methods. The first test of the theoretical framework developed in Chapter 1 comes through the application of these methods to study the effect
of EDR on turnout. The statistical analyses use individual-level survey
data from the Current Population Survey: Voter Supplement File (here-
after CPS) for presidential elections from 1972 through 2000, excluding
1976.[30] Unfortunately, the 1976 CPS does not have a variable with a

---

[30] The Voter Supplement File survey is administered in November, in both presidential
   and midterm election years. The Current Population Survey universe is the U.S. civilian noninstitutionalized population who live in households, generated from a national

unique state identifier. The greatest advantage of using data from the CPS is its large sample size of nearly 100,000 observations per year. With this sample size, even though some of the election law classifications pertain to only one state, within each state, there are a sufficient number of observations to allow for precise estimation. Consistent with my theoretical expectations, the results clearly show that the effect of EDR is not uniform across contexts. In states that adopted reform as a result of federal intervention, the laws have had little, if any, effect. Moreover, using more appropriate methods, the results demonstrate that even in the states that adopted EDR willingly and with the avowed purpose of increasing turnout, EDR has come up short on the promise of delivering substantially higher rates of turnout.

In Chapter 4, I examine motor voter policies that were implemented at the state level, and also examine the NVRA. Surprisingly, few rigorous studies of state-level motor voter laws have been conducted. The analysis presented in Chapter 4 fills this void, with findings that call into question the fervor associated with the expansion of this policy. As was the case for EDR, motor voter's influence on turnout was the strongest when it was adopted willingly by the states, rather than being mandated by the federal government. However, even when implemented through state law, motor voter did not always have an effect on turnout.

Chapter 5 provides a link from the overall effects of EDR and motor voter on turnout to how these effects vary across individual-level characteristics. Using questions recently added to the CPS, I compare registration and turnout rates for those registering before and after the NVRA was implemented, showing that turnout rates in the former group are higher than those for the latter. I also show that turnout among motor voter registrants exceeds the expectations of its critics, but is still lower than the rates of turnout among citizens who choose more costly methods of registration – e.g., registering at the clerk's office. This work revises the widely held belief that most registrants vote; rather, turnout among registrants in the post–NVRA era varies considerably with when and how one registers to vote.

probability sample of households in the United States. The Voter Supplement questions are administered only to citizens who are eighteen years or older. Responses are generated from both self-reports and proxy reports. Jennings (1990) and Highton (2005) have shown that the estimates of turnout are not affected by this procedure. I focus on presidential elections due to the wide variation in races and candidates across states during midterm elections, which could confound the results.

In Chapter 6, I extend the analyses from Chapters 3 and 4 to estimate who is most likely to respond to registration reform. Primarily, I characterize individuals based on the demographic characteristic that has received the greatest amount of attention in the literature – educational attainment – but also examine the effects by age and a measure that combines income and education. Much of the work on this question has found that the least well-off stand the most to gain from registration reform (see Wolfinger and Rosenstone 1980). More recently, however, Brians and Grofman (1999, 2001) and Huang and Shields (2000) provided a contrary claim, arguing that those who have high school degrees but no further education are the most responsive to EDR. In their study of motor voter, Highton and Wolfinger (1998) also find that high school graduates are especially responsive to changes in registration laws. At present, this more recent conclusion seems to be most in favor (Highton 2004).

The results presented here suggest a revision. Using both a traditional and a newer, more flexible, statistical approach that allows for the relaxation of an important behavioral assumption, I find that the largest effects are found among those with the least education, the youngest, and the least well-off. However, the turnout rates among these groups remain substantially lower than those at the top of the socioeconomic spectrum.

Election officials and parties play a crucial role in the implementation of election reforms. In Chapter 7, I ask: Do variations in how political parties have responded to EDR and/or failed implementation by the states provide alternative explanations for my results? Interviews with state political party leaders and state election officials suggest that they do not; somewhat surprisingly, I find a high degree of similarity across all of the EDR states in terms of both program implementation and party response. Piven and Cloward (2000) have cast aspersions on the parties, suggesting they are semi-elitist organizations that actively exclude the least well-off. My interviews with party officials show otherwise, producing results that are consistent with expectations derived from Rosenstone and Hansen (1993). That is, party officials in states with EDR, like those in other states, exist in a world of scarce resources, and thus concentrate their efforts on mobilizing those most likely to respond – that is, those who are already registered, rather than those who are eligible but not registered.

I conclude the chapter with a summary of the findings, noting the implications of my conclusions for researchers and policy makers alike. I argue that structural changes might be important as signs that the government supports participation, but movements to increase turnout must make some hard choices and take a longer view. Although I focus on EDR and motor voter, my hope is that the design employed here will serve as a model that will be applied broadly to the analysis of other (current and yet to be implemented) election laws, such as voter identification requirements, an issue that recently came before the U.S. Supreme Court.

I

Motivation and a New Theoretical Framework

America's status at the bottom of international turnout rankings has shaped the study of voter turnout in the United States. Although it should be quite obvious that a single explanation for low turnout does not exist, researchers have devoted substantial attention to the role of institutions in structuring the rules regarding who registers and votes and the norms relating to whom the parties contact. Scholars and policy experts remain attracted to institutional reforms as solutions because of the collection of concerns that arise out of the decentralized nature of election administration in the United States, coupled with the tools available to make changes.[1] After a review of the nature of these concerns, I highlight the flaws in the existing theoretical approach to the study of the effects of registration laws on voter turnout, discuss the methodological pitfalls that follow, and present a theoretical framework and research design that better reflect the complexities of political behavior in the contemporary United States.

OPPORTUNITY AND VOICE

In the United States, out of the roots of federalism, a sprawling election administration system has sprouted, with roughly 10,000 officials responsible for conducting elections at the state, county, and municipal

---

[1] In a series of articles in the June 1990 issue of *PS: Political Science and Politics*, Stephen Earl Bennett, Francis Fox Piven and Richard A. Cloward, and Curtis B. Gans debate whether or not researchers recognize the complex nature of the decision to vote and thus the need for more than one solution (see Bennett 1990a, 1990b; Gans 1990; and Piven and Cloward 1990).

levels. With the implementation of the National Voter Registration Act of
1993 (NVRA) and Help America Vote Act of 2002 (HAVA), the federal
government brought a greater degree of standardization to the electoral
process. The primary components of the NVRA – its motor voter, mail,
and agency registration provisions – led to more uniformity in the ways
citizens can register to vote. The NVRA also established a set of strict
national standards for the removal of citizens from registration lists, ending the practice of removing citizens without notice simply for their failure
to vote in the last few elections.[2] Perhaps the most recognized feature of
HAVA is its ban on punch card and lever machines, which reduced the
diversity of voting machine types used across the nation.[3] Another key
feature of HAVA was its requirement that the states implement a com-
puterized statewide voter registration database. Yet, despite these steps
by the federal government, substantial powers continue to rest with the
states, which, in turn, can delegate authority for certain features of the
electoral process to county and municipal governments.

The states also have moved toward more standardization. For example, Michigan, a state with more than 1,500 election officials, decided to
use one general type of voting system – optical scanning – and requires all
municipalities in a given county to use the same manufacturer and model.
Prior to the sweeping changes inspired by HAVA, even very similar
municipalities within the same county could have used different voting
technologies. This was the case for voters in the city of Plymouth,
Michigan, who voted on optical scan voting machines, and voters just
over the border in the surrounding Plymouth Township, who voted on
direct recording electronic (DRE) machines.

Although a variety of steps have been taken to standardize across
different levels and numerous phases of the electoral process, including
voter registration, important differences across the states remain; thus,
voters in one state may still face a different set of opportunities (or obstacles) from those in another. Consider a twenty-five-year-old citizen in
Hampton, New Hampshire. Although she cannot register to vote while
obtaining a driver's license, she can register on the day of the election at

[2] This practice is known as purging for nonvoting and its implementation varied by state.
[3] Although punch card and lever machines have been outlawed, those responsible for selecting voting machines at the state and local levels can still choose from an extensive menu
of optical scan and direct recording electronic (DRE) systems. Moreover, the language
of HAVA describes the changes as minimum requirements, thus allowing the states to
implement additional measures, provided, of course, that they do not conflict with federal
law.

her polling place. Her twin sister, in contrast, only eleven miles away in Newburyport, Massachusetts, has to register to vote twenty days or more before the election to be eligible to vote in that contest. However, she was given the opportunity to do so when getting her driver's license. Beyond the distinction between election day registration (EDR) and motor voter registration, the laws regarding the timing of registration (closing date) are not uniform even in the states that were required to implement motor voter. The only restriction on the closing date for registration is that it not exceed thirty days. For the 2000 and 2004 elections, among the NVRA states (excluding Maine, which also has EDR) the shortest closing date was eight days and the longest was thirty days, with about half of the motor voter states setting the closing date at twenty-nine or thirty days.[4] In sum, laws relating to both the method and, to a larger extent, the timing of registration continue to stop at state lines. But one might reasonably ask: Why does this matter?

Voting is generally regarded as the participatory act that provides the most level playing field. For example, in terms of the volume of the activity, Verba, Schlozman, Brady, and Nie (1993) characterize voting as "the one participatory act for which there is mandated equality: each citizen gets one and only one" (p. 304). However, additional aspects of the process reveal the potential for inequality; equality is achieved only among those who register, go to the polls, and have their vote accurately counted. The experiences from the past several decades alone – from the discriminatory Jim Crow laws applied in the South (see Rosenstone and Hansen 1993) to the well-intentioned, but confusing, butterfly ballot in the 2000 presidential election in Palm Beach County (see Wand, Shotts, Sekhon, Mebane, Herron, and Brady 2001) – provide ample reason for concern. With decision-making power over the electoral process stretched across such a wide and diverse range of individuals and contexts, the effects of this system on the equality of the vote in the United States must be given careful consideration, both theoretically and empirically. Among the set of institutional arrangements, the system of voter registration stands out as an area worthy of special attention.

Registration is the first gate through which eligible citizens must pass if they wish to vote. Thus, at some point (though perhaps just once), registration laws have the potential to influence all eligible citizens. Laws regarding the methods or timing of voting (absentee voting, early voting, vote by mail) apply only to those who are registered, and laws and

---

[4] In 2000, twenty-four states (including DC) had closing dates of twenty-nine or more days; in 2004, this number dropped to twenty-two.

procedures relating to the machinery used for voting affect only those who have both registered and then attempted to cast a ballot. Given its status as the entry point for voting, some have taken strong stances on the side of removing features that might impede registration (James 1987; Piven and Cloward 1988, 2000).

James (1987), through the lens of legal analysis, argues that pre–election day registration is a violation of the fundamental right to vote. She begins by establishing the vote as a fundamental right, citing *Yick Wo v. Hopkins* 118 U.S. 356 (1886) in which the Supreme Court asserted that voting is "a fundamental political right, because [it is] preservative of all rights" (p. 1621). She obtains additional backing from *Wesbury v. Sanders* 376 U.S. 1 (1964), in which the Court states: "No right is more precious in a free country than that of having a voice in the election of those who make the laws under which, as good citizens, we must live. Other rights, even the most basic, are illusory if the right to vote is under-mined" (p. 1618). Although James recognizes that the states have the constitutional authority to set voter qualifications, she contends that the Supreme Court has maintained that such qualifications must not conflict with the right to equal protection or any other constitutional provisions (see James 1987, p. 1618, where she cites *Williams v. Rhodes*, 393 U.S. 23 [1968]). Having concluded that only the need to protect against fraud might justify pre–election day registration as a compelling state interest, James asserts:

The constitutionality of the voter registration requirement should be challenged under the fundamental rights strand of equal protection analysis... No form of pre-election day registration is necessary when states are not making use of registration as a means to combat voter fraud [which many are not] or if an alternative election day mechanism is available to accomplish the fraud prevention purpose for which the state is actually using its registration data (p. 1640).

With the move to statewide voter registration databases, those subscribing to this view will be given additional ammunition, as it presumably will be easier to manage the registration lists, thus reducing the time necessary to prepare them for use on election day.

Of those who have championed institutional reforms, Francis Fox Piven and Richard Cloward have dominated the spotlight. In addition to their scholarly writing, their work as activists was crucial for the passage of the NVRA. Like many scholars, Piven and Cloward (2000) place voting at the "core... of democratic politics" (p. 2). Although they note that "voting itself is meaningless, unless citizens have other rights," by maintaining that "the right to vote is the feature of the democratic polity that makes all other political rights significant," they echo the sentiment from the Supreme Court in *Wesbury v. Sanders* (Piven and Cloward 2000, p. 2). The authors build from this view and take issue with the failure of the U.S. government to encourage citizens to participate, arguing that the system of voter registration procedures is the "linchpin of [our] distorted American democracy" (1988, p. 17). Moreover, according to Piven and Cloward, "remote registration sites, together with complicated forms, are de facto income and literacy tests" (1989, pp. 584–585). Although some, myself included, may object to equating post–Voting Rights Act era registration hurdles with the much more severe income and literacy tests of the past, Piven and Cloward's larger message gets to the heart of the relevance of institutional factors, especially registration laws, for understanding voter turnout in the United States. Lest one dismiss Piven and Cloward as radicals, Arend Lijphart, in his presidential address to the American Political Science Association, took the argument even further. According to Lijphart (1997), "the logical and empirical link between low turnout and unequal turnout is the functional equivalent of... discriminatory qualifications" (pp. 6–7).

If the composition of voters is a function of the system, and the system produces low and systematically unequal turnout, then political influence will also be unequal (see Lijphart 1997). Uneasiness over this is heightened in the United States, where turnout is especially low and imbalanced in favor of those who are well-off. Moreover, because the U.S. system has not been and still is not uniform, the ability of eligible citizens to express their views through the vote also is not uniform. We thus arrive at the concern forcefully conveyed by proponents of institutional reforms – especially Piven and Cloward (1988, 2000) – which is that American society has been shaped in a way that has prevented certain types of individuals from having their voice heard on policy issues that surely affect them.

Another impetus for the study and promotion of registration reform comes from the empirical generalization that the turnout rate among those who are registered is quite high (Erikson 1981; Glass, Squire, and Wolfinger 1984; Piven and Cloward 1988; Squire, Wolfinger, and Glass 1987). Squire, Wolfinger, and Glass (1987) reveal the importance of this result, claiming that:

This finding leads to a critical shift in perspective. Traditionally, scholars have asked why people don't vote. The fact that registration is virtually equivalent to voting changes the question. The problem instead is to understand why people do not register (p. 47).

As I discuss in Chapter 5, more recently, the robustness of this result in an environment now characterized by more and easier ways for citizens to register has been called into question (Highton 1997; Hanmer 2000; Brown and Wedeking 2006).

Having established the importance of the study of registration laws and turnout, I now move to a discussion of how the research enterprise went astray. The democratic dilemma of low and skewed turnout did not materialize overnight, nor will it go away overnight with the stroke of a pen on new legislation.

LESSONS FROM PREVIOUS RESEARCH

Voting is, perhaps, the most studied topic in political science. Although the immense literature has taught us much, it is easy for political scientists and students in political behavior courses to become frustrated by just how much we do not know. On even the most basic question – why do people vote? – the answer is elusive. For example, in their model of redistributive politics, Dixit and Londregan (1996) simply note: "We have no better solution than does anyone else to the question of why people vote at all when they are individually so unlikely to affect the outcome."

The rational choice paradigm has provided theoretical structure (see, for example, Aldrich 1993), but has largely failed to produce a satis-factory answer (see Blais 2000 for a superb review and interpretation of this literature). According to the rational choice approach, the deci-sion whether or not to vote boils down to a simple cost–benefit analysis. As illustrated in the "calculus of voting" model (Downs 1957), if the expected benefits exceed the costs, a rational citizen should vote, whereas if the costs exceed expected benefits, the rational citizen should abstain. Here, the benefits are described as instrumental, or focused on the out-come – electing one's preferred candidate. But the model's predictive capacity is weakened by the fact that the benefits of voting are discounted by the probability that one's vote is decisive, which is usually quite low. That is, if the probability of being decisive is low, the expected benefits, calculated as the benefits multiplied by the probability of being decisive, will also be low. Thus, when the probability of being decisive is low, the costs will overwhelm the expected benefits, which leads us to predict that a rational citizen will abstain.[5] The so-called paradox of voting arises

---

[5] This model is represented mathematically as follows, with P representing the probability of casting the deciding vote, B the benefits, and C the costs: if $P^*B > C$, the citizen votes, but if $P^*B < C$, the citizen abstains.

from the vast disconnect between the theoretical predictions of the model
and the empirical fact that millions of people vote. Although solutions to
this paradox within the rational choice framework have been attempted,
they are less than satisfying (for excellent reviews and commentary, see
Blais 2000 and Schuessler 2000).

Work on expressive voting (Brennan and Buchanan 1984; Brennan
and Lomasky 1993; Schuessler 2000; Achen 2006) moves us closer to an
answer. This literature offers an account of voting that recognizes differences between market and electoral behavior and argues that citizens,
much like sports fans, vote to express their *attachment* to the candidates,
parties, issues, outcomes, and others who behave similarly. Schuessler
(2000) points out a crucial distinction between the rational choice characterization of voters – as motivated by casting a ballot – and the expressive voting characterization of voters – as motivated by the consumption
benefits that derive from casting themselves as voters. In other words,
benefits are derived from "being" a voter, whether or not one's vote is
decisive. Though more work in this area is necessary, the incorporation of
expressive benefits into models of voting represents a significant advance
in the understanding of voter turnout.

Although rational choice has not been able to explain the level of
turnout, the structure of cost–benefit analysis provides leverage for understanding differential rates of turnout across individuals and across contexts. Yet the overemphasis on costs, without recognizing the importance
of expressive motivations and how context interacts with the costs and
benefits, clouds our understanding of the effects of registration reform
and leads us down a path of inflated expectations.

In this book, I tackle some of the more difficult issues to surface from
previous research on electoral reform. Included among the problems that
plague existing research are: 1) failure to account for the reasons underlying state-to-state variations in election laws, which leads to the extrapolation of results from one electoral context to another without consideration
for the fit between institutions and the citizenry; 2) failure to account for
the distinctiveness of EDR and motor voter policies, including the mechanisms through which they might influence turnout; 3) statistical models
that, based on an untested assumption, determine who will be the most
sensitive to changes in election laws; and 4) research designs that ignore
the ways political parties respond and adapt to electoral reforms. As a
result of these problems, our understanding of the effects of registration
laws on turnout and the composition of the electorate is fuzzy at best. A
review of previous research and a discussion of what needs to be corrected
follow.

The Effect of Registration Laws on Turnout

With regard to turnout, the general conclusion reached in the literature that emerged from Wolfinger and Rosenstone (1980) is that EDR laws, if implemented nationally, could increase turnout by five to fourteen percentage points (see, for example, Teixera 1992; Mitchell and Wlezein 1995; Rhine 1996; Highton and Wolfinger 1998; Brians and Grofman 1999, 2001; Huang and Shields 2000; Knack 2001; and Timpone 2002). The estimated effects of motor voter laws are generally more modest, ranging from no effect (Martinez and Hill 1999; Fitzgerald 2005; Brown and Wedeking 2006) to a few percentage points (Knack 1995; Rhine 1995; Franklin and Grier 1997). However, if the effects are simulated by equating motor voter to EDR, they may result in as much as a 9-percentage-point increase (Highton and Wolfinger 1998).[6]

Although expressive motivations are acknowledged in this literature, the reduction of costs to the voter is the force that drives the theoretical expectations. However, problems emerge when registration costs are treated as the primary obstacle to voting and when the fit with the social and political environment is disregarded. Some scholars have been cognizant of one or both of these issues (see especially Teixeira 1992; Highton 1997), but they have not incorporated these insights into their research design.

Earlier, I drew a distinction between laboratory experiments and the self-selection of election laws that characterizes the American states. The assumption of random assignment lies at the core of most previous studies of registration reform. That is, scholars have largely ignored endogeneity in the relationship between the decision of states to establish a set of election laws and the decision of citizens to vote or abstain. More specifically, scholars proceed by assuming that the unobservable factors that affect the

---

[6] For additional references, see Traugott (2004). In addition to the conceptual shortcomings described in the Introduction and throughout the present chapter, much of the work cited here relies exclusively on aggregate data and is thus subject to the concerns about the disconnect between the theory and data noted by Hanushek and Jackson (1977) (for additional discussion, see footnote 10). Fitzgerald (2005) exhibits yet another problem beyond the usual theoretical and methodological shortcomings common in the literature – in some cases, the classification of state laws is questionable. For example, as I discuss in Chapter 4, Colorado should not be classified as having motor voter in 1988. Moreover, the classification of states as having unrestricted absentee voting prior to California in 1978 and the classification of states as having early voting in 1970 are inconsistent with my own legal research and the literature (see, e.g., Patterson and Caldeira 1985; Stein and Garcia-Monet 1997; and Gronke, Galanes-Rosenbaum, and Miller 2007).

selection of election laws are unrelated to the unobservable forces that affect turnout. However, attitudes regarding the value of political participation, or the "taste" for participation, are clearly a force that affects turnout; thus we can expect these unobserved attitudes to play a role both in the adoption of a set of election laws and individuals' decisions whether or not to vote. In the United States, the electoral system gives expansive authority to the states to choose their system of registration laws; whereas some states take an active role in promoting participation, others do not. As shown in the figures presented in the Introduction, in the states that were first to adopt EDR, the conditions were such that they had high rates of turnout even before EDR was implemented. In other words, the unmeasured attitudes that led to high rates of participation also fueled efforts to enact laws that supported continued high rates of participation.

Achen (1986) observes that "[i]n evaluation research, many a study is carried out without randomized assignment to treatment and control groups, and the actual assignment process goes completely unspecified" (p. ix). The consequences of ignoring endogeneity are severe – one cannot distinguish between the impact of the laws and the unobserved factors that lead to their selection (see Achen 1986). That is, when the factors that lead to the selection of a particular law are not taken into account, as is the norm in this literature, estimates of the effect of the law will be biased.

To the best of my knowledge, in the literature on turnout and registration reform, Wattenberg (2002) provides the only published model with the registration closing date as the dependent variable.[7] However, when trying to explain the decline in turnout, he does not incorporate the process that led to the selection of the closing date. Further, when other empirical researchers, working in other literatures, do account for the assignment process, their statistical models often rely on assumptions that are difficult to justify. In this book, I argue that scholars must not only modify the traditional conceptualization of the effect of registration laws but also employ additional methods that account for the endogenous nature of the selection of registration laws.

---

[7] Hill and Leighley (1999) model ease of registration via an index that includes the closing date, finding that racial diversity, education, and income inequality strongly influence state-level registration laws. These findings are consistent with the view that registration laws should not be treated as exogenous. However, like Wattenberg (2002), their turnout model does not fully account for the process that leads to the mix of registration laws across the states.

Who Is Most Sensitive to Changes in Registration Laws?

There is considerable debate regarding who will be the most sensitive to relaxed registration laws, especially with respect to how the effects vary by individuals' educational attainment.[8] Most of the earlier studies (Wolfinger and Rosenstone 1980; Teixeira 1992; Nagler 1994; Mitchell and Wlezein 1995; Highton 1997) suggest that EDR leads to the largest turnout gains among those with the lowest levels of education. Nagler (1991) challenges Wolfinger and Rosenstone's results, but his own 1994 article revises his original claims; and though he argues that the mechanism differs, Nagler (1994) arrives at the same substantive conclusion as Wolfinger and Rosenstone (1980). However, Brians and Grofman (1999, 2001) and Huang and Shields (2000) offer contrary results. According to these scholars, those who have high school degrees but no further education stand the most to gain from relaxed registration laws. When studying motor voter, Highton and Wolfinger (1998) also find some of the largest effects among high school graduates. In his review of the literature, Highton (2004) seems persuaded by the new evidence indicating that the largest effects are for those with moderate levels of education. In other words, favor seems to have swung toward the more recent findings.

I contend that the jury is still out, as the estimates of the effects are sensitive to researchers' choices with respect to the statistical methods used to analyze the data. By and large, previous studies use statistical models (namely, probit or logit) that implicitly assume that the largest impact will be on those with a fifty-fifty chance of voting – that is, an initial probability of voting equal to 0.5. For this purpose, this assumption is clearly problematic; researchers do not know ahead of time who is most sensitive to changes in election laws, so this is something that scholars would want to estimate, not assume. Nagler (1994) calls attention to this issue and in an attempt to relax this assumption, uses the scobit model.[9] However,

---

[8] Because the theoretical relationship of interest exists at the individual level (that is, individuals make the decision to vote or abstain) and the data are readily available at the individual level, the literature I address here uses individual-level estimates of voter turnout. Several scholars (see, e.g., Calvert and Gilchrist 1993; Jackson, Brown, and Wright 1998; Martinez and Hill 1999; and Knack and White 2000) use data aggregated at the county or state levels and work from a slightly different perspective. These studies are discussed further in Chapter 6.

[9] The scobit model is similar to logit but is designed to provide an estimate of the point at which individuals will be most sensitive to changes in the independent variables.

as I discuss later, scobit also falls short of providing a solution (see also Hanmer 2002, 2006; Achen 2002). In sum, the inability of the research community to develop appropriate research designs is a significant obstacle, one that has driven the inability to draw firm conclusions. In order to understand current policies and advance the development of new policies, it is essential to know which types of individuals will be the most likely to benefit from various reforms. To settle this debate, research that applies more appropriate methods is necessary. I take up this task in Chapter 6.

Although critical of previous scholarship, I do not mean to suggest that this work, especially Wolfinger and Rosenstone's (1980) *Who Votes*, has not made important contributions. Notably, Wolfinger and Rosenstone, by linking individual-level survey data to administrative data on the laws from each of the states, provided an approach to data analysis that allows the effects of these laws on individual behavior to be estimated precisely. This was a giant step forward. Although studying whether or not a policy leads to larger turnout at the state level can be illuminating, the analysis should be connected to the level at which we are theorizing. Here, individual behavior in response to policy changes is of paramount interest. Individuals, not the states, decide whether to vote or abstain. Therefore, it is appropriate to study the effects of election laws on turnout at the individual level (see Hanushek and Jackson 1977).[10] Unfortunately, many who have written on the subject have relied exclusively on state-level data, and thus depict only part of the story.

The bulk of the conclusions drawn in *Who Votes* derive from an intensive analysis of survey data from 1972, a year in which only one state (North Dakota) effectively had EDR and motor voter was not yet started. Since then, tremendous change has taken place. Wolfinger and Rosenstone's (1980) work made it possible for those who have followed – myself included – to come to a deeper understanding of the complexity of the task of evaluating these laws. They provided a lens through which researchers seeking to contribute to our understanding of registration reform have been able to witness the policy transformations take place. With this experience and new analytical tools, certain issues – most

---

[10] As Hanushek and Jackson (1977) explain, it is a "fact that individual level data are usually richer than aggregate data, permit estimation of more elaborate models, and thus are to be preferred when available" (p. 180). In a footnote to that statement, they go on to say: "In simplest terms the hypotheses investigated with aggregate data often relate to the behavior of individuals. Aggregation across individuals may obscure the relationship of interest by suppressing variations in the [independent variables] across individuals" (Hanushek and Jackson 1977, p. 180).

notably the selective nature of the adoption of registration reform – are more apparent today than they were nearly thirty years ago.

Essential to overcoming the problems with our current state of knowledge are both a theoretical framework that recognizes the concerns just discussed and a research design consistent with that framework. This new approach to the study of registration reform is discussed subsequently.

THEORETICAL FRAMEWORK

I begin this section by discussing how and why EDR and motor voter registration might increase turnout. Although Teixeira (1992) and Highton and Wolfinger (1998) treated EDR and motor voter as functionally equivalent, I lay out the theoretical differences between these two registration systems. Next, I demonstrate that research in this area must confront the identification problem – that is, the fact that, at any given time, we observe the behavior of individuals only in the context in which they presently live. We cannot observe how those same individuals would behave in another context. Following this, I explain why the assumption that election laws can be treated as randomly assigned (exogenous) is problematic. Finally, I derive new hypotheses regarding the effect of registration reform on turnout. The chapter concludes with a discussion of the research design.

EDR and Motor Voter, Similarities and Distinctions

Verba, Schlozman, and Brady (1995), contend that citizens do not participate "because they can't; because they don't want to; or because nobody asked" (p. 15). Although they do not apply their approach to barriers to registration, it is straightforward to expand the scope of their insights to this arena. Using this conceptualization of non-voting allows for a more complete understanding of how EDR and motor voter laws, respectively, lead to an increase in the probability of voting and why their effects are limited.

They Can't. The literature on the effect of election laws on turnout is based on the argument that lowering the costs of voting to individuals should make voting more likely (Downs 1957). By lowering the costs of voting, EDR should primarily lead to an increase in turnout among those who fall into Verba and colleagues's "can't" category. EDR should thus lead to an increase in voting among two classes of eligible citizens: 1) those

who are interested but are unable to meet early registration deadlines; and
2) those who become interested late in the campaign. In EDR states, those
who want to vote but cannot register due to resource constraints, such as,
a lack of time and/or information regarding where to register, can more
easily overcome these constraints than if they were subject to closing dates
as early as thirty days prior to the election. With EDR, administrative
procedures that are a prerequisite to voting – that is, registration – and the
act of voting itself can be accomplished with just one trip on election day.
One need not expend the effort going to the clerk's office, downloading
or otherwise locating and returning a mail-in registration form, and so
on. In other words, although one still needs to find the correct polling
place and bring the proper identification, it is unnecessary to engage in
an administrative procedure prior to election day that carries additional
time and information costs. Additionally, because they can register and
vote on the same day, those who have the resources but not the impetus
to register until late in the campaign, when activity tends to heat up, are
also more likely to vote under EDR. Similar individuals in states that
do not allow EDR will be excluded until the next election. Because they
will not be shut out of the process due to an early closing date, recent
movers who fit into one of the aforementioned two categories also have
an increased likelihood of voting in EDR states.

Motor voter provisions, now in place in all but five states, also reduce
the costs of voting.[11] By incorporating voter registration into obtaining or
renewing a driver's license, an administrative procedure through which
nearly 90 percent of the population goes, the need to seek out the location of the clerk's office or otherwise spend time and energy to become
registered is eliminated. However, eligible citizens come into contact with
driver's license agencies infrequently (in most states, once every four to
six years). This can leave a significant time gap between the date of registration and the date of the next election, with those who obtain or
renew a license immediately after an election missing out until the next
time. Although the registration period ends as early as thirty days prior
to the election, during an election year, only some – those with license

[11] The discussion here focuses on transactions through motor vehicle offices. For the most
part, the same logic that applies to registration through motor vehicle offices applies to
public agency registration; thus, public agency registration is not discussed so as to avoid
redundancy and to simplify the discussion. Additionally, a much smaller percentage of
the population comes into contact with public agencies than with motor vehicle offices.
Mail registration is not separately discussed because it requires effort on the part of the
registrant similar to that required for registering at a government office.

renewal dates in October – will miss the opportunity to register due to an early closing date. More importantly, a separate trip to the polls is still necessary, and this requires an awareness of being registered, in addition to knowing the location of the polling place. Similar logic applies for those planning to vote by absentee ballot. Though a separate trip is not necessary, additional steps that cannot be handled by the motor vehicle offices are needed to request and cast the absentee ballot. To simplify the remaining discussion I focus on voting in person at a polling place.

Overall, with respect to those who "can't" vote, EDR and motor voter do work similarly. However, registering and voting under motor voter is a two-stop process; EDR requires only a single stop on election day. Therefore, the costs to individuals are lower in states that allow EDR than those in motor voter states, but not by much.

They Don't Want To. Simply put, on their own, neither EDR nor motor voter should be expected to change directly the likelihood of voting among those who fail to vote because they "don't want to." Whether registration is easier or even if registration were not required, individuals who do not have a sufficient level of interest in voting would maintain their status as nonregistrants and thus nonvoters. However, the availability of EDR or motor voter could change the political environment in a way that makes it more likely that individuals are mobilized and, through the process of mobilization, decide that they want to vote.[12] This brings us to Verba and colleagues' "Nobody asked" category.

Nobody Asked. As discussed earlier, under EDR, there is more time for individuals to develop and then act on an interest in voting. Although such interest might develop on its own, it seems more likely that the change in interest is sparked by some mobilization process. In EDR states, the candidates and campaigns have a longer period of time to get eligible citizens interested in voting (for them) through campaign ads, mailings, phone calls, door knocking, and so on (for research on these activities see, for example, Green and Gerber 2004; and Nickerson, Friedrichs, and King 2006). Thus, EDR can work through these mechanisms indirectly by facilitating the process by which unregistered but eligible citizens are encouraged to register and vote. In states that do not allow

---

[12] For example, another reform, the inclusion of ballot measures, has also been shown to increase interest and thus turnout (see, e.g., Smith and Tolbert 2004; Tolbert and Smith 2005).

EDR, those who passed up the opportunity to register through a driver's license transaction will not be able to act upon a late-developing interest in the election, propelled by being asked to vote, if the closing date has passed.

However, in the context of an upcoming election, citizens who register via motor voter are more likely to be mobilized than those who ultimately register on election day. Registration lists are an important tool used by political parties and candidates to identify prospective allies in the fight for victory on election day. The names of citizens who register via motor voter are placed on the lists in time for parties and candidates to seek their support. This makes it less likely that these individuals abstain because "nobody asked." Potential election day registrants, because they do not yet appear on registration lists, are more costly to identify, and therefore contact, than are those who previously registered.

However, although motor voter will place more names on registration lists, the mere presence of new names on a registration list may not be enough to generate a contact from the parties. Voter history is a key component of the databases maintained by the parties. Being on the registration list is likely to put individuals' names into the party database, but individuals without any history of voting will be viewed as more risky and thus reduce their likelihood of being contacted relative to those who have a history of voting (on the strategic nature of party contacts, see Rosenstone and Hansen 1993). For example, DeNardo (1980) notes that "peripheral voters are just as fickle inside the voting booth as they are about getting to it" (p. 418). In sum, both EDR and motor voter might increase the probability that an individual votes because somebody asked; however, the two policies differ with respect to the way this might occur.

More on Motivation. A key feature that distinguishes EDR from motor voter registration but does not fit cleanly into one of the aforementioned categories has to do with the intended targets and their respective motives. Motivation crept into some of the earlier discussion, but additional attention is warranted. EDR adds people to the rolls who, at the very least, are interested in voting in the election for which they register. EDR, like registration at a government office, is an explicitly political act. That is, election day registrants are purposeful registrants. They might never return, but to the extent that voting is habitual (Green and Shachar 2000; Plutzer 2002; Gerber, Green, and Shachar 2003), at least some portion will vote again.

Motor voter, on the other hand, casts a wide net and hits three types of people: 1) those who wanted to register in the first place and, therefore, do so; 2) those who did not initially intend to register, but do so when asked; and 3) those with absolutely no intention of registering, who choose not to register. The individuals in categories 1 and 2 might not vote for a variety of overlapping reasons. But those in group 2 are less likely to have the motivation to vote. Given their lack of motivation to register and their focus on the primary task of dealing with a driver's license transaction – an act not related to political participation – it is understandable that some will not recognize or will forget that they registered in the first place. The longer the lapse between the registration transaction and the election, which for major elections can be years, the more likely it is that a person will forget he or she has registered. As a result, although motor voter will add to the registration rolls, in order to add to vote totals, these individuals must acquire and maintain an awareness of their registration status, as well as an interest in the election and a willingness to bear the costs associated with going to the polls.

But wait, you might say, an important attribute unique to motor voter has been left out; under motor voter, individuals are *asked by a government official* if they would like to register. In this way, motor voter represents a step toward the goal of increased governmental responsibility for which Piven and Cloward and others vigorously fought. Yet this is a perspective from the outside that likely does not take on the same meaning for those on the ground. Registering to vote is not a widely celebrated event, and especially not when it is the consequence of a more pressing and nonpolitical pursuit, such as obtaining a driver's license.

In my view, other factors overwhelm any potential connection or reconnection with the government felt by motor voter registrants. For some, having to complete one more task at the department of motor vehicles might be considered yet another annoyance in an already overly bureaucratic activity. And this is putting it nicely. Although I have nothing more than anecdotal evidence on this point, I firmly believe that few, if any, would characterize their interactions with motor vehicle offices as enjoyable, and many can tell a series of horror stories. Thus, I simply do not believe that motor voter registration will be a transformative event for those who have been left out or have opted out of electoral politics. Being asked to vote by a motor vehicle clerk, through a question on a form, or even by a case worker, is not sufficient to overcome the lack of will to vote and does absolutely nothing on its own to provide the information (about the candidates, parties, issues, and other logistical matters) necessary to take the next step.

Teixeira (1992) argues that because motor voter "comes close to eliminating registration as a separate activity with its own costs," estimates of the effect of motor voter can be derived from estimates of the effect of EDR (p. 130). Highton and Wolfinger (1998) agree and use EDR as a proxy to predict the effect of the NVRA.

I have shown that there is more to the story; important distinctions between the programs require that they not be treated as substitutes. In sum, the acts themselves and their targets separate EDR from motor voter. Registering to vote on election day is a political behavior – registering to drive is not. Not all motor voter registrants will register, and among those who do, only those who overcome the psychological and other logistical barriers to vote will make the second trip on election day. However, it is true that for those who would have registered anyway, motor voter makes doing so more convenient.

I now set the study of EDR and motor voter into the broader context of treatment effects. In so doing, I will expose the nature of the random assignment assumption (a.k.a. exogenous selection).

The Identification Problem

Recent work by Manski (1989, 1990, 1994, 1995, 1997) on the study of treatment effects helps bring to light the power of traditional assumptions that are often downplayed or overlooked. As Manski (1995) notes, social scientists often ask questions in the form of: "What is the effect of ____ on ____?" (p. 21), where the first blank is filled in with some treatment and the second blank is filled in with the outcome of interest. The treatment of interest is routinely some public policy but could also take on a variety of other forms, including measures of behavioral choices such as how much education one received, family attributes such as whether one's parents divorced (Manski, Sandefur, McLanahan, and Powers 1992), being contacted by a political party, and so on. Here, the treatment of interest is the registration policy that is in place, EDR or motor voter, respectively. The explanation that follows uses EDR as the running example, but the same logic applies for electoral reforms generally, including motor voter.

The problems inherent with the data used to answer treatment-effect questions to which Manski draws attention apply straightforwardly to the study of electoral reforms, such as EDR. At any point in time, an individual either lives in a state that allows EDR or does not.[13] In the language of treatment effects, each individual receives only one of several possible treatments; here, one treatment would be living in a state that allows EDR, and another would be living in a state that does not allow EDR. Thus, with data on any one point in time, the type of data most commonly available,[14] one only observes the voting outcome for individuals in the context in which they live, and cannot observe how individuals would have acted in another context. In other words, we can observe the behavior of those who live in EDR states, but we cannot observe how those same individuals would behave if they lived in a state that does not allow EDR. Similarly and more directly related to the question of primary interest, we can observe the behavior of those who do not live in EDR states, but we cannot observe how those same individuals would behave if they lived in a state that allows EDR. This is known as an identification problem.

To help show the limitations of the data and, thus, the difficulty of estimating the effect of EDR on turnout, following Manski (1995), I now provide a series of definitions to describe what information is provided by the data so as to reveal the nature of the identification problem. The argument here excludes the equations that represent the concepts mathematically; the full details, adding in the mathematical representation of the concepts, can be found in the appendix to this chapter.[15]

Each individual can be characterized by values for their voting outcome, whether or not they receive the treatment of interest, and their individual attributes. For present purposes, the voting outcome represents information regarding whether or not each individual voted in a given election. The treatment of interest here is EDR, and each individual either lives in a state that has EDR or lives in a state that does not have EDR. The individual attributes provide descriptive information about the individuals, such as their age, education, and so on. For those who live in states with EDR, we can observe whether or not they voted when this policy was in place. Likewise, for those who live in states that do not allow EDR, we can observe whether or not they voted in the absence of

---

[13] Of course, some individuals have multiple residences. This does not complicate the analysis because only one residence can be used for voting.

[14] Although the National Election Studies panel studies are widely known and available, the samples are not drawn to be representative of state populations; plus, the number of individuals in the sample from the EDR states is small.

[15] Those interested in the discussion and mathematical representation of the concepts should turn now to this appendix and then return at the start of the next section.

this policy. Due to the identification problem, for each individual, we do not have information about how he/she would have behaved if the policy in his/her state had been different. In other words, as stated earlier, we are unable to observe how citizens in states that do not allow EDR would have behaved had EDR been allowed in their state.

Using the available information, the overall goal is to estimate the effect of EDR on the probability of voting. With data generated from a single election, the task boils down to a comparison of those living in states with EDR and those living in states that do not allow EDR. However, care must be taken to understand what the data reveal and what assumptions are necessary in order to obtain credible estimates. Before estimating the overall effect of EDR, two intermediate steps are necessary: 1) understanding how to estimate the probability of voting for individuals with some set of individual attributes if EDR were adopted in all states; and 2) understanding how to estimate the probability of voting for individuals with these attributes if EDR were not available in any of the states. Once these estimates are obtained, the effect of EDR can be estimated.[16]

The first intermediate step examines the probability that an individual will vote under the EDR treatment. There are four components that, when put together, provide an estimate of the probability of voting if EDR were available in all states. These components are:

1) the probability of voting for those living in EDR states;
2) the probability of living in a state that allows EDR (known as the selection probability);
3) the probability of voting for those who do not live in states that allow EDR, if they instead lived in a state that did allow EDR (here, this is the counterfactual probability); and
4) the probability of living in a state that does not allow EDR (known as the censoring probability).

Data from a sample of individuals living in states with EDR and without EDR will reveal components 1, 2, and 4 but will *not* reveal component 3. That is, component 3 represents how those living in states that do not allow EDR would behave if they were to live in a state that allows EDR, which, because they did not actually live in such a state, we are unable to observe.

[16] In the interest of simplicity, the discussion that follows ignores any conditioning based on individual attributes; see the appendix to this chapter for the inclusion of this information.

Using the law of total probability, the probability of voting if EDR were in place in all of the states can be specified using these four components. We know that in this situation we are dealing with just two scenarios – one either lives in a state that allows EDR or does not. Thus, we can think of the overall probability of voting that would result from the adoption of EDR in all states as the average of the probability of voting among those who live in states with EDR and the probability of voting among those who do not live in states with EDR, if they did have EDR available, weighted by the respective probabilities of living in each scenario. To obtain our estimate, we would first take the probability of voting among those who live in states with EDR and multiply this by the probability of living in a state with EDR. Both of these components can be obtained from the available data. This result would then be added to the result obtained by multiplying the probability of voting among those who live in states that do not allow EDR if they instead lived in states that allowed EDR by the probability of living in a state that does not allow EDR. However, as noted earlier, we are unable to observe the probability of voting among those who live in states that do not allow EDR if they instead were to live in states that allow EDR. Because the data reveal whether an individual voted or not under only one of the treatments (here, living in a state with EDR), more of the same type of data would not eliminate the identification problem (Manski 1995). After a brief discussion of the next intermediate step, I will discuss how researchers typically deal with this considerable problem.

The next intermediate step addresses the probability that an individual will vote if none of the states allowed EDR. The process discussed in detail earlier concerning the probability of voting under the EDR treatment applies here as well. As such, I will jump to the use of the law of total probability in order to demonstrate the problem with obtaining an estimate of the probability of voting if EDR were not available in any of the states. The data will reveal the probability of voting for those who live in states that do not allow EDR, and the respective probabilities of living in a state with EDR and a state without EDR. However, the data will *not* identify the probability of voting in the absence of EDR for those who actually live in states that allow EDR. In other words, we do not know how those living in EDR states would behave if EDR were not available. Again, more of the same type of data will not solve the problem.

The previous discussion reveals that without prior information or assumptions, neither the probability of voting if EDR were available in all states, nor the probability of voting if EDR were not available in any of the states can be identified. Thus, the classical treatment effect (here-after CTE), which reveals the effect of EDR on the probability of voting, and is simply the difference between these two probabilities, also is not identified. Manski (1995) discusses and evaluates how most researchers deal with the identification problem:

> The conventional practice is to invoke assumptions strong enough to identify the exact value of [the parameters of interest]. Even if these assumptions are not plausible, they are defended as necessary for inference to proceed. Yet identification is not an all-or-nothing proposition. Weaker and more plausible assumptions often suffice to bound parameters in informative ways (p. 8).

Specifically, the assumption commonly employed, most often implicitly, is that selection of the treatment is random (exogenous). But Manski's call for a shift in the way social scientists approach inference problems should be taken seriously. In the chapters that follow, I explore a num-ber of identifying assumptions. Here, as a final step in exposing the limitations in the traditional approach to this problem, I demonstrate the implications of the exogenous selection assumption, the assumption used in the literature to identify the effect of EDR on the probability of voting.

In order to identify the probability of voting if all states were to adopt EDR, researchers simply assume that if non-EDR states adopted EDR, those who live in them would have the same probability of voting as those who currently live in states with EDR. In other words, researchers assume that the process of selecting a given set of registration laws can be ignored, and thus, the social and political contexts that brought about the implementation of EDR in the states that already have it are not directly or indirectly associated with an individual's probability of voting. To bring the point to life, consider two 18-year-olds, identical on all demographic factors except the state in which they and their respective families were born and raised, with one calling Minnesota home and the other, Mississippi. When it comes to electoral politics, I contend that these individuals should not be treated as identical. They were socialized in distinct environments, those around them are not alike, and the rules that governed registration and voting for their grandparents and even their parents were vastly different.[17] Whereas Minnesota has a tradition of encouraging participation, Mississippi is stained by its history of actively

---

[17] One might argue that family history can be controlled for but such information is rarely available in traditional surveys.

seeking to prevent certain segments of the population, most obviously blacks, from voting. Moreover, even if Mississippi were to adopt EDR, to achieve outcomes similar to those in Minnesota, one would have to assume that the other institutional arrangements as well as the general level of support for participation among the citizenry would also shift to resemble Minnesota. Thus, not only should it be expected that the states in which these two individuals live would adopt a dissimilar set of laws, but even if the same law is implemented, individual responses to it should be expected to differ.

Similar logic applies to the probability of voting if none of the states allowed EDR. Here, it is assumed that if EDR were not allowed in states that currently have EDR, citizens would have the same probability of voting as those who do not live in EDR states. By making assumptions about the missing pieces from each of the intermediate steps, the effect of EDR can be determined by taking the difference between the probability of voting if all states were to adopt EDR and the probability of voting if none of the states allowed EDR. It turns out that when one assumes that the selection of registration laws is random (exogenous selection), the effect of EDR is simply the difference between two of the quantities that are revealed by the data – the probability of voting among those living in states that allow EDR and the probability of voting among those in states that do not allow EDR.

To recap, based on the theoretical explanations just provided, EDR is expected to have a positive impact on the probability of voting, such that the probability of voting when EDR is allowed should be greater than the probability of voting when EDR is not allowed. Under the exogenous selection assumption, the CTE is estimated to be the difference between the observed probability of voting among those in states with EDR and those in states that do not allow EDR. However, this requires one to believe that the effect found in one context *will be the same* when EDR is exported to other contexts. This is a strong and erroneous assumption. To conclude this section, I now turn to an examination of why one should expect the size of the effects to be conditioned by social and political context.

Why the Assumption Fails

We know that in the not-so-distant past, some states erected election laws with the purpose of keeping certain types of individuals away from the polls. We also know that the states that put forth these policies differed systematically from those that did not erect such laws. Even with the eradication of blatantly discriminatory practices, such as literacy tests and poll taxes, the states continue to chart different courses. The states that have adopted reforms that welcome voters represent the tastes of the citizens in those states for easier access to the voting booth. In the states that have failed to increase access, similar sentiments are less abundant, if not absent. Thus, not only do the states have distinct histories, systematic differences among the states persist, though the magnitude of the differences is surely smaller than it was prior to the Voting Rights Act of 1965. When the states that have a history of restricting access ease barriers to registration and turnout, the fit between institutions and the citizenry, at least initially, remains different from the fit found in states that traditionally promote participation, especially when the shift in policy is handed down from the federal government. I contend that this will have consequences for the effectiveness of the laws.

Piven and Cloward (1988) decry efforts to explain the rise and fall of turnout due to political stimuli, asserting that "political context determines whether [demographic or social psychological] factors will have a significant effect on participation, and just what those effects will be" (p. 117). They further contend that education, urbanization, and income should not be used as controls in studies of the impact of election laws on turnout because these factors determine the laws. This claim represents, on one hand, recognition that election laws are determined endogenously and, on the other hand, failure to understand how statistical methods can be used to assess the impact of these laws. Just because these variables have an impact on the choice of election laws does not prohibit them from having a subsequent impact on turnout. For example, it has long been established that as education increases, so too does the probability of voting. If elected officials, when deciding on the system of election laws, take the citizenry's education into account, the role education plays in the decision to vote at the individual level is not necessarily eliminated. However, as Piven and Cloward suggest, the effect of education on turnout is conditioned by the extent to which education is considered in the legislative process. A more accurate way to express the concern would be to say that in traditional models, the demographic and psychological variables included in the model are not adequate controls for the purposeful selection of election laws, thus resulting in misleading estimates of the effects of the independent variables on turnout (see Achen 1986). Although there appears to be confusion with regard to the details, Piven and Cloward are correct in suggesting that traditional approaches are inadequate. Further, recognizing that the rules that govern electoral behavior are not exogenous is a necessary first step toward improving our understanding of the effect of election laws on turnout.

Drawing on insights presented by March and Olsen (1984) helps complete the argument. March and Olsen (1984) contend that:

The distribution of political resources is ... partly determined endogenously. Political institutions affect the distribution of resources, which in turn affects the power of political actors, and thereby affects political institutions. Wealth, social standing, reputation for power, knowledge of alternatives, and attention are not easily described as exogenous to the political process and political institutions (p. 739).

Applying this to the issue at hand, one should expect that attention to politics, knowledge of alternatives, and interest in politics should be higher in places that tend to facilitate participation. In other words, attachments to the democratic system and the political parties will be deeper in such places. Thus, when administrative hurdles are removed, a larger pool of citizens will seek to take advantage of the easier procedures.

Prior to doing so, the states that originally adopted EDR were already high turnout states known for their participatory culture and, thus, had the most favorable conditions for responsiveness to EDR. When this policy is exported to other contexts, where connections to democratic norms are less strong, smaller effects should be expected. That is, whereas the room for improvement in states with already high levels of registration and turnout is smaller, those outside the system in states with low levels of registration will likely need more than the removal of an administrative hurdle to get them to the polls. Similarly, in states that adopted motor voter without having it imposed by the federal government, it should be expected that the passage and active implementation of state-level motor voter laws reflect the demand for easier access, and thus, a better fit between the institutions and the citizenry than when the federal government forces the issue into places where it was not in demand. Reflecting back on the discussion of the insights drawn from the categorization of Verba et al. (1995), I contend that the pool of those who "don't want to" vote, relative to those who "can't" vote, is expected to be smaller in states with stronger participatory traditions. The two primary hypotheses derived from this framework can be written as follows:

Hypothesis 1: The forces that lead to the selection of election laws condition their effect, such that the effect when controlling for endogeneity is smaller than when endogeneity is ignored.

Hypothesis 2: When states that already have a history of facilitating participation relax registration laws, the effects will be larger than those found in other contexts.

These two hypotheses might strike some as counterintuitive. Should not the largest effects be found where there is the most to gain (see Knack 2001)? My answer is no. I agree that there is greater potential in states with 60 percent registration as opposed to 80 percent registration, but there is little reason to expect that simply removing a relatively small barrier will open the flood gates of participation in places that have not shown a commitment to participation. Although EDR and motor voter differ in a number of respects, an important similarity is that if they work to increase turnout, they do so primarily through a reduction in the costs of voting. However, a reduction in costs is insufficient to increase turnout. The key ingredient to participation is motivation. Altering the costs does not alter motivation. Because voting is an expressive act, a prerequisite for these laws to have an effect on any given individual is for that person to form an attachment to the electoral system or some component of it, such as one of the parties. That is, these policies provide easier access for those who are already interested or who might become interested in voting; those with no interest in voting will remain on the outside. The size of the effects is thus a function of the proportion of citizens who have been prevented from registering but who have formed an attachment such that they desire to be a voter, or who, through the campaign, might come to do so. In turn, the proportion of citizens fitting this description is determined by the social and political contexts. These hypotheses are tested in Chapters 3 and 4.

IMPLEMENTING A NEW DESIGN

Following from my theoretical framework, any design seeking to assess the effect of registration laws on turnout must integrate multiple quantitative and qualitative methods. With respect to the quantitative analyses, I make methodological contributions through the use of statistical procedures that consider the purposeful nature of the selection of registration laws and allow for the critical evaluation of traditional assumptions about voting behavior that have not been given sufficient scrutiny. The qualitative analyses are crucial for demonstrating the reasons underlying the adoption of EDR across contexts, understanding implementation and party response, and ruling out alternative explanations.

The difference in difference approach (see Card 1992; Gruber 1994; Ruhm 1998; Besley and Case 2000) can be used to estimate the effects of a policy when one is concerned that the unobserved factors that lead to the selection of the policy and the outcome of interest are related.[18] This method employs data across multiple time periods, and takes endogeneity into account through the selection of control groups. Here, the treatment group is made up of individuals in states that adopt registration reform (EDR, or motor voter, respectively) and the control group is made up of individuals in *similar* states who do not experience the shift in policy.[19]

The difference in difference approach is not without critics. Besley and Case (2000), for example, study workers' compensation benefits in the construction industry and are cautious about recommending this approach. However, I believe their worries have more to do with the topic they study and their selection of states than the method itself.[20] The primary point of their critique, with which I agree, is that the estimates are sensitive to the choice of control states. Thus, prior to estimation, tremendous care must be taken to select credible control states.

Some scholars complain that little can be learned from the lessons of a single state, yet happily generalize the effects of a few states across the entire nation. I take a different approach. As noted earlier, it would be easier to estimate the effect of registration laws if researchers could randomly assign registration procedures across a variety of states, but that is impossible. So, we are, instead, left with the task of trying to figure out the effects when states selectively choose to make a change. The first step, in my view, is to determine what the effect was in the places adopting

[18] Timpone (1998) provides a model that recognizes voting as a two-stage process, arguing that registrants are not a random sample of eligible citizens. Although I find the argument compelling, I take the selection of the laws rather than individual selection into registration as being the more serious concern. Furthermore, the assumptions necessary to estimate a Heckman (1979) type model, as is used by Timpone, requires identification assumptions that utilize aggregate-level instruments. Achen (2008) provides a critique of the use of selection models for the study of registration and voting, and suggests that, for now, modeling turnout directly is the best strategy. Moreover, when using the difference in difference approach to estimate the effect of an aggregate-level variable, the model cannot be identified by using aggregate-level instruments.

[19] As applied here, the difference in difference approach is similar in spirit to matching techniques. Due to its transparency and simplicity, I prefer the difference in difference approach. One might also consider techniques that account for the clustering of the data, but in the present application, there are too few clusters to provide reliable estimates (Primo, Jacobsmeier, and Milyo 2007).

[20] Among the comparisons used by Besley and Case (2000) are Montana and Kentucky. I see little to recommend these two states as being comparable in terms of responsiveness to changes in workers' compensation benefits.

the new procedures. With this information in hand, the process of determining what would happen in other contexts can begin. This should be treated as serious business. Plugging new values into a probit equation is not enough. At the very least, the output needs to be evaluated in light of what we know about the real world as well as the methods and data used in our attempt to make sense of the real world. Through the careful interpretation of his results, Teixeira (1992) provides an excellent example of this. However, now that we have more experience and better tools, why not make some of these judgments before going to the data? I argue we should.

The nonparametric bounds approach, developed by Manski (1989, 1990, 1994, 1995, 1997), represents another alternative to traditional approaches that ignore endogeneity.[21] It is also quite flexible in that it does not make functional form or distributional assumptions, and thus relaxes the assumptions implicit in probit and logit models – most importantly, that the largest impact will be on those with a fifty–fifty chance of voting. Furthermore, the logic of the approach dictates that analysis begins with minimal assumptions and proceeds by explicitly layering on stronger assumptions. Thus, the power of various identifying assumptions can be examined. Additionally, the estimates from nonparametric models can then be used to test the predictions of traditional parametric models (Manski et al. 1992; Pepper 2000; Hanmer 2007).

The logical starting point for analysis is the investigation of the circumstances surrounding the implementation of registration reforms. I take the reasons for adoption to be a reflection of the attitudes toward participation in these states, and thus the conduciveness to increased turnout via relaxed registration laws. To establish the selective nature of the adoption of registration reform, I conducted archival research in the states that allowed EDR as of the 2000 election.[22] I use this information to construct legislative histories that provide insight into the intent of the laws. Not only do the legislative histories shed light on the partisan interest in EDR laws, they reveal that the adoption of EDR is not always motivated purely by concerns with increasing citizen participation.

---

[21] Instrumental variables approaches were considered but, as explained in Chapter 3, were not used. A state and year fixed-effects model is used to evaluate the NVRA.

[22] Piven and Cloward (2000) have, in large part, addressed the adoption and implementation of state motor voter laws as well as the NVRA. Moreover, because the NVRA was passed nearly 20 years after the first state motor law went into effect, the states that did not adopt at the state level can be assumed to have been less concerned with reducing the costs of voting than those that moved on motor voter prior to the NVRA.

To explore the possibility that differences in the underlying reasons for adopting EDR led to variations in implementation, I conducted interviews with officials in state elections divisions. During these interviews, I asked about efforts made to disseminate information about the laws, problems that arose, costs of implementation, the perceived effectiveness of EDR, and recommendations they would give to other officials who might consider instituting EDR.

Not only do election laws structure individual behavior, but they also structure party behavior. For example, Patterson and Caldeira (1985) note that when California moved to unrestricted absentee voting, the parties sought to promote the new law among their respective supporters. Although research on party responses is in short supply, Stein (1998) and Gronke, Galanes-Rosenbaum, Miller, and Toffey (2008) provide a discussion of the ways in which parties might respond to changes in reforms aimed at those who are already registered. Unfortunately, the dearth of empirical research is explained in large part by a lack of readily available data. Through interviews with party chairs in the states allowing EDR, I examined the ways in which political parties responded to this reform. I obtained information regarding mobilization strategies for registered as well as unregistered citizens, the perceived effectiveness of EDR, and how their strategies would change if EDR were not available. Because party behavior surrounding EDR has not been previously investigated, this work fills an important gap in our understanding of the effects of registration reform.

CONCLUSION

This chapter described the theoretical framework and analytical tools I use in the remainder of the book. It began by demonstrating the importance of the system of voter registration in the United States, both theoretically and normatively. With the exception of North Dakotans, all those who vote in the United States must first go through the process of registering to vote, a process that imposes a series of costs on the citizenry. Because these costs vary considerably and systematically across the states, concerns emerge regarding the equality of opportunity and, in turn, the equality of the outcomes. The failure of previous research to acknowledge properly the purposeful nature of self-selected registration laws has obscured our understanding of how registration reforms have worked in the places that have adopted them and how these reforms would work if adopted on a wider scale.

I next offered a theoretical framework that represents a new approach to the study of electoral reforms in the United States. By examining the mechanisms by which EDR and motor voter might increase turnout, with attention to the targets of the reforms and their motivations, I demonstrated that the theoretical difference between these institutional reforms requires that they not be treated as proxies for one another. Whereas election day registrants are primarily motivated by an interest in voting, this is not necessarily true for motor voter registrants, who are primarily engaging in a nonpolitical act – completing a driver's license transaction. Motivation, the key ingredient for expressive voting, has been overlooked in other ways as well. Because attitudes toward participation have been differentially cultivated in the states, reflected in their history of participation and policies to promote or discourage participation, doubt has been cast on the traditional assumptions applied to the study of electoral reforms. Using a simple mathematical model, this chapter exposed the power of the exogenous selection assumption. I have argued that it is erroneous to assume that the selection of registration laws is a random process; rather, the selection of registration laws is related to social and political contexts. Drawing on the insights from March and Olsen (1984) leads to the expectation of an endogenous relationship between participatory tradition and the effects of electoral reforms, such that the proportion of citizens who will respond when institutional reforms are introduced is conditioned by the social and political contexts. In other words, the effects of the reforms in one context should be expected to vary when the reforms are exported to other contexts.

This chapter concluded with the specification of two hypotheses that have not been previously tested, and a research design that combines quantitative and qualitative methods that have not yet been applied to this line of inquiry. Having called into question the exogenous selection assumption, it is necessary to provide evidence in support of my claim. Chapter 2 takes up this task.

Appendix

The information provided here uses as a base the text from the section on the *Identification Problem*, adding to it the mathematical representation of the concepts. Those choosing to read this appendix, upon completion, should return to the section on *Why the Assumption Fails*.

All individuals can be characterized by values for their voting outcome, whether or not they receive the treatment of interest, and their individual attributes. This information can be represented using the following variables: y_1, y_0, t, and x. The variable t represents whether or not an individual received the treatment in question; t is a binary variable – that is, it takes on one of just two values, either 1 or 0. For those living in states that allow EDR, the treatment of interest, t, is set to a value of 1, and for those living in states that do not allow EDR, t is set to 0. The variable x represents the covariates of interest that describe an individual, such as his/her age, education, and so on. The variable y_1 is defined as the voting outcome if an individual were to live in a state with EDR; y_1 takes on a value of 1 if such individuals vote, and y_1 takes on a value of 0 otherwise. The voting outcome if an individual lived in a state that does not allow EDR is represented by the variable y_0; y_0 takes on a value of 1 if such individuals vote and y_0 takes on a value of 0 otherwise. Due to the identification problem, for each individual, only one of the voting outcome variables, y_1 or y_0, is observed. One observes y_1 for those who actually live in states that allow EDR and one observes y_0 for those who live in states that do not allow EDR. That is, when $t = 1$, one observes a value for y_1, and when $t = 0$ one observes a value for y_0. In other words, as stated earlier, we are unable to observe how citizens in states that do not allow EDR would have behaved if EDR were allowed in their state.

From these definitions, a series of equations that expose the importance of the identification problem can be specified. The overall goal is to estimate the effect of EDR on the probability of voting. With data generated from a single election, the task boils down to a comparison of those living in states with EDR and those living in states that do not allow EDR. However, care must be taken to understand what the data reveal and what assumptions are necessary in order to obtain credible estimates. Before estimating the overall effect of EDR, two intermediate steps are necessary: 1) understanding how to estimate the probability of voting for individuals with some set of attributes, represented by x, if EDR were adopted in all states; and 2) understanding how to estimate the probability of voting for individuals with attributes x if EDR were not available in any of the states. Once these estimates are obtained, the effect of EDR can be estimated.

The first intermediate step examines the probability that a person with individual attributes x will vote under the EDR treatment. Employing the definitions given earlier, this can be represented as $P(y_1 = 1 \mid x)$, where P stands for probability. There are four components that, when put together, provide an estimate of the probability of voting if EDR were available in all states. These components are:

1) the probability of voting for those with individual attributes x living in EDR states, which can be expressed as $P(y_1 = 1 \mid x, t = 1)$;
2) the probability of living in a state that allows EDR given individual attributes x, $P(t = 1 \mid x)$ (known as the selection probability);
3) the probability of voting for those with individual attributes x who do not live in states that allow EDR, if they instead lived in a state that did allow EDR, $P(y_1 = 1 \mid x, t = 0)$ (here, this is the counterfactual probability); and
4) the probability of living in a state that does not allow EDR given individual attributes x, $P(t = 0 \mid x)$ (known as the censoring probability).

Data from a sample of individuals living in states with EDR and without EDR will reveal components 1, 2, and 4 but will *not* reveal component 3. Component 3 represents how those living in states that do not allow EDR would behave if they lived in a state that allows EDR. Given that they did not actually live in such a state, we are unable to observe their behavior.

Using the law of total probability, the probability of voting, given the individual level characteristics of interest, if EDR were in place in all of the states, $P(y_1 = 1 \mid x)$, can specified using these four components. We know that in this situation we are dealing with just two scenarios, one either lives in a state that allows EDR or does not. Thus, we can think of the overall probability of voting that would result from the adoption of EDR in all states as the average of the probability of voting among those who live in states with EDR and the probability of voting among those who do not live in states with EDR, if they were to have had EDR available, weighted by the respective probabilities of living in each scenario. To obtain our estimate, we would first take the probability of voting among those with attributes x who live in states with EDR and multiply this by the probability of living in a state with EDR among those with attributes x. Both of these components can be obtained from the available data. This result would then be added to the result obtained by multiplying the probability of voting among those with attributes x who live in states that do not allow EDR if they instead lived in states that allowed EDR by the probability of living in a state that does not allow EDR among those with attributes x. However, as noted earlier, we are unable to observe the probability of voting among those with attributes x, who live in states that do not allow EDR if they instead were to live in states that allow EDR. Because the data reveal whether an individual voted or not under only one of the treatments (here, living in a state with EDR), more of the same type of data would not eliminate the identification problem (Manski 1995). The process we are seeking to understand can be expressed mathematically as follows:

$$P(y_1 = 1 \mid x) = P(y_1 = 1 \mid x, t = 1)^* P(t = 1 \mid x)$$
$$+ P(y_1 = 1 \mid x, t = 0)^* P(t = 0 \mid x). \qquad (1)$$

After a brief discussion of the next intermediate step I will discuss how researchers typically deal with this considerable problem.

The next intermediate step addresses the probability that an individual, with attributes x, will vote if none of the states allowed EDR. This can be represented as $P(y_0 = 1 \mid x)$. The process discussed in detail earlier concerning the probability of voting under the EDR treatment applies here as well. As such, I will jump to the use of the law of total probability in order to demonstrate the problem with obtaining an estimate of the probability of voting if EDR were not available in any of the states, $P(y_0 = 1 \mid x)$, which can be expressed as:

$$P(y_0 = 1 \mid x) = P(y_0 = 1 \mid x, t = 0)^* P(t = 0 \mid x)$$
$$+ P(y_0 = 1 \mid x, t = 1)^* P(t = 1 \mid x). \qquad (2)$$

The data will reveal the probability of voting for those with attributes x who live in states that do not allow EDR, $P(y_0 = 1 \mid x, t = 0)$; and the respective probabilities, among those with attributes x, of living in a state with EDR and a state without EDR, $P(t = 1 \mid x)$ and $P(t = 0 \mid x)$, as they were defined earlier. However, the data will *not* identify the probability of voting, among those with attributes x who live in states that allow EDR if they instead lived in states without EDR, $P(y_0 = 1 \mid x, t = 1)$. In other words, we do not know how those living in EDR states would behave if EDR were not available. Again, more of the same type of data will not solve the problem.

The previous discussion reveals that without prior information or assumptions, neither the probability of voting if EDR were available in all states, $P(y_1 = 1 \mid x)$, nor the probability of voting if EDR were not available in any of the states, $P(y_0 = 1 \mid x)$, can be identified.[23] Thus, the classical treatment effect (hereafter CTE), which reveals the effect of EDR on the probability of voting, and is simply the difference between these two probabilities [that is, the CTE can be defined as $P(y_1 = 1 \mid x) - P(y_0 = 1 \mid x)$], is also not identified. Manski (1995) discusses and evaluates how most researchers deal with the identification problem:

> The conventional practice is to invoke assumptions strong enough to identify the exact value of [the parameters of interest]. Even if these assumptions are not plausible, they are defended as necessary for inference to proceed. Yet identification is not an all-or-nothing proposition. Weaker and more plausible assumptions often suffice to bound parameters in informative ways (p. 8).

Specifically, the assumption commonly employed, most often implicitly, is that selection of the treatment is random (exogenous). But Manski's call for a shift in the way social scientists approach inference problems should be taken seriously. In the chapters that follow, I explore a number of identifying assumptions. Here, as a final step in exposing the limitations in the traditional approach to this problem, I demonstrate the implications of the exogenous selection assumption, the assumption used in the literature to identify the effect of EDR on the probability of voting.

---

[23] In the interest of simplicity and flow, though it still applies, I now eliminate the language related to the individual attributes x. However, it should be noted that all of the discussion and equations would remain valid if the individual attributes were not included.

In order to identify the probability of voting if all states were to adopt EDR, $P(y_1 = 1 \mid x)$, researchers simply assume that if non-EDR states adopted EDR, those who live in them would have the same probability of voting as those who currently live in states with EDR. In other words, researchers assume that the process of selecting a given set of registration laws can be ignored and, thus, the social and political contexts that brought about the implementation of EDR in the states that already have it are not directly or indirectly associated with an individual's probability of voting. To bring the point to life, consider two 18-year-olds, identical on all demographic factors except the state in which they and their respective families were born and raised, with one calling Minnesota home and the other, Mississippi. When it comes to electoral politics, these individuals should not be treated as identical. They were socialized in distinct environments, those around them are not alike, and the rules that governed registration and voting for their grandparents and even their parents were vastly different.[24] Whereas Minnesota has a tradition of encouraging participation, Mississippi is stained by its history of actively seeking to prevent certain segments of the population, most obviously blacks, from voting. Moreover, even if Mississippi were to adopt EDR, to achieve outcomes similar to those in Minnesota, one would have to assume that the other institutional arrangements as well as the general level of support for participation among the citizenry would also shift to resemble Minnesota. Thus, not only should it be expected that the states in which these two individuals live would adopt a dissimilar set of laws, but even if the same law is implemented, individual responses to it should be expected to differ.

With respect to the probability of voting if none of the states allowed EDR, $P(y_0 = 1 \mid x)$, similar logic applies. Here, it is assumed that if EDR were not allowed, those who currently live in EDR states would have the same probability of voting as those who now do not live in EDR states. By making assumptions about the missing pieces from equation (1) and equation (2), the effect of EDR can be determined by taking the difference between the probability of voting if all states were to adopt EDR and the probability of voting if none of the states allowed EDR. It turns out that when one assumes that the selection of registration laws is random (exogenous selection), the effect of EDR is simply the difference between two of the quantities that are revealed by the data – the probability of

---

[24] One might argue that family history can be controlled for but such information is rarely available in traditional surveys.

voting among those living in states that allow EDR and the probability of voting among those in states that do not allow EDR.

The previous discussion regarding the exogenous selection assumption and its implications for the calculation of the effect of EDR can be summarized mathematically as follows:

$$P(y_1 = 1 \mid x) = P(y_1 = 1 \mid x, t = 1) = P(y_1 = 1 \mid x, t = 0); \quad \text{and}$$
$$P(y_0 = 1 \mid x) = P(y_0 = 1 \mid x, t = 0) = P(y_0 = 1 \mid x, t = 1).$$

Because the data reveal $P(y_1 = 1 \mid x, t = 1)$ and $P(y_0 = 1 \mid x, t = 0)$, and it is assumed that the former stands in for the missing piece from equation (1) and the latter for the missing piece from equation (2), this assumption serves to identify $P(y_1 = 1 \mid x)$ and $P(y_0 = 1 \mid x)$. Once those quantities are identified, the CTE can be identified as follows:

$$CTE = P(y_1 = 1 \mid x) - P(y_0 = 1 \mid x)$$
$$= P(y_1 = 1 \mid x, t = 1) - P(y_0 = 1 \mid x, t = 0). \tag{3}$$

To recap, based on the theoretical explanations provided, EDR is expected to have a positive impact on the probability of voting, such that the probability of voting when EDR is allowed should be greater than the probability of voting when EDR is not allowed, $P(y_1 = 1 \mid x) > P(y_0 = 1 \mid x)$. Under the exogenous selection assumption, the CTE is estimated to be the difference between $P(y_1 = 1 \mid x)$ and $P(y_0 = 1 \mid x)$. However, this requires one to believe that the effect found in one context *will be the same* when EDR is exported to other contexts. This is a strong and erroneous assumption.

2

The Purposeful Adoption of Election Day Registration

That laws, and election laws specifically, are adopted purposefully seems noncontroversial. Yet the literature on the impact of electoral reform has failed to take this into account. To gain a complete understanding of the effect of election day registration (EDR) on turnout, it is first necessary to explore the reasons behind the adoption of EDR. Toward this end, I created legislative histories that are important descriptively, but more essentially serve to provide insight into legislative intent and the political environment that existed when EDR was adopted.

I approached the task of discerning legislative intent the same way in each state. Information required for the legislative histories *cannot* be obtained through commonly used legal research methods such as Lexis-Nexis or library work in a single state. Thus, I traveled to the capitals of each state that currently allows EDR and conducted archival research in a variety of locations, including state historical societies, state archives, state law libraries, state libraries, and legislative services offices.

My general approach can be described as follows. First, using the annotated revised statutes, I located the current version of the law as it relates to voter registration and traced its history. Upon reaching the law that first put EDR into effect, I examined the *House* and *Senate Journals*.[1] When available, I then examined the relevant committee folders, drafting records, and statements of purpose. Other official documents as well as newspaper reports were also examined. To assess the partisan make-up of the votes, I also collected rosters from the state legislative

---

[1] In Maine, the *Legislative Record* serves the same purpose as the *House* and *Senate Journals*.

houses and matched them with the legislative documents in which the "ayes" and "nays" were recorded. Although the approach was the same, some pastures were greener than others. Like election laws, legislative record keeping varies from state to state. Copious records are kept in some states – for example, New Hampshire – but little is available in others.

This chapter is structured straightforwardly. I begin chronologically, with analysis of the states that broke new ground by adopting EDR in the 1970s – Minnesota, Maine, and Wisconsin – and finish with the states that backed into EDR in 1993 and 1994 – Wyoming, New Hampshire, and Idaho. Ultimately, the results provide unambiguous support for my claims that the adoption of registration reform is purposeful and that the circumstances leading to the adoption of EDR in Maine, Minnesota, and Wisconsin differ substantially from those in Wyoming, New Hampshire, and Idaho. In other words, for the study of EDR, the exogenous selection assumption is indefensible.

EARLY AND ENTHUSIASTIC ADOPTERS (MINNESOTA, MAINE, AND WISCONSIN)

Minnesota (Blondes and Blue Ears Have More Fun Voting)

In 1973, Minnesota became the first state to allow EDR at polling places. This marked the first year (according to records dating back to 1951) during which the Democrats (called Democratic-Farmer-Labor or DFL in Minnesota) controlled the State Legislature; Democrats held 57 percent of the sixty-seven seats in the Senate and 58 percent of the 134 seats in the House. In addition, the Governor was a Democrat. As will be clear from the analysis that follows, this proved advantageous for the Democrats, who were supportive of EDR. Although audiotapes of floor sessions are currently available, the sessions were not recorded in 1973.[2] Minutes from House and Senate committee hearings, Journals of the House and Senate, Minnesota Statutes, and newspaper accounts[3] were used to trace the history and gain insight into the intent behind the adoption of EDR in Minnesota.

The 1973, the Minnesota Legislature considered two bills with provisions to establish EDR. At the time, the closing date for registration

---

[2] Audiotapes for sessions from 1985 to present are available.
[3] The Minnesota Legislative Reference Library maintains clipping files containing newspaper articles on a variety of topics. The articles cited here were obtained using the elections subject files.

in Minnesota was twenty days prior to the election.[4] The possibility of establishing EDR in Minnesota was among nine topics discussed during the January 29, 1973 meeting of the House's General Legislation and Veterans Affairs subcommittee on Elections. Unfortunately, details of the dialogue between the three DFL and two Republican members of the subcommittee were not recorded. Shortly thereafter, on February 15, 1973, five DFL members in the State House of Representatives introduced House File (HF) 605 (also known as Senate File [SF] 648). The bill was limited in scope; it proposed allowing EDR only at polling places in areas that had a permanent registration system. HF 605 was considered in a joint session of the Elections subcommittees in both chambers, and later, with amendments related to how eligible citizens could provide proper identification, was re-referred to the full Committee on General Legislation and Veterans Affairs, where it died. Two DFL members and one Republican in the State Senate introduced SF 1246 (also known as HF 1395), a more encompassing bill than HF 605, on March 15, 1973.[5] It is important to note that on April 7, both HF 605 and SF 1246 were amended such that the EDR provisions from HF 605 were incorporated into SF 1246.

With respect to discerning legislative intent, the minutes from a special joint Senate-House subcommittee on Elections, on April 3, 1973, are especially informative. During this meeting, both HF 605 and SF 1246 were discussed, with SF 1246 garnering the most attention. The minutes related to HF 605 indicate that Democratic Senator John Milton explained the foundation for his support of EDR, arguing that exercising one's citizenship via voting was difficult in the United States. Bob Meek, co-chairman of the Governor's Voter Participation committee, provided comparable testimony on SF 1246. The records indicate the committee was "appointed to try to improve voter participation in Minnesota" and that Mr. Meek contended that the "voter registration process itself blocks personal participation in elections" (p. 3). Among his recommendations was a provision for EDR, but with a penalty to election day registrants in the form of a separate line for registration transactions. Not everyone supported EDR. A representative from the League of Women Voters and the Republican Secretary of State were supportive of some of the bill's other provisions but expressed concern with EDR. The League of Women Voters submitted a letter suggesting that EDR was not necessary,

---

[4] Until 1984, registration was not required in all of Minnesota's political subdivisions.
[5] As discussed subsequently, just after passage of SF 1246 in the Senate, the Republican author, Senator Robert Brown, had his name removed as a co-author.

might cause delays on election day, and that devoting more resources to preregistration would be more effective. Disappointingly, the nature of the Secretary of State's concerns was not documented. The joint meeting is also noteworthy because the first of several documented differences between the parties emerged during the meeting. The Associate Chairs of the Republican and Democratic parties both voiced their opinions on EDR, with the Republican speaking against EDR and the Democrat for EDR.

Additional information is provided in the minutes for the April 19 meeting of the Senate's Transportation and General Legislation committee. At this meeting, Senator Stephen Keefe, a Democrat and one of the main authors of SF 1246, revealed his view that "the bill would reduce incidents of fraud and make it easier to vote" (p. 2). Although Republican Senator Robert Brown, also a co-author of the bill, moved to delete the bill's EDR sections, the motion failed to pass. All six of the votes against deletion were from DFL members and Republicans cast all three of the votes for deletion. This was the first of several votes that followed party lines.

On April 23, 1973, the full House General Legislation and Veterans Affairs committee received SF 1246. During the meeting, Representative David Cleary, a Republican, offered an amendment to require that EDR apply only to those political subdivisions that elect to adopt the EDR provisions. Partisan differences surfaced yet again. The vote closely followed party lines and the amendment failed. Nine voted for the amendment (all Republicans) and fourteen (thirteen DFLers and one Republican) voted against the amendment.

May 10 was a busy day for SF 1246 in the Senate. A number of amendments were proposed, including one by Republican Carl Jensen to remove EDR from the bill. The EDR sections were kept in the bill on a vote of twenty-nine for their removal and thirty-four against their removal. Only one Democrat voted to remove EDR whereas twenty-eight Republicans did so; all of those voting against the removal of EDR were Democrats. The third reading of SF 1246 in the Senate also took place on May 10. The bill passed, with thirty-six voting for passage, all but one of whom were Democrats, and twenty-eight against, only two of whom were Democrats. However, the bill did not move directly to the House; the next day, Senator Harmon Ogdahl, the lone Republican to have voted for passage, moved to reconsider the vote. On the vote whether to reconsider, the number of Senators present differed from the previous day; three Republicans who were absent for the vote on May 10 voted on May 11, and one Democrat who voted on May 10 was absent, and thus did not vote. This gave the Republicans a better chance to defeat EDR. Although the Republicans were united, only one Democrat voted with them and the motion to reconsider failed (thirty-one voted to reconsider and thirty-four voted against the motion to reconsider). Among those present for both votes, with the exception of two Senators, the vote matched the original vote for passage. Those who voted against passage on May 10 voted to reconsider on May 11 and those who voted for passage on May 10 voted against reconsideration on May 11.

Several newspaper articles covered the passage of SF 1246 in the Senate. The articles present the arguments from both supporters and opponents of the bill and EDR specifically. In a May 11 article by Dave Giel, a staff writer for the *St. Paul Pioneer Press*, Senator Brown was quoted as saying that EDR offered "a clearcut invitation to corruption" and that during the debate he asserted: "I've never seen a piece of legislation make me so sick in the four seasons I've been here." In light of these comments, it is not surprising that Senator Brown had his name as one of the co-authors removed. Also on May 11, two newspaper articles provided information from interviews with Senator Keefe regarding SF 1246's goals and purposes. In the *Minneapolis Tribune*, staff writer Robert Franklin quotes Senator Keefe as saying: "It's up to government and us as elected officials to do everything in our power to help people vote." Dave Giel, in the *St. Paul Pioneer Press*, reported that, according to Senator Keefe, SF 1246 would lead to increased turnout, would provide improved protections against fraud, and would "treat voting as a right not a privilege and [was] designed to make voting as easy as possible." As mentioned earlier, the Republicans thought there were ulterior motives. In the articles by Franklin and Giel, the Republicans claimed the bills would put rules into place that would favor the Democratic party and would also encourage fraud. The battles over EDR were not quite over; EDR still had to make it through the House.

Perhaps fueled by their colleagues in the Senate, Republicans in the House sought to prevent the adoption of EDR. Two attempts to thwart EDR were made on May 16. First, Republican Representative John Johnson moved to delete the sections of SF 1246 that dealt with EDR. The motion failed on a vote of fifty-two for the deletion of EDR and seventy-three against the deletion of EDR. Fifty of fifty-two Republicans voted to delete EDR and seventy-one of seventy-three Democrats voted to keep EDR. Although he failed in committee, Representative Cleary tried one more time to leave the decision to adopt EDR up to the municipalities.

Again the vote was divided along party lines, and again Cleary's attempt failed. The vote was fifty-two for his motion and seventy-six against it; one Democrat and fifty-one Republicans voted in the affirmative, and one Republican and seventy-five Democrats voted in the negative. The House ultimately passed SF 1246 on a seventy-seven-to-forty-two vote, with seventy-three of the seventy-seven votes for passage coming from Democrats and thirty-nine of the forty-two votes against cast by Republicans.

According to an article appearing in the *Fergus Falls Daily Journal* on August 16, 1973, by Associated Press writer Gerry Nelson, Secretary of State Erdahl recommended that the Governor veto SF 1246. Notwithstanding the advice of the Republican Secretary of State, the Democratic Governor signed the bill into law on May 24, 1973 and it was implemented for the 1973 elections.

Minnesota is widely known as a state that encourages participation and has clean elections. The avowed purpose of SF 1246, to make voting easier in Minnesota, fits with that tradition. However, as the bill neared passage, members of the Republican party asserted that the Democrats sought to use provisions of the bill, such as EDR, to extend their newfound control of the legislature. If this were their intention, one surely would not expect them to admit to it. However, even if the Democrats intended to use SF 1246 to maintain or enhance their control, increasing turnout was the mechanism by which this would have occurred. Certainly, this is a less pure motivation, but nonetheless, increased turnout was an important goal. In the spirit of Minnesota's tradition, Gerry Nelson, in the article cited earlier, reported that Secretary of State Erdahl encouraged county clerks, who largely opposed the law, not to seek changes in the 1974 legislative session.

Maine (the Way Voting Should Be)[6]

Maine extended EDR to all eligible citizens in the state in the same year Minnesota established EDR. Unlike Minnesota (discussed earlier) and Wisconsin (discussed subsequently), the Republicans controlled the legislature that adopted EDR in Maine.[7] Although, in Maine, floor

---

[6] Upon entering Maine by car, one might see welcome signs with the words "Welcome to Maine: the Way Life Should Be."

[7] In 1973, there were eleven Democrats and twenty-two Republicans in the Senate and seventy-two Democrats and seventy-nine Republicans in the House.

debates are transcribed in the *Legislative Record* and Statements of Fact were kept in 1973, records of committee proceedings or other such documents that might indicate intent were not available. With respect to the expansion of EDR throughout the state, little was recorded.

On February 1, 1973, Elden Shute, a Republican in the State Senate, presented a bill, Legislative Document (LD) 556 (known as Senate Paper 206, amended as LD 1535, and adopted as LD 1916), to revise election laws. The bill was signed into law as Chapter 414 of 1973 with an effective date of October 3, 1973. According to the Statement of Fact, section 631 of LD 556 standardized registration schedules in all municipalities. Specifically, this section provided for EDR in all municipalities. Previous law set the closing date to vary by municipality size, with EDR allowed only in municipalities with 2,500 people or less.[8] It is important to note that registration transactions on election day were not (and are still not) always processed at the polling places.

In the *Legislative Record* for March 26, Senator Shute explained that LD 556 resulted from a study committee made up of clerks, legislators, citizens, and boards of registration to "[bring the laws] up to date in the light of changes brought on by congressional edict or by the Supreme Court" (1228). Although a number of provisions, for example, changing the residency requirement, resulted from changes at the national level, this was not the case for EDR. However, EDR is certainly consistent with the climate of making voting easier.

Although there was discussion in the legislature relating to EDR, it was not contentious. Rather, most of the statements relating to EDR served to provide clarification. On April 5, Republican Representative Rodney Ross explained that whereas the original version of the bill in the House allowed EDR in special elections, he meant for EDR to be allowed in regular elections, too. In addition, on April 9, he noted that the Senate version provided for EDR at all elections, but maintained variations in the closing date prior to the election based on municipality size. By establishing a statewide standard, Representative Ross said he "went a little too far" because "the needs for keeping the office hours vary from town to town" (*Legislative Record*, April 9, 1973, p. 1487). As a result, amendments allowing EDR at all elections and maintaining local variation in office hours were presented. These amendments were

---

[8] Dating back to the 1800s, registration on election day was possible in municipalities with fewer than 500 voters. Since 1961, EDR has been available in municipalities with a population of 2,500 or fewer.

subsequently adopted.[9] Wrangling over a number of issues, not including EDR, delayed the bill's progress, much to the chagrin of Senator Shute, who, on May 17, expressed his irritation with the length of time the bill spent in the House. Senator Shute did not have to wait much longer, as the bill was sent to the Governor, Democrat Kenneth Curtis, for signature on May 24, 1973 and was signed into law the next day.

Because considerable debate regarding other features of the bill took place, the lack of debate on EDR suggests that the expansion of EDR in 1973 was widely desired. However, by 1977, support for EDR had diminished somewhat. This was evidenced by the introduction of LD 197 by two Republicans and two Democrats in the House. The initial draft of LD 197 scaled back EDR considerably, allowing EDR only for those who became eighteen within thirty days prior to the election or those "who [became] eligible to vote in the municipality within 30 days prior to election day" (February 2, 1977, p. 2). The Statement of Fact notes that EDR was burdensome to boards of registration and registrars, and made it possible for people to commit fraud by registering and voting in more than one place without being noticed.

On June 7, two competing drafts emerged out of the Committee on Election Laws; LD 1864 was supported by the majority and maintained EDR, whereas LD 1865 was the minority's version and kept the limits on EDR that were part of the first draft. Whereas partisanship did not seem to play a role in 1973, in 1977, the parties were split on EDR. Six Democrats and one Republican signed the majority report; five Republicans and one Democrat signed the minority report. On June 8, the House adopted the majority version on a seventy-nine to fifty-five vote, thus keeping EDR. The vote closely followed party lines, with 91 percent of the votes for the majority version coming from Democrats and 87 percent of the votes against coming from Republicans.

The Senate also considered both LD 1864 and LD 1865. During the debate on the floor of the Senate, Republican Bennett Katz argued against EDR. Senator Katz asserted that if the government were to become unstable due to civil unrest, widespread fraud would be easier under EDR and that although he

[did not] want to take anyone's rights away, . . . American citizens . . . have responsibilities and [he was] equally concerned that Americans today do not necessarily live up to their responsibilities as much as they should (*Legislative Record* June 17, 1977, p. 1779).

---

[9] When requested and agreed to by one fifth of those present and voting, roll call votes were recorded; for these motions, such a request was not made.

Also speaking on June 17 was Democratic Senator Peter Danton. He began by expressing his hope that the issue not be made a partisan one.[10] Senator Danton went on to say he talked with local officials and made it clear that "if they thought there wasn't going to be any registration on election day, they were just kidding themselves" but that the process could be made easier, something LD 1864 sought to do. On a vote of sixteen for and nine against, LD 1864 prevailed. Without further delay, LD 1864 passed through the Legislature, was sent to the Governor, Independent James Longley, on June 22, and was signed on July 1, becoming Chapter 431 of 1977.

The analysis just provided indicates that in the spirit of making voting easier, Maine made a number of changes to the laws governing registration and voting. Although one might argue that EDR was simply the byproduct of a concern with establishing a statewide standard, further analysis fails to support such a view. Establishing a statewide standard was surely an important goal, but it could have been accomplished in two ways: 1) by eliminating EDR in municipalities with 2,500 or fewer people; or 2) by expanding EDR to all eligible citizens. If increased participation was not a central concern, option 1) or maintaining the status quo could have been chosen. In addition, because differences in the dates for closing registration prior to its reopening on election day were preserved, applying a single standard could not have been the primary motivation.

Wisconsin (EDR Moves Forward in America's Dairyland)

Wisconsin was the third state to adopt EDR, doing so in 1975.[11] The analysis that follows is based on records from the *Journal of the Assembly*, the *Journal of the Senate*, Wisconsin Session Laws, and public hearing reports.

Upon a request from the Democratic Governor, Patrick J. Lucey, twelve Democratic State Senators and one Republican, along with three Democrats in the State Assembly, introduced Senate Bill (SB) 234 of 1975,

---

[10] The 1977 Senate was made up of twelve Democrats and twenty-one Republicans, and the House was composed of eighty-seven Democrats and sixty-four Republicans. Senator Danton alluded to the advantage held by the Democrats in the House, asserting that if LD 1846, with its modifications to current law that would ease the burden of EDR on local officials, did not pass, the House would surely just allow the status quo to prevail.

[11] Election administration in Wisconsin is handled at the municipal level. Prior to the Help America Vote Act's statewide registration database requirement, municipalities with fewer than 5,000 people did not have to require voter registration. The previous closing date in municipalities requiring registration was thirteen days.

a bill to reform voter registration laws in Wisconsin. A key component of this bill was a provision to allow EDR.

Partisan battles over SB 234 were waged in both chambers. The Democrats controlled the legislature; the Senate was made up of nineteen (58 percent) Democrats and fourteen (42 percent) Republicans, and the Assembly had sixty-three (64 percent) Democrats and thirty-six (36 percent) Republicans. When the bill passed the Senate, the vote was eighteen for passage and fourteen against; all of the votes for passage were from Democrats, with a lone Democrat voting no and one Republican not voting. Republicans in the Assembly fought the bill to the end. After consideration of all amendments, four attempts to prevent passage were made by Assembly Republicans. Each attempt was thwarted, with voting along party lines at each turn. The bill ultimately passed with a sixty-one to thirty-one vote; fifty-eight of fifty-nine Democrats voted for passage and thirty of thirty-three Republicans voted against.

Statements regarding the intent of the law can be found in the records of the public hearing, in the text of the law, and in a message from Governor Lucey. Each presents similar sentiments. Records from the Addendum to Bill History, prepared by the Legislative Council Staff, document the arguments that were raised in favor and against SB 234 at the public hearing. Because there were not any appearances against the bill, there were not any arguments against it. Among the arguments raised in favor of the bill were that it "would rectify many of the shortcomings and inequities in our present voter registration laws" and that the "bill is designed to remove all unreasonable impediments to voting and to insure that all qualified electors will be afforded ample opportunity to register and vote" (Addendum to Bill History, 1975 Senate Bill 234, p. 3).

The intent is also captured in the text of the law, and perhaps most clearly:

The legislature finds that the vote is the single most critical act in a democratic system of government; that voter registration was not intended to and should not prevent voting; that registration should simply be a remedy against fraud and its burden be placed upon administrators, not the electorate ... and that the act of personal registration is a major cause of limited electoral participation. Therefore, pursuant to the policy of this state and nation to ensure all people the right to vote, the legislature finds it imperative to expand voter registration procedures (Wisconsin Session Laws 1975, c. 85, § 1).

Governor Lucey, in a letter to the Senate on October 9, 1975, presents a positive view of the EDR component of SB 234:

By providing for postcard registration and registration at the polls on election day, it will remove some of the artificial barriers which have discouraged voter participation in past elections. The bill is in the best tradition of our democratic form of government and it has my enthusiastic support (*Journal of the Senate*, 1975, p. 1474).

He goes on to address concerns with fraud as well, noting that "the bill is carefully drafted and provides necessary safeguards against abuse" (*Journal of the Senate*, 1975, p. 1474).

The sentiment in Wisconsin can be summarized as follows. Registration laws were recognized as an impediment to voting, and although fraud was a concern, it was viewed as the responsibility of election officials, not the citizenry, to prevent it. Simply put, Wisconsin sought to increase participation by removing administrative hurdles faced by its eligible citizens.

Although the records in Minnesota and Maine do not make the case as clear cut as it is in Wisconsin, these three states were pioneers in the realm of registration reform. I now turn to states that chose not to adopt EDR until they were faced with the prospect of implementing motor voter, a law they considered an unfunded federal mandate and a threat to local control.

RECENT AND RELUCTANT ADOPTERS (WYOMING, NEW HAMPSHIRE, IDAHO)

Wyoming (Circling the Wagons against Federal Intervention)

Since 1951, Wyoming has allowed EDR at primary elections. On March 5, 1993, Mike Sullivan, the Democratic Governor of Wyoming, approved House Bill (HB) 312 of 1993, which expanded EDR to general elections and exempted Wyoming from the NVRA. At the time, the NVRA had not yet passed and the NVRA's nonapplicability clause, section 4(b)(2), allowed states with EDR at polling places an exemption from the NVRA's requirements. Prior to Wyoming's adoption of EDR, Section 4(b) was written as follows:

(b) NONAPPLICABILITY TO CERTAIN STATES. – This Act does not apply to a State described in either or both of the following paragraphs:

(1) A State in which there is no voter registration requirement for any voter in the State with respect to an election for Federal office.

(2) A State in which all voters in the State may register to vote at the polling place at the time of voting in a general election for Federal office (H.R. 2 1993, February 18).

The first paragraph of section 4(b) was written to apply to North Dakota, the only state that does not have a voter registration system; and the second section applied to Minnesota and Wisconsin.[12]

Soon after Wyoming passed EDR, on March 16, 1993, U.S. Senator Wendell Ford of Kentucky offered an amendment, with language drafted by U.S. Senator Al Simpson of Wyoming, that inserted a cutoff date into the nonapplicability clause. In the *Congressional Record* for March 16, Senator Ford, in response to a question from Senator Simpson, noted that the addition of the cutoff date was intended to address the situation in Wyoming. Specifically, the amendment added that states that had a law allowing EDR at polling places that was "in effect continuously on and after March 11, 1993, or that was enacted on or prior to March 11, 1993" were exempt (42 U.S.C. 1973gg-4(b)(2)).[13] The amendment passed and the final version of the bill that was signed into law maintained this cutoff date.[14]

Gathering information regarding legislative intent in Wyoming proved to be somewhat more difficult than in other states. Floor debates are not recorded, statements of intent are uncommon, and records of committee testimony are not available. However, the name of the sponsor, drafting files that contain research materials, and roll call votes at the committee level and on the floor are available. The Wyoming Legislature's Web site also suggests that reports by other state officials and newspaper accounts are often helpful in the construction of legislative histories of Wyoming laws.[15] In the case of the expansion of EDR in Wyoming, this was certainly true. Evidence from the Secretary of State, and newspaper accounts, supplemented the limited information provided in legislative documents.

---

[12] Maine did not fit under this paragraph because not all polling places allow for registration on site.

[13] As noted, states without a registration system were exempted under 42 U.S.C. 1973gg-4(b)(1). The amendment added the March 11, 1993 cut-off date to such states as well.

[14] An amendment to an appropriations bill in 1995, by Senator Gregg of New Hampshire, changed the cut-off date to August 1, 1994.

[15] See http://legisweb.state.wy.us/leginfo/hiswylaw.htm, accessed March 2003.

Although little can be learned about intent from the legislative documents related to the adoption of EDR in Wyoming, the drafting file for HB 312 of 1993 and the *House Journal* for the 1993 session provide insight into the process. The first finding of note is that a Republican in the State House of Representatives, Les Bowron, introduced the bill. The initial version of HB 312 was based on Senate File 252 of 1989, which was introduced by three Democratic State Senators; the 1989 attempt to establish EDR died in committee. In the House Committee on Corporations, Elections, and Political Subdivisions, made up of six Republicans and three Democrats, HB 312 was recommended to the full House with nine votes for and zero against. The roll call vote for the third reading of HB 312 in the House indicated that it passed by a vote of fifty-four to six. Coding of the "ayes" and "noes" by party fails to indicate a partisan difference in the votes; thirty-seven of forty-one Republicans (90 percent) and seventeen of nineteen Democrats (89 percent) voted for passage. Clearly, Democrats and Republicans in the House both in committee and on the floor did not view the adoption of EDR as a partisan issue.

In the Senate, the five-member (three Republicans, two Democrats) Committee on Corporations, Elections, and Political Subdivisions recommended the bill to the full Senate on a five to zero vote. Partisan differences emerged in the Senate after Republican Senator, Charles Scott, introduced an amendment to repeal EDR at general elections if the national motor voter legislation failed to pass by November 1, 1994. Although the amendment was adopted, at the third reading, Republican Senator Jim Geringer offered an amendment to delete the section of the Scott amendment relating to the repeal of EDR for general elections in the event that the NRVA did not pass. Geringer's attempt to remove this section, and thus keep EDR even if the NVRA failed, was not successful. Twelve voted for Geringer's amendment and eighteen voted against; ten of the twelve votes for the Geringer amendment were from Democrats and all eighteen of the votes against the amendment were from Republicans. The Senate ultimately passed the bill to allow EDR at general elections on a twenty-two to eight vote. The Republicans were decidedly for the bill, with only two, Geringer and Scott, voting against its passage. The Democrats were split; four voted for passage and six voted against passage.

On March 2, 1993, the House passed the bill with the Senate amendments fifty-six to four. As noted earlier, the Governor signed HB 312 into law a few days later. Although EDR was expanded to general elections in Wyoming, it would have been repealed if the NVRA failed to pass. Section 2 of the law indicates the following:

The provisions of this act shall not be enforced and shall only become effective following the passage of federal legislation from HR2 from the 103rd Congress or substantially similar legislation prior to November 1, 1994. If no such legislation is passed, this act shall be repealed November 1, 1994 (Session Laws of the State of Wyoming 1993, c. 172, § 2).

This points strongly toward the conclusion that the intent behind the expansion of EDR to general elections in Wyoming was not focused on increasing participation. Information provided by the Secretary of State provides additional support for this conclusion.

In her 1993 Annual Report, Secretary of State Kathy Karpan, a Democrat, claimed that "[t]he general election day registration bill was the most important piece of election related legislation passed this session" (p. 14). She went on to reveal the intent of the legislation, stating: "This legislation was passed solely in response to the federal legislation commonly known as 'motor voter.'" The report also noted that Wyoming's county clerks were opposed to the national motor voter bill because it would have been expensive and would have boosted registration while having a trivial effect on turnout. In an article by staff writer Tom Zoellner on February 9, 1993, published in the *Wyoming Eagle*, Secretary of State Karpan also noted her concern with federal intervention in state election laws. In the article, Karpan is quoted as saying: "We have a phrase in America: 'Don't make a federal case out of it.' We believe as a matter of philosophy that states should have the ability to regulate their own election laws" (p. 3). The article also revealed that Wyoming's congressional delegation, made up entirely of Republicans, opposed the NVRA. Representative Craig Thomas is quoted as saying the NVRA bill "is something only Washington could write – the dreams of special interests and political consultants" (p. 3).

By utilizing the nonapplicability clause contained in the NVRA, Wyoming circled the wagons to avoid federal intrusion. Surely, increased turnout was a concern; but the evidence is consistent with the argument that avoiding the costs associated with the NVRA and maintaining state control over elections were a larger priority in Wyoming. As shown earlier, had the NVRA not been enacted, Wyoming's thirty-day closing date for registration prior to general elections would have remained intact. Without the threat of the NVRA, one can safely conclude that EDR would not have been expanded to general elections in Wyoming.

New Hampshire (Live Free [of Federal Mandates] or Die)

To research the passage of EDR in New Hampshire I used a number of sources, including the *Journal of the House*, the *Journal of the Senate*, New Hampshire Session Laws, and various committee folders. Not only did I find extensive coverage of the debate surrounding EDR's adoption in New Hampshire, but, as will be shown subsequently, the debate was quite lively.

The NVRA was enacted on May 20, 1993, and required that states implement its provisions by January 1, 1995. New Hampshire, under Republican Governor Stephen E. Merrill, and with Republican majorities in the State Senate and State House of Representatives, approved HB 1506 on May 23, 1994, establishing EDR in New Hampshire.[16] A key provision was that the law was retroactive to March 10, 1993. With this provision, New Hampshire took advantage of the NVRA's nonapplicability clause, section 4(b)(2). As noted earlier, this clause included a cutoff date of March 11, 1993 (added after Wyoming adopted EDR in anticipation of the NVRA).

New Hampshire Secretary of State William Gardner, a Democrat, was a staunch and vocal opponent of the NVRA. During the debate in Congress on the NVRA, Secretary of State Gardner provided a statement expressing his objection to the NVRA. Among the arguments presented by Mr. Gardner were that the NVRA: 1) would not necessarily increase turnout; 2) would lead to large expenses for the benefit of a few; and 3) might require two registration lists, meaning that "[c]haos would reign at the polling place." He noted that: "Most troublesome is the potentially excessive cost required to benefit very few in [New Hampshire]" (*Congressional Record*, Senate, March 11, 1993). Although Secretary of State Gardner conveyed a concern with making voting easier and preserving the right to vote, he contended that citizens must bear a burden of responsibility. He then goes on to say:

This bill attempts to describe those voting age citizens who haven't taken the time to register to vote as victims of a system which has deliberately attempted to make it difficult for them to vote. We, on the other hand, would ask, why should the 80% of the eligible voters in New Hampshire who have made the effort to register spend their tax dollars on the 20% who have not done so, especially when in our depressed economy we have so many other serious needs (*Congressional Record*, Senate, March 11, 1993).

---

[16] The previous closing date for registration was ten days prior to the election.

Uneasiness with the cost of the NVRA was echoed when New Hampshire introduced legislation to implement EDR.

Testimony by the primary sponsor[17] of HB 1506, Representative Gary Gilmore, a Democrat, as well as the text of the law itself, make clear that the NVRA was the impetus behind the adoption of EDR in New Hampshire. At the first public hearing on HB 1506, Representative Gilmore stated that adopting EDR would be the "best way to implement the [NVRA] at the least amount of cost and [would] best serve the state" (New Hampshire General Court, January 11, 1994). In testimony before the Senate Committee on Public Affairs, Representative Gilmore revealed that the town and city clerks stood in strong opposition to the NVRA and its associated costs. He also argued that fraud has not been an issue in states that have EDR and that EDR would be more likely to increase turnout than would the NVRA. These issues were incorporated into the text of the bill.

Representative Gilmore noted that the Declaration of Purpose for HB 1506 was "largely lifted, plagiarized if you will, from the [NVRA]" (New Hampshire General Court, March 2, 1994). The NVRA's findings and purposes are:

> (a) Findings. The Congress finds that
>   (1) the right of citizens of the United States to vote is a fundamental right;
>   (2) it is the duty of the Federal, State, and local governments to promote the exercise of that right; and
>   (3) discriminatory and unfair registration laws and procedures can have a direct and damaging effect on voter participation in elections for Federal office and disproportionately harm voter participation by various groups, including racial minorities.
> (b) Purposes. The purposes of this Act are –
>   (1) to establish procedures that will increase the number of eligible citizens who register to vote in elections for Federal office;
>   (2) to make it possible for Federal, State, and local governments to implement this Act in a manner that enhances the participation of eligible citizens as voters in elections for Federal office;
>   (3) to protect the integrity of the electoral process; and
>   (4) to ensure that accurate and current voter registration rolls are maintained (42 U.S.C. §1973gg-2).

As can be seen from the Declaration of Purpose for HB 1506, which follows, not all of the purposes were lifted from the text of the NVRA.

---

[17] Five Democrats and three Republicans sponsored the bill.

Declaration of Purpose:

I. The general court finds that the right of citizens of New Hampshire to vote is a fundamental right. The general court further finds that it is the duty of state and local government to promote the exercise of the right to vote. Discriminatory and unfair registration procedures can have a direct and damaging effect on voter participation in elections, and can disproportionately harm voter participation by various groups.
II. The purposes of this act, therefore, are to:
   (a) establish procedures that will increase the number of eligible citizens who vote in elections for state and federal offices.
   (b) Protect the integrity of the electoral process.
   (c) Ensure that accurate and current voter registration rolls are maintained.
   (d) Make it possible for state and local government to enhance voter participation in elections for federal and state office, while avoiding unnecessary confusion and excessive expense necessitated by federal legislation.
   (e) Enable New Hampshire to comply with the nonapplicability section of the National Voter Registration Act of 1993, as provided in section 4(b)(2) of that act, by making the provisions of section 2 of this act retroactive to March 10, 1993 (New Hampshire Session Laws 1994, c. 154, § 1).

Sections I and II a-c, as Representative Gilmore suggests, closely follow the language used in the NVRA. Section II(d) and Section II(e) stand out.

As with the language in the NVRA, a clear interest in increased turnout is stated. However, the New Hampshire law takes jabs at the federal government and the NVRA itself. Not only does the purpose make it plain that the New Hampshire legislature found the NVRA costly and confusing, but the loophole that seemed closed by the inclusion of a specific date is exploited by making the EDR section of the law retroactive. According to Gilmore's testimony before the Senate Committee on Public Affairs, this was "a sort of legislative thing that we do at times" (New Hampshire General Court, March 2, 1994).

During public hearings and debate, concerns about the intent of the legislation were paramount. In a memo to the members of the Committee on Constitutional and Statutory Revision, the League of Women Voters provided written testimony in opposition to HB 1506. According to the letter, the failure to enact the NVRA was a sign that New Hampshire would be ranked first in terms of complicated registration procedures "with no other state even close to our contempt for our citizens' rights" (New Hampshire General Court, January 11, 1994). The letter went on to note that although EDR would be easier in one sense, maintaining the system that allows each town to determine what sort of proof of identification is needed would lead to confusion and might lead some towns to make the process difficult. Representative Martha Fuller Clark, a Democrat, although a co-sponsor of the bill, argued that both EDR and motor voter provisions should be implemented. Despite these concerns, the bill passed out of committee by a twelve to one vote. In the Statement of Intent included in the Committee Report, Representative LeRoy Dube, writing on behalf of the committee, stated that the bill "is intended to exempt New Hampshire from the National Voter Registration Act and the large costs and confusion associated with it" (Committee Bill file, January 20, 1994). Representative Dube's statement of intent fails to mention increasing voter turnout.

When the bill reached the floor of the House, Representative Fuller Clark offered an amendment to delete the retroactive clause. This attempt failed, with 91 votes for deletion of this clause and 262 against. The Democrats tended to support the amendment; 73 (61 percent) voted for it and 46 (39 percent) voted against. And the Republicans were decidedly against it; 212 of 229 (93 percent) Republicans voted against the amendment.[18] The bill, with the retroactive clause intact, passed through the House and was sent to the Senate.

Representative Fuller Clark also expressed her concerns with HB 1506 before the Senate Committee on Public Affairs. She noted that she sponsored a bill, HB 212, in 1993 that would have allowed EDR, but that it died in committee. The *House Journal* for February 4, 1993 revealed that HB 212 was voted down in the House Committee on Constitutional and Statutory Revision by a vote of fifteen to two. The report out of the Committee revealed that although the spirit of the bill was "respected," it "would cause confusion at the polling places and extra work for the supervisors of the checklist on election day . . . [It] would also leave the election process vulnerable to abuses" (*House Journal* February 4, 1993, 81). This bill included a requirement that an oath be signed and added an address verification provision to safeguard against fraud. Interestingly, only the former is included in HB 1506. Representative Fuller Clark noted that she was "outraged" that those who failed to support her bill supported EDR as a means to avoid the NVRA.

In her testimony, Representative Fuller Clark proposed an interesting empirical project. She contended that a review of the testimony on the

---

[18] One Independent voted for the amendment and four Libertarians voted against it.

1993 EDR bill, if compared to that of the 1994 bill, would reveal that those who opposed the 1993 bill supported the bill in 1994 because it would allow New Hampshire to avoid implementation of the NVRA. Not all Committee members testified, but my investigation of the composition of the committee in 1993 and 1994 and the votes in committee confirmed Representative Fuller Clark's basic argument. Eighteen members of the House Committee on Constitutional and Statutory Revision in 1994 were also on the Committee in 1993, with eleven members voting on both bills in committee; nine of the ten members who voted for passage of EDR in 1994 voted against in 1993, including Representative Gilmore, whereas one member voted for EDR both times. She also contended that local clerks opposed the NVRA out of fears that they would lose control (New Hampshire General Court, March 2, 1994). Despite these objections, the bill was sent to the floor of the Senate. Further objections relating to the intent of the bill were not raised in the legislature. It is important to note that accusations about changes in political power that might result from a change in the composition of the electorate were absent from the recorded debate.

The signing into law of HB 1506 did not eliminate the question of New Hampshire's exemption from the NVRA. The retroactive passage of EDR and the failure to implement the NVRA led to a legal battle between citizen groups and state officials in the United States District Court, District of New Hampshire (*League of Women Voters et al. vs. Stephen E. Merrill et al.*, Docket No. C-95-232-JD). The New Hampshire League of Women Voters, New Hampshire AFL-CIO, and New Hampshire Citizens Action sued the Governor, the Secretary of State, and other state officials seeking to have the provisions of the NVRA implemented in New Hampshire. In the event that New Hampshire would have to comply with the NVRA, HB 333 of 1995 was signed into law as Chapter 289. The law stated that, if ordered to do so, New Hampshire would implement the NVRA provisions, but for federal elections only, thus establishing two registration systems. In the two-system plan, those registering through NVRA provisions would be registered to vote for federal offices only.[19] In addition, the law had provisions to repeal EDR and increase

---

[19] Chapter 289 of 1995, section 7 indicates that Title 2 U.S.C. 431(3) defines "federal office" as "the office of President or Vice-President, or of Senator or Representative in, or Delegate or Resident Commissioner to, the Congress" (Laws of the State of New Hampshire, 1995, p. 509).

the closing date for registration to thirty days prior to elections for federal offices. The issue was resolved in New Hampshire's favor when U.S. Senator Judd Gregg, of New Hampshire, added an amendment to an appropriations bill (H.R. 2076 of 1995) that changed the cutoff date in the NVRA's nonapplicability clause (section 4(b)(2)) to August 1, 1994.

The evidence just presented is consistent with the argument that although increasing the opportunities to register was a consideration in New Hampshire, avoiding the NVRA and its associated costs outweighed this concern. The failure to pass EDR out of committee in 1993, less than one year prior to the introduction of EDR as a means to become exempt from the NVRA, is strong evidence on its own. When coupled with the Statement of Intent and provisions set to go into place had the court ruled in favor of the League of Women Voters et al. (i.e., that EDR be repealed, the closing date set to thirty days prior to federal elections, and that NVRA registrants register with their local clerk in order to vote in all elections), little doubt is left on this question. Without the threat of the NVRA, the evidence reveals that EDR would not have been implemented in New Hampshire. The "Live Free or Die" motto is more than space filler on the state quarter and license plate – the conviction remains alive and well.

Idaho (Passing on a National Hot Potato)

Although floor debate is not recorded in Idaho, a rich collection of resources, including statements of purpose and summaries of testimony in committee, was available for researching the adoption of EDR in the state. Information regarding the intent of the law was found across several sources. As I demonstrate subsequently, each indicates a concern with voter participation, but it is clear that the NVRA prompted the change from the status quo.

House Bill 603, to establish EDR in Idaho, was sponsored by Republican Representative Pam Ahrens. It was introduced on January 25, 1994 and with little difficulty passed through both houses. On March 7, 1994 HB 603 was approved by the Democratic Governor, Cecil Andrus. The legislature was predominantly Republican; twenty-three of the thirty-five (66 percent) Senators were Republicans and fifty of the seventy (71 percent) Representatives were Republican. However, a look at the votes recorded makes it obvious that both parties supported the passage of EDR in Idaho. In the House, only one vote was cast against passage of

HB 603;[20] at the third reading, HB 603 passed on a vote of sixty-three to one with six members absent and excused. Unanimous support among those present was expressed for HB 603 in the Senate; the vote at the third reading in the Senate was thirty-three to zero with two members absent and excused.

The same general message regarding why EDR was adopted in Idaho was expressed throughout the legislative process. For example, the Statement of Purpose declared that:

The purpose of this legislation is to provide for more access to Idaho's voter registration system...Implementation...by the State should exempt the State from having to implement the unfunded federal mandates of the National Voter Registration Act of 1993 (52nd Idaho Legislature 1994).[21]

In committee, Republican Secretary of State Ben Ysursa, who was listed as the sponsor, presented the bill and provided testimony in its favor. Summaries regarding the purpose of the legislation, consistent with the excerpt just given, are contained in the minutes from the House State Affairs Committee on January 25, 1994 as well as those from February 8, 1994, and the minutes from the Senate State Affairs Committee from February 23, 1994. The summary of testimony by the Deputy Attorney General for the Department of Health and Welfare expressed support for the bill, noting that the NVRA would require the department "to address the registration process over 300,000 times during the course of a year" (State Affairs Committee from February 23, 1994, p. 2). Although the summary does not go into further detail, it seems safe to infer that this represents concern with the costs that would be imposed by the NVRA.[22] The ideas just discussed were incorporated into the text of the legislation itself, as well.

As can be seen by a comparison with the findings and purposes contained in the New Hampshire legislation, those from HB 603 in Idaho are

[20] According to Penny Ysursa, a thirty-year employee in the office of the Idaho Secretary of State, Democratic Representative Kenneth Robison voted against the bill because he wanted it to be more permissive.

[21] The House State Affairs Committee Highlights used identical language.

[22] Although concerns were raised about proof of residence requirements, that the bill did not allow EDR at local elections, and that it increased the number of days before the election that one could register at a clerk's office, there is no record to suggest that concerns regarding shifts in the partisan composition of the electorate were brought up. Expansion to local elections was added in 1995, and a County Clerk, who represented the Association of Counties as well as the Clerks Association, noted that the increase in the time period at a clerk's office was due to the mail-in registration provision included in the bill.

quite similar. The findings and purposes, displayed here, are contained in section 1 of HB 603.

Section 1. The Legislature of the State of Idaho finds that the right of the citizens of Idaho to vote is a fundamental right. The Legislature further finds that it is the duty of state and local government to promote the exercise of the right to vote.

The purposes of this act, therefore, are:

(1) To establish procedure that will increase the number of eligible citizens who vote in elections for state and federal offices;
(2) To protect the integrity of the elector process;
(3) To ensure that accurate and current voter registration rolls are maintained;
(4) To make it possible for state and local government to enhance voter participation in elections for federal and state office, while avoiding unnecessary confusion and excessive expense necessitated by federal legislation; and
(5) To exempt Idaho from compliance with the National Voter Registration Act of 1993, as provided in section 4(b)(2) of that act (General Laws of the State of Idaho 1994, c. 67, § 1).

Whereas New Hampshire modified the text from the NVRA relating to the adverse effects voter registration procedures can have, Idaho removed them completely. Otherwise, there are only minor differences in the New Hampshire and Idaho versions of the findings and purposes. The text of section 8 of HB 603, presented subsequently, indicates that the portions of the law that relate to establishing EDR would take effect retroactively.

An emergency existing therefor, which emergency is hereby declared to exist, the provisions of Sections 1 and 5 of this act shall be in full force and effect on and after passage and approval retroactively to March 10, 1993 and the remaining Sections of this act shall be in full force and effect on and after January 1, 1995 (General Laws of the State of Idaho 1994, c. 67, § 8).

In addition, the *Daily Data Final Edition*, which provides a summary of the actions and votes on bills, reveals that the bill was adopted "in order to achieve compliance with the spirit of the National Voter Registration Act of 1993 and to gain an exemption from certain specific requirements" (52nd Idaho Legislature 1994). Like the New Hampshire General Court, the Idaho Legislature points out the importance of voter participation, but also makes it apparent that the NVRA and the "unnecessary confusion and excessive expense" that come with it motivated this concern.

CONCLUSION

Although the reasons differ across states, EDR was adopted with clear purposes in mind. The states that adopted EDR in the 1970s did so during a period in which suffrage was being expanded by federal mandate. By adopting EDR, these states chose to take an additional step that would make voting easier. In the 1990s, when the federal government made another push to increase participation, via the NVRA, three states responded to federal mandates by taking advantage of a loophole. Whereas the first three states to adopt EDR were enthusiastic in their push for increased participation, Wyoming, New Hampshire, and Idaho were reluctant to change the status quo. They did so, but only to avoid what was viewed as a more costly and potentially chaotic system. This should not be taken to imply that anything pernicious was afoot. Although some might argue that motor voter does more to actively engage citizens, especially the least well off, than does EDR, the decision to circumvent the NVRA did not come down to installing barriers or knocking them down; rather, it came down to finding the least costly way to comply with federal legislation while maintaining an independent state ethos.

Other states considered adopting EDR as a way out of the NVRA, too, but ultimately accepted the NVRA. An investigation seeking to discern why they did not preempt the NVRA by adopting EDR is beyond the scope of this project. Such a study would require an in-depth analysis of legislative records from the states, which may or may not contain enough information to determine the reason(s) behind their decision to adopt the NVRA, rather than EDR. Having read through the legislative records in the new EDR states, as well as Congressional testimony on the NVRA, and conducted interviews with some of the people who influenced their states' decision, I can speculate as follows. First, EDR was least viable in states with large populations, where the threat of wide-scale fraud was most serious. States that did not have a history of clean elections would also have had a harder time promoting EDR over the NVRA. On these grounds, for example, Illinois is ruled out; even the staunchest proponent of EDR would recognize that without sufficient measures to prevent fraud, EDR in Illinois could be a nightmare. The fight from local governmental agencies to prevent the NVRA would also have been less severe in states with more centralized service delivery. A final decisive factor relates to partisan control in the state legislature. Given the strong campaign for the NVRA from the national Democratic party, states with legislatures controlled by the Democratic party would have felt pressure from the national party not to go the way of Idaho, New Hampshire, and Wyoming.

The fact that so few states allow EDR suggests that not all feel as strongly about encouraging participation as do those in states such as Minnesota and Wisconsin. The recent failure of ballot measures that would have allowed EDR in California and Colorado indicates that even in these relatively progressive states, voters are not ready to place a higher priority on reducing barriers to registration.

In sum, the comparison of the early adopters with the recent adopters provides strong evidence against the treatment of election laws as exogenous forces. Based on the theoretical framework set out in the previous chapter, it should be expected that EDR would be less effective in states that adopted for reasons of cost and avoidance of federal intervention (the recent and reluctant adopters) than in states that adopted mainly as a means to increase participation (the early and enthusiastic adopters). I take the legislative process as an indicator of the participatory culture of the state at the time of adoption. That is, as a proxy for the degree to which unregistered citizens will be motivated to vote when the costs of doing so are decreased. As discussed in Chapter 1, only those interested in participating will be responsive to lower costs. Thus, when there is demand for reform, I hypothesize that the effect reform has on turnout will be more pronounced. The statistical analyses reported in Chapter 3 test whether or not this is the case, showing that it is.

3

Election Day Registration by Choice and by Federal Mandate

When studying the effect of electoral reform, including election day registration (EDR), in order to obtain point estimates of the effect of the policy program, researchers impose the exogenous selection assumption, which treats the selection of election laws as a random process.[1] Thus, it follows that once the new laws are implemented, citizens in states with traditionally low levels of participation (and thus low levels of factors that affect participation, such as political interest) will act the same as those in states with high levels of participation. As discussed in Chapter 1, this view is flawed. However, researchers have attacked the study of electoral reform without full recognition of the consequences of imposing such an assumption.

When using individual-level data to study EDR, one usually proceeds in four steps: 1) run a traditional logit or probit model on a binary dependent variable coded as 1 for those who voted and 0 for those who did not vote, with a variable for closing date and perhaps an indicator variable for EDR as the key independent variables; 2) set the values of the variables to indicate that EDR applies for all and calculate a predicted probability of voting for each individual; 3) set the values of the variables to indicate that EDR does not apply to anyone and calculate a predicted probability of voting for each individual; and 4) subtract the result obtained in step 3) from the result obtained in step 2) and then take the average to

---

[1] Although one could argue that the usual approach treats the selection of the laws as random once other factors associated with the selection process have been controlled for, as I argued earlier, the usual approach fails to account for the unobservable factors that influence both the selection of the laws and turnout and thus remains problematic.

obtain an estimate of the effect of EDR.[2] *Implicit in this procedure is the imposition of the exogenous selection assumption.* Because, as demonstrated in Chapter 2, EDR is chosen purposefully, this method will produce biased estimates of the effect of EDR. The difference in difference approach and the bounds approach address these issues and allow for tests of the hypotheses derived from my theoretical framework.[3]

In this chapter, I employ both the difference in difference and bounds methods to study the effect of EDR on turnout. I begin with an explanation of the difference in difference approach and then apply it to EDR as implemented in states where individuals are most likely to be responsive (Minnesota and Wisconsin). I compare these results to those using the traditional approach, made fashionable by Wolfinger and Rosenstone (1980). The results confirm my first hypothesis that once endogeneity is accounted for, the effect of EDR is estimated to be lower than when endogeneity is ignored. Next, I investigate EDR in the states that reluctantly changed the status quo and adopted EDR in order to avoid motor voter (Idaho, Wyoming, and New Hampshire). On their own, these results also provide confirmation for my first hypothesis. Together with the results from Minnesota and Wisconsin, the hypothesis that the effect of EDR is higher where the citizenry is more engaged is supported.

The second half of the chapter explains and then utilizes Manski's (1995) nonparametric bounds approach. Because the bounds approach

---

[2] This describes the procedure used in Wolfinger and Rosenstone (1980, see Appendix C).
[3] One might argue for an instrumental variables or state fixed effects approach to the problem of endogeneity. For present purposes, a variant of two-stage least squares, known as instrumental variables probit, might be used. Instrumental variables estimation of the system found here (the system here is triangular) requires that two conditions be met: 1) one must identify a variable that has an effect on the adoption of a set of election laws but does not affect turnout; and 2) this variable must not be correlated with the unobserved factors that influence turnout. Finding credible instruments is always difficult (Bartels 1991), and is perhaps more difficult than usual in the present context. Political variables, such as those relating to the composition of state legislatures and variables relating to constitutional provisions, have been suggested in recent studies (see for example, Besley and Case 2000; and Knight 2000). Given the close relationship between the laws that govern the ability to vote and the decision to vote, these political variables do not prove to be plausible instruments in this context, mainly due to the violation of the second condition discussed earlier. A number of instruments were examined, but none was deemed credible. Using a fixed state effects model (essentially this involves including dummy variables for each state) to capture time-invariant unobserved attitudes toward participation is another option for confronting endogeneity. However, this is insufficient if attitudes toward participation within states change over time. Changes in the closing date for registration over time suggest that attitudes toward participation do change within states. Thus, a fixed effects model will not eliminate bias, but it will reduce it.

dictates that analysis begins with minimal assumptions and proceeds by explicitly layering on stronger assumptions, the power of various, often implicit, identification assumptions must be confronted. This process is perhaps the most significant contribution of this work, as it forces us to expose the theoretical motivation of the assumptions, and the meaning of each with respect to our substantive understanding of voting behavior. Using the bounds approach, I provide a series of estimates of the effect of EDR and demonstrate that the sharpness of the estimates depends on the assumptions one is willing to maintain.

DIFFERENCE IN DIFFERENCE ESTIMATION

Besley and Case (2000) show that the difference in difference approach can be used to deal with policy endogeneity. One begins with the selection of the treatment groups. This is straightforward, as the treatment groups are made up of those who are subject to the change in policy; here, individuals in states with EDR make up the treatment groups. A crucial element for this work is the selection of control groups. The control groups should be made up of individuals in similar circumstances who do not experience a change in the policy under study, nor other changes that might influence the outcome of interest. Here, individuals in states without EDR make up the pool of possible control groups. However, given the rather unique features of the states that adopted EDR, in order to avoid the problems produced by endogeneity, only those in states that are similar to the states that adopted EDR should be included as controls. The groups are compared before and after the change to EDR; and the difference in the probability of voting between the two groups from before to after the change to EDR represents the effect of EDR.

The large samples in the Current Population Survey: Voter Supplement File (CPS) make this approach possible.[4] The samples are drawn to be representative of each state, and even in the case of the relatively low population EDR states, there are hundreds and even thousands of individuals in the sample in a given survey.

I chose control states based on region (using states in close proximity to one another), population, and demographic composition – that is,

---

[4] As noted in Chapter 1, the Census collects demographic, employment, and voting data in November of each election year from a sample of the civilian noninstitutionalized population in all fifty states and the District of Columbia.

factors that influence turnout.[5] By using states close to one another I hope to control for variations in migration patterns, the economy, and other factors that might influence the development of the states' social and political environments. Thus, as is important for providing credible estimates of the effect of the change in the law on turnout, the treatment and control groups also have similar pretreatment patterns of turnout. Eligible citizens living in Minnesota and Wisconsin make up the first treatment group, with those living in Iowa and South Dakota serving as the control group. The new EDR states are broken up by region as well. Montana serves as the control for Idaho and Wyoming,[6] whereas turnout in New Hampshire is compared with turnout in Vermont.[7] Overall, the respective treatment and control states are similar in terms of their population, median income, and percentages of racial minorities, noncitizens, high school graduates, and population over age sixty-five. All of the states considered have small populations and have small percentages of racial minorities and noncitizens, and larger than average percentages of people with at least a high school degree. Appendix B contains descriptive statistics by decade, from 1970 to 2000, for these states. As discussed in the previous chapters, I expect that the largest effects will be found in the

---

[5] Although any classification is subject to scrutiny, the evidence in the appendices as well as the pre-adoption plots of turnout in the states I have chosen for comparison are supported further by Hero's (1998) classification of states based on measures of racial/ethnic diversity; for the most part, the states I use as comparisons are in the same quadrant and those that are not are still quite close to one another. Hero's (1998) extensive review of the literature reveals a number of the theoretical and empirical criticisms of Elazar's (1966) work on political culture. Hero shows racial/ethnic diversity to be a driving force behind political culture.

[6] Utah was also considered as a control for Idaho and Wyoming. Utah dropped from contention due to a change in instrumentation in anticipation of the NVRA. The massive purge of the registration lists that took place prior to the implementation of the NVRA had the effect of pushing the measure of turnout down dramatically. This instrumentation confound renders Utah ineligible as a control.

[7] Because North Dakota eliminated registration requirements in 1951, prior to the availability of CPS data, North Dakota is excluded from the analysis. Choosing a control state for Maine proves to be difficult. New Hampshire and Vermont are the most viable candidates, but 1972 turnout in Maine, the last presidential election prior to the implementation of EDR, was especially low, thus introducing the possibility of a regression to the mean effect. Vermont changed its closing date during this period, which violates one of the identification assumptions (see later discussion), thus removing it as a potential control state for Maine. The situation with Maine reveals an important limitation of the difference in difference method; without suitable controls, the method fails to provide an improvement over other methods. The results are included in Appendix C and should be viewed with caution, especially because Maine did not conduct all EDR transactions at the polling places.

states that adopted EDR with the primary goal of increasing participation. That is, EDR should lead to larger increases in turnout in Minnesota and Wisconsin than in Idaho, New Hampshire, and Wyoming.

Aggregate Patterns

Before explaining the statistical model and presenting its results, an examination of the patterns of turnout in the respective EDR and control states helps justify the selection of control states and hints at the expected effect of EDR on turnout. The figures presented subsequently are based on data from the Federal Elections Commission and calculate turnout as a percentage of the voting age population (VAP). Although the VAP measure is problematic in that it includes some who are not eligible to vote, most notably noncitizens, and excludes some who are eligible (McDonald and Popkin 2001), I use these data because they allow for an examination of turnout over a longer time span than do other data sources.

Figure 3.1 plots turnout in presidential elections from 1960 to 2000 for Iowa, Minnesota, Wisconsin, and South Dakota. Recall that Minnesota and Wisconsin adopted EDR between the 1972 and 1976 elections. The dark vertical line separates turnout into pre- and posttreatment categories. Note that Minnesota and Wisconsin are shown with dark, solid lines and solid markers, whereas Iowa and South Dakota are lighter, with dashed lines and open markers.

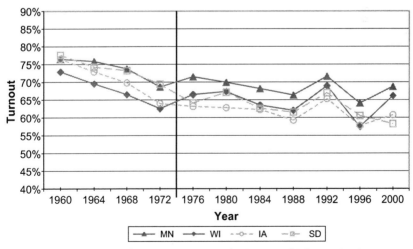

FIGURE 3.1. Presidential year turnout and EDR in high motivation states (Minnesota and Wisconsin vs. Iowa and South Dakota) 1960–2000 (Source: FEC).

Distinct pre- and posttreatment patterns are evident. From 1960 through 1972, turnout was in a state of decline. Turnout rates were the highest and extremely similar in South Dakota and Minnesota, with Iowa a few points below and Wisconsin lower still. The 1960 to 1972 patterns make it evident that Iowa and South Dakota make good controls for Minnesota and Wisconsin; although the level of turnout varied, the change in turnout from election to election was comparable across all four states. After EDR was implemented, both Minnesota and Wisconsin saw a modest increase in turnout, while turnout in Iowa and South Dakota dropped. The gain in turnout in Wisconsin pushed turnout there above Iowa and South Dakota for 1976. Over the rest of the series, the gap between Minnesota and the rest of the states remained intact and for the most part, so did the similarity in turnout for Wisconsin and South Dakota, the 2000 election being an exception. Thus, in summary, turnout in Minnesota and Wisconsin increased after the implementation of EDR; but the increases were not earth shattering. The increases are certainly not as large as advocates of reform, such as Piven and Cloward, would expect and do not appear as large as those found in previous studies. In fact, the increases in turnout from 1988 to 1992, across all four states in Figure 3.1, were larger than the increases in turnout after EDR went into effect in Minnesota and Wisconsin. As is well known, the 1992 election was a hotly contested race among George Bush, Bill Clinton, and Ross Perot. The closeness of the race and the presence of an interesting third-party candidate pushed up turnout across the nation. This underscores the point that turnout is influenced by a variety of factors.

Turnout in Idaho, Montana, and Wyoming is displayed in Figure 3.2. Again, the states that adopted EDR during this period, Idaho and Wyoming, are shown with dark, solid lines and solid markers, and Montana is displayed with a light, dashed line and open markers.

For this grouping, the period between 1960 and 1992 represents the pretreatment period with 1996 and 2000 as the posttreatment years. Beginning in 1972, turnout tended to be the highest in Montana. Wyoming closed the gap on Montana in 1992 and, after adopting EDR for general elections, closed the gap further. The drop in Idaho from 1992 to 1996 was on par with the drop in Montana, but Idaho also experienced a drop, albeit a small one, from 1996 to 2000. It appears that EDR in Idaho did little to increase turnout.

It is important to recall that turnout dropped in 1996 across the nation, largely as a result of the lackluster contest among Clinton, Dole,

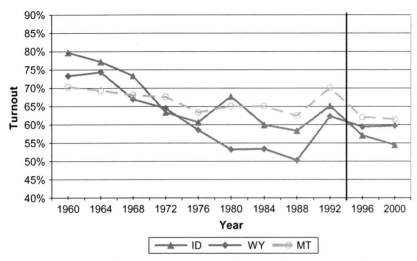

FIGURE 3.2. Presidential year turnout and EDR in low motivation states (Idaho and Wyoming vs. Montana) 1960–2000 (Source: FEC).

and Perot. Theoretically, EDR might have boosted turnout in Idaho and Wyoming between 1992 and 1996. Given the overall pattern of turnout from 1992 to 1996, a more sympathetic position would treat EDR as a mechanism working to stem the decline in turnout. That is, national trends overwhelmed any increase in turnout that might have been felt as a result of EDR. In summary, EDR appears to have had a lesser effect in this pair of states that adopted it only in response to federal mandates.

The last set of comparisons involves New Hampshire (shown with a dark, solid line and solid markers) and Vermont (shown in a lighter, dashed line and open markers). Figure 3.3 presents the results. From 1960 to 1980, turnouts in these two states were extremely similar, with New Hampshire slightly edging out Vermont. Vermont crept above New Hampshire from 1984 to 1992, with New Hampshire seeming to close the gap after adopting EDR. As was the case with Wyoming and Idaho, the first presidential election for which EDR was available in New Hampshire was in 1996. Again, the effects of EDR were not sufficient to lead to increased turnout, but might have helped keep turnout from declining further.

On the whole, any gains in turnout as a result of EDR seem small. Furthermore, the patterns of turnout suggest that the states being compared to the EDR states represent credible controls.

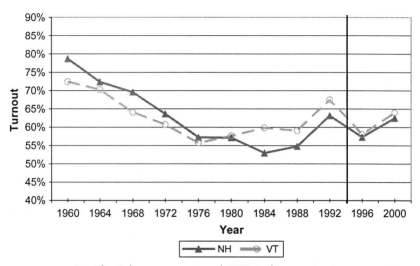

FIGURE 3.3. Presidential year turnout and EDR in low motivation states (New Hampshire vs. Vermont) 1960–2000 (Source: FEC).

Statistical Model and Results

Although the figures presented earlier are instructive, it is necessary to control for forces that affect turnout and that might explain some of the patterns found in the graphs. Results using the difference in difference approach can be obtained by estimating the following equation via probit:

$$P(\text{VOTE}_{ist}) = a + \gamma \text{TS}_i {}^* \text{TY}_t + b\text{TS}_i + c_1 X_{ist} {}^* \text{TS}_i$$
$$+ c_2 X_{ist} {}^* (1 - \text{TS}_i) + d\text{TY}_t + e_{ist}$$

where P stands for probability, the subscript i for the individual, the subscript s for state, and the subscript t for year. The dependent variable is a binary variable equal to 1 if an individual voted and equal to 0 if the individual did not vote. Included in the analysis are all eligible citizens who responded with an answer of "yes" or "no" to the question on voting; that is, citizens 18 years of age or older who either voted, were registered but did not vote, or were not registered.[8] Living in the treatment state (here, the treatment is EDR) after the treatment is implemented is represented by $\text{TS}_i {}^* \text{TY}_t$, where TS_i represents living in a treatment state

---

[8] Those who refused to answer or responded by saying they "don't know" if they voted were dropped from the analysis.

and TY_t represents being in a time period after the treatment was put into place. Thus, TS_i equals 1 if an individual lives in a state that adopts EDR over this period, and equals 0 otherwise; and $TY_t = 1$ for years after EDR has been implemented and $TY_t = 0$ for years prior to the change to EDR. When multiplied together, TS_i*TY_t is an indicator variable equal to 1 for those in EDR states after the treatment and 0 otherwise. The coefficient γ, represents the effect of EDR after controlling for the mean difference in the probability of voting between those in the EDR states and those in the control states (b), the mean change in the overall probability of voting before and after the adoption of EDR in at least one of the states under consideration (d), and the effect of the other independent variables (c_1 and c_2). This model also allows the independent variables, X,[9] to have different effects based on whether the state is in the treatment or control group.

Besley and Case (2000) note that two assumptions are necessary for identification. These are: 1) "apart from the control variables included (X), there are no other forces affecting the treatment and control groups pre- and post-treatment"; and 2) "the composition of the treatment group and control group must remain stable over this period" (p. F686). Here, these assumptions are not problematic.[10]

The analysis begins with an investigation of EDR in Minnesota and Wisconsin, states that adopted EDR as a means to increase turnout. As

---

[9] These include education, age, age squared, income quartile, and mobility (when available). Coding of the independent variables appears in Appendix A.

[10] Given that one would not expect migration patterns to change as a result of election laws, the second identification assumption is easily satisfied. Assumption 1 presents some complications. EDR was certainly the primary electoral reform put into place in the states that adopted it during the 1990s. However, the legislation that established EDR in Minnesota and Wisconsin did more than add EDR. The other key provisions were establishing postcard registration and reducing the residency requirement (from six months to twenty days in Minnesota and to ten days in Wisconsin). These other reforms simply do not stack up theoretically when compared to EDR. Postcard registration still requires information costs not required by EDR, which makes voting a one-stop process. Although the effect of postcard registration and EDR cannot be separated, I am willing to assume that postcard registration accounts for a negligible portion of the effect. Even without accounting for endogeneity, Wolfinger and Rosenstone (1980) find that registration by mail has little, if any, effect. As a result of the Voting Rights Act of 1970, residency requirements for voting for president and vice president were eliminated. Furthermore, South Dakota and Iowa, the states to which I compare Minnesota and Wisconsin, completely removed their residency requirements in 1974 and 1973 respectively. Because the changes occurred across all four states, the coefficient for the change to EDR cannot be picking up the influence of the change in the residency requirements. That is, the first identification assumption is satisfied.

TABLE 3.1. *Difference in Difference Probit Estimates of the Effect of EDR on Turnout (MN and WI compared to IA and SD, 1972 and 1980)*

Variable	Coefficient	Standard Error	z	p value
EDR Effect	0.1625	0.0597	2.72	0.007
MN and WI	0.4850	0.2079	2.33	0.020
Education * MN and WI	−0.0860	0.0269	−3.20	0.001
Age * MN and WI	−0.0003	0.0080	−0.04	0.968
Age Squared * MN and WI	0.0000	0.0001	−0.47	0.638
Income * MN and WI	−0.0363	0.0279	−1.30	0.194
Education	0.3776	0.0210	17.99	0.000
Age	0.0590	0.0062	9.56	0.000
Age Squared	−0.0004	0.0001	−6.39	0.000
Income Quartile	0.1638	0.0220	7.45	0.000
1980	−0.1301	0.0490	−2.66	0.008
Constant	−2.7310	0.1634	−16.71	0.000

$N = 11,948$.
Log likelihood $= -5961.37$.
Source: 1972 and 1980 CPS.

was demonstrated earlier, Iowa and South Dakota are similar to Minnesota and Wisconsin in terms of the factors that affect turnout and are used as the control states. Table 3.1 presents the results from difference in difference estimation of a probit model using data from 1972 and 1980.[11] Even with just two election years and four small states, there are nearly 12,000 observations. The independent variables included in the model are education, age, age squared, and income, all of which are known to be related to the probability of voting. The coefficient representing the effect of EDR is positive, as expected, and is statistically significant. As expected, education, age, and income have a positive and statistically significant impact on the probability that an individual will vote. The coefficient for 1980 is negative and significant, indicating that turnout was lower in 1980 than it was in 1972.

In order to gain greater insight into the effect of EDR, I calculated the predicted probability of voting for each individual under two scenarios: 1) if the EDR treatment did not apply to anyone; and 2) if all were to receive the EDR treatment. The difference in these two probabilities

[11] As was noted in Chapter 1, the 1976 CPS do not allow one to determine respondents' state of residence. The two-election-year period is used to reduce the chance that other changes influence the results. Analyses using the entire CPS time series from 1972 to 2000 for each of the state groupings do not produce substantively different results.

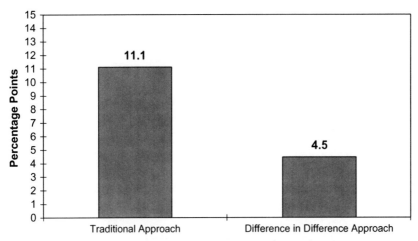

FIGURE 3.4. Percentage point increase in turnout due to EDR in high motivation states (Minnesota and Wisconsin) by statistical approach.

represents the effect of EDR.[12] I am interested not only in the estimated effect of EDR from this approach, but also in the comparison to the effect produced using the traditional approach that does not account for the nonrandom selection of election laws (that is, endogeneity). Thus, I also estimated probabilities of the effect of EDR using the traditional approach (popularized by Wolfinger and Rosenstone [1980]), run on the pooled 1972 and 1980 CPS samples. Figure 3.4 presents the overall effect using the two methods.

For the model based on the traditional approach, the other states that have EDR during this period – Maine, North Dakota, and Oregon – are eliminated from the sample because the effect of EDR in these states might differ from that in Minnesota and Wisconsin.[13] An additional control for living in Southern states is included in the traditional model.[14] Reducing the closing date from any value but not allowing for EDR increases the time available to register but still requires a second trip at a later date in order to cast a vote. In order to account for the difference between reducing closing date from, say, fifteen to fourteen days, and from one to zero days, an indicator variable for EDR (set to 1 if EDR is allowed

---

[12] The procedure discussed at the beginning of this section was followed, replacing the traditional model estimates in step 1 with the difference in difference model estimates.

[13] Similar considerations are taken when examining the other sets of comparison states.

[14] This was excluded from the difference in difference model because none of the Southern states appears in the treatment or control groups.

and set to 0 otherwise) is included in addition to closing date (see Brians and Grofman 1999, 2001). The coefficient estimates all have the expected signs and are statistically significant. The estimates from the traditional model appear in Appendix E.

The results presented in Figure 3.4 are striking. Consistent with my argument, controlling for endogeneity leads to smaller estimates of the effect of EDR. The failure to control for endogeneity (traditional model) leads to an estimated effect 2.5 times larger than the effect obtained when endogeneity is accounted for (difference in difference approach). Using the traditional model that treats election laws as exogenous, EDR is estimated to increase turnout by 11 percentage points overall. By way of contrast, the difference in difference estimates suggest an overall increase in turnout of 4.5 percentage points.[15] In the traditional model, the coefficients on closing date and the EDR dummy soak up the unobserved factors associated with both the selection of EDR and turnout, such as attitudes toward participation, and improperly attribute them to the effect of EDR.

The previous analysis can be extended to study the effect of EDR in the states that implemented EDR only after their hands were forced by federal legislation. Here, when the difference in difference method is employed, as was the case in the section on aggregate patterns, Montana serves as a control state for the treatment states of Wyoming and Idaho, and Vermont acts as the control state for New Hampshire. Following the process used for the first set of comparisons, for these two groups of comparisons, other states that allowed EDR were excluded from the traditional model. Thus, analysis of EDR using the traditional approach for Idaho and Wyoming excludes New Hampshire, Maine, Minnesota, North Dakota, and Wisconsin. Likewise, analysis of EDR using the traditional approach for New Hampshire excludes Idaho, Wyoming, Maine, Minnesota, North Dakota, and Wisconsin. Using the same computational methods as were used for the analysis of Minnesota and Wisconsin, Figure 3.5 presents the results for Idaho and Wyoming, and Figure 3.6 presents the results for New Hampshire (the coefficient estimates are displayed in Appendix E, Tables E.2 and E.3 and E.4 and E.5, respectively). The analyses were performed using data from the 1992 and 1996 CPS.[16] Looking first at the comparison of Idaho and Wyoming to Montana, in Figure 3.5, again

---

[15] Bootstrapped confidence intervals were computed for both predicted probabilities showing that they are statistically different from one another at $p < 0.02$.

[16] A variable for geographic mobility, that was not available in the 1972 CPS, is included in the analysis using the 1992 and 1996 CPS.

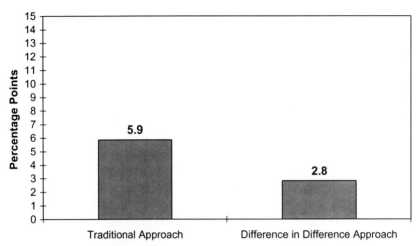

FIGURE 3.5. Percentage point increase in turnout due to EDR in low motivation states (Idaho and Wyoming) by statistical approach.

the traditional approach leads to larger estimates of the effect of EDR than the difference in difference approach. The difference in difference estimates are about half as large as the estimates from the traditional approach. However, regardless of the estimation strategy, the effect of EDR in Idaho and Wyoming cannot be statistically distinguished from zero ($p = 0.133$ for the traditional model, and $p = 0.168$ for the difference in difference model).

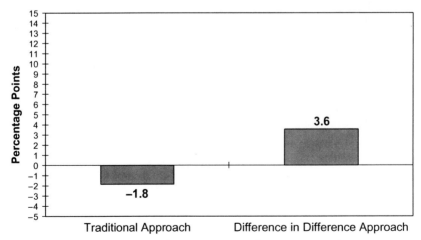

FIGURE 3.6. Percentage point change in turnout due to EDR in a low motivation state (New Hampshire) by statistical approach.

The adoption of motor voter in Montana prior to the 1992 election is a possible confounding factor. Although turnout in 1992 rose in Montana (see Figure 3.2), it also went up across the nation, including in Idaho and Wyoming, due to the excitement of the race among Clinton, Bush, and Perot. Furthermore, again like the rest of the nation, turnout dropped in Montana in 1996. In order to test whether motor voter had any effect in Montana, I ran a difference in difference model using data from the 1988 and 1992 CPS. Although the coefficient for the effect of motor voter is positive (0.047), it is substantively small, and not statistically significant ($p = 0.519$), so the effect cannot be distinguished from zero. Even if motor voter had an effect on turnout in Montana, because all but North Dakota and the EDR states have motor voter, comparing EDR to motor voter is certainly worthwhile. However, this might suggest that motor voter could wash away the larger effect of EDR in Minnesota and Wisconsin. This is not the case. As noted earlier, the estimated effects of EDR are not substantively different when the models are run on the entire 1972 to 2000 series. When all years, including those after Iowa and South Dakota adopted motor voter, are included, the estimated effect of EDR for Minnesota and Wisconsin is statistically significant ($p = 0.005$) and remains at about 4 percentage points.

When investigating EDR in New Hampshire, the two approaches considered thus far lead to substantially different conclusions. Before reviewing the results, it is important to note that, due to issues related to Vermont's Voter Oath provision, Vermont delayed full compliance with the NVRA until July 1, 1997.[17] Thus, possible effects from the implementation of motor voter are not a concern for the difference in difference estimates. However, the coefficient on the EDR effect dummy in the traditional model is negative and is statistically significant, suggesting that EDR led to a drop in turnout in New Hampshire. As shown in Figure 3.6, the traditional approach estimates suggest that the predicted change in the probability of voting due to EDR in New Hampshire is −1.8 percentage points! This represents another reason for concern with the traditional approach. Although I have highlighted concerns with previous research regarding the size of the effect of EDR, the debate should be about effect sizes of zero and above. Theoretically, EDR could not lead to a decrease in the probability of voting. EDR might not increase turnout much, but it is simply illogical to attribute a decrease in the probability of voting to

---

[17] In order to implement the NVRA, the Vermont Constitution had to be amended.

EDR; something else must be going on. It appears other factors present in the other states, perhaps even motor voter, play a role in this. That is, the coefficient for EDR soaks up the influence of factors that depressed turnout in New Hampshire relative to the other states in the analysis, whether or not they were comparable to New Hampshire. A more reasonable estimate is obtained using the difference in difference technique; the effect of EDR in New Hampshire is estimated to be small and positive, but cannot be statistically distinguished from zero ($p = 0.223$).

The estimates in Figures 3.4, 3.5, and 3.6 also provide evidence in support of my second hypothesis, which states that the effects should be largest where motivation is the highest. By examining EDR separately across contexts, it is obvious that EDR did not have as large an impact in Idaho, New Hampshire, and Wyoming as it did in Minnesota and Wisconsin. The effects in Minnesota and Wisconsin, states that adopted EDR on their own initiative to boost turnout by making voting easier, are small but are statistically significant. In contrast, the effects in the newer EDR states, states that adopted EDR primarily to avoid the NVRA, which they viewed as an expensive intrusion from the federal government, cannot be distinguished from zero.

THE BOUNDS APPROACH

Manski's (1995) nonparametric bounds approach can also be used to provide estimates of the effect of EDR. Through this approach, I reveal the power of various identifying assumptions and am able to relax the functional form and distributional assumptions implicit in traditional probit and logit models. I first explain how the bounds approach works and then apply it to obtain estimates of the effect of EDR on turnout, producing direct estimates of equations (1), (2), and the classical treatment effect (CTE) under various assumptions (as defined in Chapter 1 and reproduced subsequently).[18]

---

[18] See Chapter 1 and the appendix to Chapter 1 for the mathematical details of the basic bounds set up. It should be noted that this is a cross-sectional technique. Although it has advantages, this is surely a limitation. Because the change to EDR is not under direct investigation, all states that had EDR for a given year enter the analysis. For the 1980 election, ME, MN, ND, OR, and WI are coded as having EDR. Although ND does not have a registration system, like those in states with EDR, in order to vote, eligible citizens do not need to perform administrative tasks prior to election day. Removing ND and/or OR does not alter the conclusions. The bounds software is available free from Charles Manski's homepage: http://faculty.econ.northwestern.edu/faculty/manski/.

I report estimates using the bounds approach for 1980, 1996, and 2000 using data from the CPS. The 1980 election is the first presidential election after EDR was adopted for which individual level CPS data are available by state.[19] For 1980, there are two treatments, living in a state with or without EDR, whereas for 1996 and 2000 there are three treatments, living in a state with mature EDR (that is, a state that had EDR in place at least since the 1970s), living in a state with newly implemented EDR, and living in a state that does not allow EDR.[20] For 1980, EDR was available for those living in the states of Maine, Minnesota, North Dakota, Oregon, and Wisconsin; citizens in these states are compared to those living in all other states. For 1996 and 2000, two sets of comparisons are made: 1) between those living in states with mature EDR[21] and those in states without any EDR and 2) between those living in states with newly implemented EDR and those in states without any EDR.

Worst Case Bounds

The logic of the bounds approach dictates that analysis begins by assuming nothing at all about the processes that determine the selection of registration laws and turnout (more generally, selection into the treatment and the outcome of interest). As discussed in Chapter 1, the usual approach begins with assumptions strong enough to identify point estimates of treatment effects. Without any assumptions, the probability of voting if all had EDR, the probability of voting if none had EDR, and the CTE are not identified.[22] However, even without assuming anything about the process that determines the selection of registration laws and turnout, we know that the respective counterfactual probabilities – the probability of voting with EDR for those in states that do not currently allow EDR, and the probability of voting without EDR in states that currently allow

---

[19] Analyses using data from other presidential election years (1984, 1988, and 1992) do not substantively alter the conclusions.

[20] For the 1996 and 2000 elections, ME, MN, ND, and WI are coded as having mature EDR programs and ID, NH, and WY are coded as having newly implemented EDR programs.

[21] Whereas ME and MN also had versions of motor voter in 1996 and 2000, the effect of this program is not thought to be responsible for differences in turnout between EDR and non-EDR states. Analyses excluding these two states are consistent with those presented here.

[22] That is, equations (1), (2), and (3) in the appendix to Chapter 1 are not identified.

EDR – must each lie in the interval $[0, 1]$. Using this information, one can estimate worst case bounds (called worst case because they use the least amount of information and will be the widest possible set of bounds) for the probability of voting if all had EDR, and the probability of voting if none had EDR. To calculate the lower bound for the probability of voting if all had EDR, the counterfactual probability – the probability of voting under EDR for those who did not live in EDR states – is set to 0; to calculate the upper bound, the counterfactual probability is set to 1. That is, the lower bound is derived by proceeding as if none of those who lived in states that did not allow EDR would have voted had they instead lived in states that allow EDR, and the upper bound is derived by proceeding as if all of those who lived in states that did not allow EDR would have voted had they instead lived in states that allow EDR. Similar logic applies for the calculation of the bounds on the probability of voting if none had EDR.[23] These bounds are functions of quantities identified by the sampling process alone, and thus can be calculated without imposing any assumptions on the process that generates the voting outcomes and the EDR treatment. It is important to note that the width of the bounds in the equation predicting voting when all have the EDR treatment is the probability of living in a state that does not allow EDR[24] (called the censoring probability), and the width of the bounds in the equation predicting voting when none have the EDR treatment is the probability of living in a state that allows EDR (called the selection probability).

---

[23] Recall that the probability of voting if EDR were available in all states is represented by:

$$P(y_1 = 1 \mid x) = P(y_1 = 1 \mid x, t = 1) * P(t = 1 \mid x) + P(y_1 = 1 \mid x, t = 0) * P(t = 0 \mid x); \quad (1)$$

and the probability of voting if EDR were not available in any states is represented by

$$P(y_0 = 1 \mid x) = P(y_0 = 1 \mid x, t = 0) * P(t = 0 \mid x) + P(y_0 = 1 \mid x, t = 1) * P(t = 1 \mid x). \quad (2)$$

The worst case bounds for (1) and (2) are formally defined as follows:

For (1), $P(y_1 = 1 \mid x, t = 1) * P(t = 1 \mid x) \leq P(y_1 = 1 \mid x)$

$$\leq P(y_1 = 1 \mid x, t = 1) * P(t = 1 \mid x) + P(t = 0 \mid x). \quad (1a)$$

And for (2), $P(y_0 = 1 \mid x, t = 0) * P(t = 0 \mid x) \leq P(y_0 = 1 \mid x)$

$$\leq P(y_0 = 1 \mid x, t = 0) * P(t = 0 \mid x) + P(t = 1 \mid x). \quad (2a)$$

[24] As was the case in the later parts of Chapter 1, implicit in the description is conditioning on the covariates of interest, x.

Worst case bounds on the CTE can also be estimated.[25] Once the data
are employed, the bound on the CTE, without making any assumptions,
necessarily has a width of 1; in the absence of data, the CTE would have
a width of 2 and would lie between −1 and 1.

Before moving to the results, a note on the use of the individual
attributes (covariates) is necessary. In the traditional approach, individual
attributes are used to control for treatment assignment. With the bounds
approach, controlling for treatment assignment is not relevant so individual attributes are used to designate subpopulations of interest. Manski
and Nagin (1998) provide further explanation:

> Researchers commonly assert that there is some minimal set of "correct" covariates to use in the analysis of treatment effects and that "omitted variable bias"
> may occur if one conditions on only a subset of these covariates. These statements
> relate to use of covariates to control for treatment assignment. A set of covariates
> is said to be "correct" if treatment assignment is random conditional on these
> covariates; "omitted variable bias" is said to occur if one conditions only on a
> subset of these covariates and treatment assignment is not random conditional on
> this subset. We do not assume that treatment assignment is random conditional
> on any set of covariates. Hence, the concepts of "correct" covariates and "omitted
> variable bias" are not germane to [the] analysis (p. 107).

Thus, regardless of the specification of covariates, the following question
is well posed: Among individuals with the selected covariates, what would
be the difference in the probability of voting if all such individuals were
assigned one treatment rather than the other?

Table 3.2 presents information revealed by the sampling process for
1980, 1996, and 2000, without conditioning on any covariates.[26] In each
of the years, those who lived in states with EDR (column 1, $P(y_1 = 1 \mid t = 1)$) turned out at higher rates than those in states without EDR (column
2, $P(y_0 = 1 \mid t = 0)$). In both 1996 and 2000, those in mature EDR states
turned out at the highest rates, followed by those in states with newly
implemented EDR. Table 3.2 also reveals that the proportion of people
who lived in states with EDR (column 3, $P(t = 1)$), either mature or

---

[25] The lower bound on the CTE is calculated by subtracting the upper bound of (2a) from
the lower bound of (1a) and the upper bound on the CTE is calculated by subtracting
the lower bound of (2a) from the upper bound of (1a). More formally:

$$[P(y_1 = 1 \mid x, t = 1)^* P(t = 1 \mid x)] - [P(y_0 = 1 \mid x, t = 0)^* P(t = 0 \mid x) + P(t = 1 \mid x)]$$
$$\leq \text{CTE}$$
$$\leq [P(y_1 = 1 \mid x, t = 1)^* P(t = 1 \mid x) + P(t = 0 \mid x)] - [P(y_0 = 1 \mid x, t = 0)^* P(t = 0 \mid x)].$$

[26] Those who did not provide an answer of "yes" or "no" to the question asking whether
or not the individual voted were eliminated from the sample.

TABLE 3.2. *Estimated Probabilities of Voting and Residing in a State with EDR (%)*

Year and Category	Probability of Voting in EDR States $P(y_1 = 1 \mid t = 1)$	Probability of Voting in Non-EDR States $P(y_0 = 1 \mid t = 0)$	Probability of Living in an EDR State $P(t = 1)$
1980	76	65	8
$N = 113,123$			
1996 Mature EDR	71	63	6
$N = 75,116$			
1996 New EDR	67	63	4
$N = 73,902$			
2000 Mature EDR	76	67	6
$N = 71,127$			
2000 New EDR	69	67	4
$N = 69,899$			

Source: 1980, 1996, 2000 CPS.

newly implemented, was quite small; as mentioned earlier, this will have important consequences for the width of the bounds.

Table 3.3 presents the worst case bounds for 1980, 1996, and 2000.[27] Given that the probability of living in a state with EDR (the selection probability), $P(t = 1)$, is small for each year and scenario, the bounds on the probability of voting if all had EDR (mature or newly implemented) are enormous; thus, in the absence of prior information or assumptions, very little about the effect of EDR can be learned. However,

---

[27] An illustration of the bounds approach follows. In 1980, 76 percent of those living in states with EDR voted whereas 65 percent of those living in states that did not allow EDR voted. Only 8 percent of the 113,123 respondents lived in EDR states; thus 92 percent of the respondents lived in states that did not allow EDR. Driven by the size of the selection probability, $P(t = 1)$, the bounds on $P(y_1 = 1)$ are extremely wide whereas the bounds on $P(y_0 = 1)$ are quite narrow. As shown subsequently, without making any assumptions, the probability of voting under the EDR treatment lies between 0.06 and 0.98. Obviously, without making any assumptions, very little can be said about the probability of voting if all states were to have had EDR in 1980. The calculation follows: $0.06 = 0.76*0.08 \leq P(y_1 = 1) \leq 0.76*0.08 + 0.92 = 0.98$. The worst case bounds on the probability of voting if none of the states allowed EDR are much more informative. The calculation that follows reveals that the probability of voting under this scenario is at least 0.60 and at most 0.68: $0.60 = 0.65*0.92 \leq P(y_0 = 1) \leq 0.65*0.92 + 0.08 = 0.68$. Having calculated the bounds for $P(y_1 = 1)$ and $P(y_0 = 1)$, bounds on the CTE can also be derived: $-0.62 = 0.06 - 0.68 \leq CTE \leq 0.98 - 0.60 = 0.38$. These figures can then be multiplied by 100 to get percentages.

TABLE 3.3. *Worst Case Bounds on the Probability of Voting (%)*

	Probability of Voting if All States Allowed EDR		Probability of Voting if No States Allowed EDR		Classical Treatment Effect (CTE)	
	$P(y_1 = 1\|x)$		$P(y_0 = 1\|x)$		$P(y_1 = 1\|x) - P(y_0 = 1\|x)$	
Year and Category	LB	UB	LB	UB	LB	UB
1980	6	98	60	68	−62	38
1996 Mature EDR	4	98	60	65	−61	39
1996 New EDR	3	99	61	65	−62	38
2000 Mature EDR	5	99	63	69	−64	36
2000 New EDR	3	99	64	68	−65	35

Note: LB indicates the lower bound and UB indicates the upper bound.
Source: 1980, 1996, 2000 CPS.

the worst case bounds on the probability of voting if none of the states allowed EDR are quite narrow. Because of the size of the selection probability, these bounds do not allow one to determine the sign of the effect of EDR (our main interest) and, thus, are not especially informative. Using 1980 as an example, the bounds on the CTE indicate that EDR might reduce the probability of voting by as much as 62 percentage points and might increase the probability of voting by as much as 38 percentage points. It is crucial to note that the actual value can lie anywhere within the bounds. A larger negative value does not imply that a negative value is more likely than a positive value. Although the results say little about the effect of EDR, an important point emerges: In order to tighten the bounds, and thus learn more about the effect of EDR, assumptions are necessary. As discussed earlier, the bounds approach is appealing because it requires the recognition of the importance of various assumptions, the clear statement of those assumptions, and serious evaluation of the assumptions. The next section introduces two assumptions aimed at providing additional insight into the effect of EDR, one that serves to tighten the lower bound (the ordered outcomes assumption), and one that tightens the upper bound (the capped outcomes assumption).

Intermediate Assumptions: Ordered Outcomes and Capped Outcomes

The ordered outcomes assumption (see Manski 1995, 1997; and Pepper 2000) provides a middle ground between the worst case bounds and the exogenous selection assumption.[28] This assumption implies that EDR can do no harm; that is, the probability of voting for those in non-EDR states would not decrease if EDR were made available. Having an EDR program available would presumably reduce the costs of voting, and at worst should not deter any of those who voted in its absence to abstain in its presence. In this context, the ordered outcomes assumption is noncontroversial as it fits cleanly with the theoretical expectations provided by Downs (1957).[29] By definition, the lower bound on the CTE is set to 0; thus, this assumption serves to identify the sign of EDR's effect. The CTE upper bound remains the same as in the worst case scenario.

As discussed earlier, the states that first adopted EDR are known for their tradition of encouraging participation and status as high turnout states. An assumption within the bounds framework can be constructed to account for the argument that the effect of EDR is expected to be lower when transported to new contexts. That is, this assumption captures the contention that if EDR were adopted in states with different social and political contexts than found in the states that were first to adopt EDR, the effects in these new contexts would not be any higher. In terms of the model, one can reduce the worst case upper bound by assuming that the outcome in new contexts, for example, states that adopted EDR to avoid the NVRA, would not exceed the outcome found in the states that adopted EDR without having their hand forced by the federal government.[30] I will refer to this assumption as the capped outcomes assumption.[31] Given that

---

[28] Because the primary concern is what would happen if EDR were adopted more widely, the focus of the remainder of the chapter is on $P(y_1 = 1 \mid x)$.

[29] Formally, the ordered outcomes assumption implies that:

$$P(y_1 = 1 \mid x, t = 0) \geq P(y_0 = 1 \mid x, t = 0).$$

To compute bounds for $P(y_1 = 1 \mid x)$, set $P(y_1 = 1 \mid x, t = 0)$ – the counterfactual probability – to $P(y_0 = 1 \mid x, t = 0)$ – the estimated probability of voting for those in non-EDR states – rather than zero, to get the lower bound; the upper bound does not change.

[30] Formally, this implies that: $P(y_1 = 1 \mid x, t = 0) \leq P(y_1 = 1 \mid x, t = 1)$.

[31] Those uncomfortable with this assumption should recognize that the only difference between the probit and bounds approach on this matter is that when using probit one does this to obtain a point estimate but here this is part of the construction of the bounds. When one estimates the probability of voting if EDR were available everywhere with, say, a probit model, one sets the values of those who did not receive this treatment to the estimated value of those who did receive the EDR treatment. That is, one does not assume that the effect will be less than or greater than that estimated from what was observed in the data from those in the treatment condition but assumes that the effect, if EDR were adopted elsewhere, would be equivalent to the effect observed in the places currently using this policy. In addition, note that any assumption to capture the possibility that the effect would be greater than the effect found in places currently

TABLE 3.4. *Combined Ordered Outcomes and Capped Outcomes Bounds if All States Allowed EDR (%)*

Year and Category	Probability of Voting if All States Allowed EDR $P(y_t = 1\|x)$		Classical Treatment Effect $P(y_t = 1\|x) - P(y_0 = 1\|x)$	
	LB	UB	LB	UB
1980	66	76	0	16
1996 Mature EDR	64	71	0	12
1996 New EDR	63	67	0	6
2000 Mature EDR	67	76	0	13
2000 New EDR	67	69	0	5

Notes: The ordered outcomes assumption tightens the lower bound; the capped outcomes assumption tightens the upper bound. LB indicates the lower bound and UB indicates the upper bound.
Source: 1980, 1996, 2000 CPS.

this assumption will not change the worst case lower bound, the bounds on the probability of voting if all had EDR will remain relatively wide. However, it stands to reason that if one were to accept this assumption as plausible, he/she would also accept the more innocuous ordered outcomes assumption. When combined, these two assumptions serve to tighten both the lower and upper bounds.

Table 3.4 presents the bounds on the probability of voting and the CTE if all had EDR under the combined ordered and capped outcomes assumptions. The width of the bounds under these two assumptions compared with the worst case bounds is reduced substantially, by as much as 98 percent for the year 2000 newly implemented EDR scenario. The bounds are reduced by 89 percent for 1980, by 92 percent for 1996 mature EDR, by 96 percent for 1996 newly implemented EDR, and by 91 percent for 2000 mature EDR. The less controversial ordered outcomes assumption provides the greatest portion of the reduction; the width of the bounds with the ordered outcomes assumption alone is reduced by 65 percent in 1980, by 63 percent for both EDR categories in 1996, and by 67 percent for both EDR categories in 2000.

Although, by assumption, the sign of the treatment effect is identified, because the bounds on the CTE overlap, these assumptions do not allow one to identify whether the impact of mature EDR is greater than the

in the treatment condition, in either the bounds or probit set up, would necessarily be arbitrary. That is, rather than using the data, one would have to assume the effect is some fixed amount higher, but such an exercise defeats the entire research enterprise.

TABLE 3.5. *Estimates of the Classical Treatment Effect (CTE) under the Exogenous Selection Assumption,* $P(y_1 = 1 \mid x) - P(y_0 = 1 \mid x)$, *(with 90% Confidence Interval) (%)*

Year & Category	5% Quantile	CTE	95% Quantile
1980	10	11	11
1996 Mature EDR	7	8	9
1996 New EDR	2	4	5
2000 Mature EDR	8	9	10
2000 New EDR	0	2	4

Source: 1980, 1996, 2000 CPS.

impact of newly implemented EDR, nor whether the impact in mature EDR states declined since 1980. The potential effect under these two assumptions is higher for mature EDR but the estimated effect may lie anywhere within the bounds. To identify these effects, the much stronger exogenous selection assumption (the assumption implicitly maintained in the literature, which treats registration laws as if they were randomly assigned) will have to be imposed. Although serious doubt has been cast on the exogenous selection assumption, it is useful to examine what is gained when it is imposed.

The Exogenous Selection Assumption

Estimates derived under the exogenous selection assumption, along with the 90 percent confidence interval around the estimates, are presented in Table 3.5. The 90 percent confidence interval for each estimate was computed using the bootstrap method (see Manski et al. 1992, Pepper 2000). To compute the 90 percent confidence intervals, first a sample of size N (where N is equal to the size of the sample of interest in the dataset) is drawn with replacement. Next, the estimates of interest are computed for this sample. To create a bootstrapped distribution of the estimates, the process is then repeated T times (here T is set to 200). The 0.05 quantile and the 0.95 quantile of the resulting distribution are reported to form the 90 percent confidence interval.[32]

---

[32] Bootstrapped confidence intervals for the results in Table 3.3 and Table 3.4 can be found in Appendix F Table F.1 and Table F.2, respectively. As Manski and Nagin (1998) note, with sufficiently large samples, the identification problem is much more severe than the problem of sampling variation. This can be seen most clearly by inspecting Appendix F Tables F.1 and F.2. The estimated bounds are quite large whereas the confidence intervals around those bounds are only slightly larger.

With the exogenous selection assumption, we can obtain point estimates for the probability of voting if EDR were available to all eligible citizens $(P(y_1 = 1 \,|\, x))$ the probability of voting if EDR were not available anywhere $(P(y_0 = 1 \,|\, x))$ and the effect of EDR (the CTE, where: CTE $= P(y_1 = 1 \,|\, x) - P(y_0 = 1 \,|\, x))$. Under the exogenous selection assumption, the estimated effect of EDR based on those in the states that first adopted EDR is as high as 11 percentage points in 1980, whereas the largest effect of newly implemented EDR in states that reluctantly changed the status quo is only 4 percentage points. That the effect is larger in the mature EDR states is consistent with the substantive conclusion from the difference in difference approach. In both 1996 and 2000, the effect of mature EDR is greater than the effect of newly implemented EDR, with the largest gap occurring in 2000. Whereas the impact of mature EDR appears to have diminished only slightly over time, the estimated effect of newly implemented EDR drops substantially from 1996 to 2000. One of the following might help explain the drop for new EDR states: 1) for the new EDR states, a novelty effect boosted turnout in 1996; and/or 2) the implementation of motor voter in all non-EDR states over the 1996-to-2000 period boosted turnout in the comparison states more so in 2000 than in 1996. Because mature and newly implemented EDR are compared to the same base, the second explanation seems less plausible, as the estimated effect of mature EDR did not decrease from 1996 to 2000.

Because the effect of EDR in the states that adopted it via a loophole in the NVRA is estimated to be lower than that found in mature EDR states (even more than thirty years after its initial implementation), this approach also casts serious doubt on the assumption that the effects of registration laws can be extrapolated across contexts. The difference in the estimates for mature EDR and newly implemented EDR demonstrate the need to examine the effects of the policy across the two sets of contexts separately. If, as is commonly done, states that adopted EDR prior to 1980 had been grouped with states that adopted in the 1990s to avoid the federal motor voter law, the effect of EDR for the new EDR states would have been overestimated. As I show later, when one examines the effects across different subpopulations (with a focus on education and age) the differences become more pronounced (see Chapter 6). Because more interesting differences surface once conditioning on covariates, such as education and age, is done, I also save the comparison of the bounds and probit estimates until then.

SUMMARY AND PREVIEW

Both the difference in difference and bounds estimation strategies used in this chapter can be used to deal with endogeneity. The key to the difference in difference approach is finding plausible control states. With the bounds approach, all assumptions are made explicit, but in order to avoid the exogenous selection assumption, one must accept more ambiguity. That is, under weaker but more credible assumptions, point estimates cannot be obtained. Together, the results demonstrate that the effect of EDR differs across contexts; in the states that adopted EDR primarily to avoid the NVRA and its expected costs and confusion, the effect is lower than that found in the states that led the way to one-stop voting in the 1970s. With the ordered and capped outcomes assumption, the bounds approach produces estimates of the effect of EDR that range from 0 to 16 percentage points for mature EDR states and from 0 to 6 percentage points for states that recently adopted EDR. The difference in difference estimates indicate that the effects will be closer to the lower bound than to the upper bound, especially for the new EDR states.

Although the difference in difference approach controls for endogeneity and provides point estimates, it still requires functional form and distributional assumptions. As I demonstrate in Chapter 6, based on the bounds approach results for Minnesota and Wisconsin, these assumptions do not appear problematic. Both estimation techniques suggest that the least educated in these states saw the largest increases in turnout. However, for the states of Idaho, New Hampshire, and Wyoming, the functional form and distributional assumptions are suspect. Further research is necessary to identify where these models go wrong.

CONCLUSION

The results presented here are consistent with the hypotheses derived from my theoretical framework. EDR was adopted in two sets of states under different circumstances, with important consequences for the effect of this program across these contexts. The states that adopted EDR in the 1970s did so on their own, with substantial weight placed on reducing burdens faced by citizens and enhancing voter participation. The states that adopted EDR in the 1990s would have chosen to maintain the status quo had the federal government not required implementation of the NVRA or (via a loophole) EDR and chose EDR because it was believed to be less costly to administer than the NVRA.

The central finding is that the effect of EDR is smaller than reformers would hope and previous studies suggest; making registration easier will have only small effects. Overall, this will likely be viewed as bad news. Even under the most favorable conditions, EDR leads to increases in turnout of about 4 percentage points. In places that have a history of burdensome registration procedures, unless the political parties engage in large-scale mobilization campaigns, even smaller effects should be expected, especially if the change to a new system of registration laws is imposed by the federal government, rather than chosen independently by the state. As discussed in Chapter 7, evidence from interviews with political party leaders in the states that currently have EDR suggests that expanded registration campaigns are unlikely; EDR has done little to change the allocation of resources toward voter registration. The party leaders indicate that their focus is on mobilizing registered voters thought to be sympathetic to their party's positions. Simply put, going after the unregistered is generally viewed as too expensive and too risky.

If an argument is to be made for reducing barriers to registration, it will have to be made on normative grounds, such as those expressed by James (1987) and Piven and Cloward (1988, 2000), rather than on empirical grounds. On its own, making registration easier only leads those who are already interested in voting to take advantage of the new procedure. Facilitation of mobilization efforts by political parties, an indirect avenue through which EDR can increase turnout, has not led parties to devote more resources toward registering eligible citizens. Thus, in order to boost turnout, longer-term strategies geared toward engaging the citizenry will be necessary.

This chapter has exposed the deficiencies of traditional approaches and has established that the difference in difference and bounds approaches apply straightforwardly to the study of changes in election laws. When it can be shown that the conditions across states are similar, the difference in difference approach can be used to estimate the effect of changes in election laws. The results from the bounds approach illustrate that without making any assumptions, very little, if anything, can be learned about the effect of EDR. In contrast to the approach taken in previous studies, rather than starting by imposing an assumption strong enough to identify this effect, the bounds approach begins with minimal assumptions and then applies increasingly strong assumptions that serve to provide more informative bounds as well as point estimates. Laying out the assumptions clearly should not only spark discussion regarding the credibility of the assumptions, but should also guide the search for additional information that can be used to evaluate further the assumptions, and improve our understanding of the process being studied.

As researchers move to the study of other election laws, such as those resulting from the Help America Vote Act of 2002, it will be important to take into account the factors that motivated change. The evidence presented here suggests that outcomes may differ when states make a change on their own compared with when states make a change due to federal intervention.

In Chapter 4, I turn my attention to motor voter. Given the small effects of EDR, a law that theoretically should produce larger increases in turnout than motor voter, the reader will not be surprised to find that overall, motor voter does little to increase turnout.

4

Motor Voter by Choice and by Federal Mandate

In Chapter 3, I demonstrated that the effect of election day registration (EDR) differs across social and political contexts. In the already high turnout states of Minnesota and Wisconsin, EDR led to a small but significant increase in turnout. The effect of EDR in Idaho, New Hampshire, and Wyoming, states that adopted EDR to avoid federal motor voter legislation, fell short of expectations based on previous studies and the mark set by Minnesota and Wisconsin. These conclusions were derived primarily by using the difference in difference method, a method that aims to control for endogeneity by comparing turnout over time in comparable states. The purpose of this chapter is to estimate the effect of motor voter as implemented via state law and via the National Voter Registration Act of 1993 (NVRA). The states with pre-NVRA laws that were deemed suitable for analysis are Michigan, Minnesota, Nevada, and North Carolina.

As discussed in Chapter 1, although some scholars have treated EDR and motor voter as substitutes (Teixeira 1992; Highton and Wolfinger 1998), the policies must be investigated separately. EDR and motor voter policies differ mainly in terms of the costs imposed on voters, but also in terms of the likelihood that interest in voting drives the decision to register, and the ease with which political parties and candidates can contact registrants, all of which lead to differential expectations with respect to the respective policy's effect on turnout. Because two trips are required – one to register and another, at a later time, to vote – motor voter is more costly than EDR. Moreover, motor voter policies register some who were not initially interested in doing so. That is, motor voter presents an opportunity to register to vote to those who initially set out to obtain a driver's license, register their car, or, in the case of those in need of public assistance, get help meeting basic needs; thus, the primary intention of the trip likely had nothing to do with electoral politics.

Whereas those two features suggest motor voter registration should be less effective than EDR, motor voter policies have slightly *more* promise than does EDR with respect to the prospects for mobilization by parties and candidates in an upcoming election. Unlike EDR, motor voter gets registrants' names to the political parties in time for the next election via their inclusion on registration lists, thus opening the door to potentially larger mobilization effects than one would expect from EDR, as EDR registrants obviously do not appear on the registration lists until after the present election. However, as noted earlier, those who do not have a history of voting are not likely to generate much attention from the parties.

My expectations with respect to state implementation of motor voter prior to the NVRA and the effect of the NVRA are: In the states that adopted pre-NVRA motor voter laws, motor voter should have a positive yet small effect on voter turnout. Motor voter certainly captures eligible citizens who might not otherwise register, but these new registrants will still have to make another trip to vote, in many cases, years after the registration transaction takes place. In addition to concerns that one might forget their registration status, as noted earlier, the interest in political participation of these individuals is highly uncertain, thus calling into question the effectiveness of the policy to register citizens who will then have sufficient interest to take the next step and show up at their polling place or obtain an absentee ballot. Although the NVRA is more far reaching than the early motor voter laws, as was the case with the states that were the first to adopt EDR, I expect motor voter to be most effective in states that adopted it without prompting by the federal government. That is, to the extent that motor voter has a positive influence on turnout, I expect the pre-NVRA motor voter programs that were willingly adopted through state legislative processes to have a larger effect than the NVRA, a law that was viewed by some states as an unfunded federal mandate.

The analysis begins with a brief look at motor voter programs that were put into place prior to the NVRA. As I noted in the Introduction, scholars have devoted surprisingly little attention to these pre-NVRA programs. To account for the nonrandom selection of the state motor voter policies (endogeneity), I employ the difference in difference approach when studying the pre-NVRA motor voter programs, as I did in Chapter 3.

I then turn to an evaluation of the NVRA. For this analysis, a different approach is needed. In 1995, the NVRA was implemented in all but seven states, the states with EDR (Idaho, Minnesota, New Hampshire, Wisconsin, and Wyoming), North Dakota, which does not require registration, and Vermont, which delayed implementation in order to resolve conflicts with the state's Voter's Oath provision.[1] This far-reaching policy shift complicates analysis using the difference in difference approach. For example, if one wanted to estimate the effect of the NVRA in New York, one would likely compare New York to, say, New Jersey and Pennsylvania, but both of these states were subject to the NVRA as well; thus, all three states fall into the treatment group and leave the control group empty. Without at least one viable control state, the difference in difference model cannot be estimated. Moreover, with a law that has a national scope, the relevant task changes to an evaluation of the impact of the NVRA on national turnout, rather than turnout in a handful of states, thus alleviating concerns related to the extrapolation of results to states with dissimilar social and political contexts. Thus, for this analysis, I use a model with state and year fixed effects.[2] As noted in previous chapters, models with state and year fixed effects are not without problems. However, such models fit this purpose better than they do others.

PRE-NVRA MOTOR VOTER LAWS

The first motor voter law was enacted in Michigan and went into effect in October, 1975. Anyone who has spent time in Michigan will not find it surprising that registration reform was associated with automobiles. In Michigan, the car is king; it seems everyone has at least one. The intertwining of voter registration and driver's license transactions was proposed by Secretary of State Richard Austin, passed the Democratic-controlled legislature, and was signed into law by Republican Governor William G. Milliken. Letters regarding the legislation from Austin and his staff, as well as the Legislative Analysis, reveal the intent of Michigan's move to motor voter was to promote registration and assist clerks with list maintenance. Remarkably, hardly any attention has been given to the effect of Michigan's motor voter program.

---

[1] Although Maine had EDR, because EDR transactions were not required to take place at the polling places, Maine was not exempt from the NVRA. In 1990, G. William Diamond, the Maine Secretary of State, authorized motor voter registration in the state's twelve motor vehicle registries.

[2] Throughout the chapter, data from the Current Population Survey (CPS) are used for the estimation of the difference in difference and fixed effects models.

A number of scholars have studied motor voter programs (Knack 1995; Rhine 1995, 1996; Franklin and Grier 1997; Knack and White 1998; Highton and Wolfinger 1998; Knack 1999; Martinez and Hill 1999; Parry and Shields 2001; and Brown and Wedeking 2006) as implemented prior to the NVRA and immediately after the NVRA, but a consensus regarding how best to classify the pre-NVRA motor voter states has not been reached; each study codes the states differently. In large part, the difficulties stem from variations in implementation and the difficulty of assessing implementation by researchers, especially when doing so years, and even decades, after the laws were passed. Reviewing state laws is necessary but not sufficient, as the laws were often not implemented at all or were only partially implemented (see Piven and Cloward 2000). For example, in some states, registration forms were simply placed somewhere in the motor vehicle offices; although one often has a good deal of time waiting to be called by the motor vehicle clerk, it is unlikely that many would wander around the often large and crowded waiting rooms and stumble upon the registration forms. The organization founded by Piven and Cloward, Human SERVE, in their push to promote voter registration, collected extensive information on state-level motor voter laws and the degree to which they were implemented, thus providing an important service to the research community.

Given its attempt to assess implementation, Human SERVE is the most appropriate source for information regarding which states had active motor voter programs.[3] Hence, I follow the criteria set forth by Piven and Cloward. In a critique of a Congressional Research Service Report examining state motor voter laws as of 1988, Piven and Cloward argue that:

[a]n adequate evaluation of the impact of motor voter reform would have limited the states to those with combined forms that were *operational* over a *four-year* [driver's license renewal] *cycle*, and that, in addition to new applicants, registered both *in-person and mail renewals* (emphasis from original, Piven and Cloward, 2000, p. 237).

---

[3] A note of caution is appropriate. A comparison of two documents, a 1993 pamphlet, "Motor Voter, The National Voter Registration Act: Including All Americans in Our Democracy" and a November 1992 release, "'Motor Voter' States Had Highest Registration and Turnout Increases in 1992 Elections" reveals that not all of the information provided by Human SERVE is consistent. The 1993 pamphlet suggests that the District of Columbia, Hawaii, Maine, Michigan, Minnesota, Montana, Nevada, North Carolina, Oregon, Texas, and Washington had "model programs," whereas the 1992 document excludes Hawaii altogether, and notes that Colorado is excluded because motor voter transactions were not recorded. Personal communication with Jo-Anne Chasnow, during her time as Executive Director for Human SERVE, and elections officials in Hawaii led me to treat Hawaii and Colorado as having "model programs" as of 1992.

They go on to say that only Michigan "more or less met these criteria" (Piven and Cloward 2000, p. 237).[4] On these points, especially in light of the NVRA, I agree with Piven and Cloward. Driver's license renewals make up the bulk of driver's license transactions; thus, motor voter in states that did not allow motor voter registration for renewals miss most of the potential registrants. In situations such as this, motor voter would be expected to have a miniscule effect at best. A limitation of motor voter is that the full effect will be felt only after all eligible citizens are given the opportunity to register while renewing their driver's license. The renewal cycle in most states is four years long; thus, reserving judgment of motor voter until at least four years after implementation is appropriate.

By 1992, three additional states meet the criteria established by Piven and Cloward: Minnesota, Nevada, and North Carolina, though there is some controversy surrounding these classifications. Highton and Wolfinger (1998) contend that motor voter was passive in Nevada and was active in Colorado. I defer to Human SERVE's classifications and my conversation with the organization's Executive Director, Jo-Anne Chasnow, who expressed serious concern with Wolfinger and Highton's treatment of Colorado as having an active motor voter program. It is important to note that although they rate Colorado as active, Highton and Wolfinger take a cautious view of their analysis of Colorado, stating the results are "no more than suggestive" (1998, p. 85). Although motor voter in North Carolina was active in 1984, it was more or less dormant under a Republican governor from 1985 to 1988. Up through the implementation of the NVRA, both Nevada and North Carolina had requirements that driver's licenses be renewed in-person, thus eliminating concern that those renewing by mail would be excluded.[5] The other states with "model programs" do not meet the criteria until the NVRA was in place, thus making it impossible to sort out the effect of the pre-NVRA motor voter programs from the effect of the NVRA in these states.

---

[4] Michigan sent registration applications with driver's license renewal forms but with a few exceptions, required that voter registration take place in person. The application indicated that registration had to be completed in person and when the forms were mailed to the Secretary of State's office in error, the forms were returned with "a gentle reminder that voter registrations must be completed in person" (Richard H. Austin, "A New Approach to Voter Registration," 1985, p. 18).

[5] Exceptions were allowed under rare circumstances: in North Carolina, exceptions were made for armed services personnel stationed out of state and residents living out of state for thirty continuous days; and in Nevada exceptions were made if good cause could be shown along with proof that the applicant recently passed an eye exam.

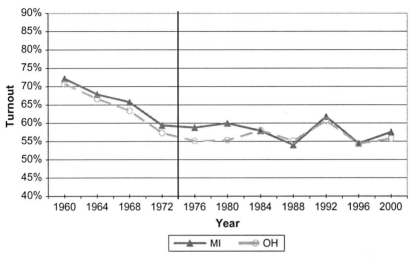

FIGURE 4.1. Presidential year turnout and motor voter in Michigan (compared to Ohio) 1960–2000 (Source: FEC).

In the rest of this chapter, I provide estimates of the effect of pre-NVRA programs on turnout in Michigan, Minnesota, Nevada, and North Carolina. The chapter concludes with an evaluation of the effect of the NVRA on national turnout.

Michigan (Paving the Way for Motor Voter)

Sometimes, those who are most similar to us are those we like the least. Michigan and Ohio, which have a history of political, economic, territorial, and college football rivalries, fit this characterization well.[6] Figure 4.1 reveals that patterns of voter turnout in Michigan, shown with a dark solid line and solid marker, and Ohio, shown with a light dashed line and open marker, from 1960 to 2000 were quite similar. This stems from the similarity of these two states on a variety of factors that influence turnout (see Appendix D). Prior to the adoption of motor voter in Michigan, that is, the portion of the graph to the left of the dark vertical line, turnout in these two states was nearly identical. As turnout declined from 1960 to 1972, turnout in Michigan was barely higher than that in Ohio. In terms of turnout rank, the two states were near

---

[6] Ohio had motor voter on the books as of 1977 but it was not implemented. Neither state ever implemented EDR.

the middle of the pack over the 1960-to-1972 period. Michigan had the eighteenth highest level of turnout in 1960 and the twenty-sixth highest in 1972, whereas Ohio ranked twenty-fourth and twenty-ninth respectively. After Michigan adopted motor voter in 1975, Michigan's turnout dropped slightly in 1976 and then rose slightly in 1980. On their own, the small changes in Michigan's turnout rate do not appear noteworthy. When compared with turnout in Ohio, however, which saw its turnout rate drop in 1976 and remain virtually unchanged in 1980, it seems motor voter played a positive role in Michigan. In 1972, Michigan's turnout rate was 2.1 percentage points higher than Ohio's and in 1980, after a full driver's license renewal cycle, the turnout gap increased to 4.7 percentage points in Michigan's favor. Moreover, Michigan had the twelfth highest rate of turnout in 1980, while Ohio ranked twenty-fifth. The effect of motor voter, though, unlike the effect of EDR in Minnesota and Wisconsin, appears short-lived; by 1984, and continuing through 2000, turnout rates in Ohio again matched Michigan's turnout rates.

These results hold up when the difference in difference model is estimated on pooled cross-sectional data from the 1972 and 1980 Current Population Survey Voter Supplement Files (CPS), with Ohio acting as a control state for Michigan.[7] As can be seen from Table 4.1, the coefficient on the motor voter effect variable is positive and statistically significant. The predicted effect of motor voter, calculated using the same method as described in Chapter 3, is 5.4 percentage points. Surprisingly, this initial effect is on par with the effect of EDR in Minnesota and Wisconsin. However, when moving beyond the short-term effects, by extending the analysis to include the entire series prior to the NVRA (1972–1992), the effect disappears. That is, the effect is not very durable. The coefficient on the motor voter effect over this period is small, 0.03, with a p value = 0.38. Although in Figure 4.1, the effect of motor voter appears to vanish after 1980, once factors that influence turnout are controlled for, a small (2.5 percentage points) and statistically significant effect remains through 1984.[8]

---

[7] The traditional approach produces similar results. With Minnesota and Wisconsin, the coefficient on the effect of EDR soaks up the unmeasured forces that affect turnout and thus the decision to adopt EDR. There, the issue of endogeneity is more serious because these unmeasured forces pushed Minnesota and Wisconsin to especially high rates of turnout even before they adopted registration reform.

[8] The coefficient for the effect of motor voter is 0.08 with a p value = 0.038.

TABLE 4.1. *Difference in Difference Probit Estimates of the Effect of Motor Voter on Turnout (MI compared to OH, 1972 and 1980)*

Variable	Coefficient	Standard Error	z	p Value
Motor Voter Effect in MI	0.1770	0.0453	3.91	0.000
MI	0.3280	0.1726	1.90	0.057
Education * MI	0.0035	0.0220	0.16	0.874
Age * MI	−0.0100	0.0067	−1.48	0.138
Age Squared * MI	0.0001	0.0001	1.37	0.171
Income * MI	−0.0339	0.0225	−1.51	0.132
Education	0.3425	0.0146	23.52	0.000
Age	0.0628	0.0045	13.99	0.000
Age Squared	−0.0004	0.0000	−9.37	0.000
Income Quartile	0.1822	0.0153	11.93	0.000
1980	−0.1719	0.0301	−5.71	0.000
Constant	−2.9926	0.1150	−26.02	0.000

$N = 15,345$.
Log likelihood $= -8449.24$.
Source: 1972 and 1980 CPS.

Minnesota (Blondes and Blue Ears Have More Options)

As a sign of continued efforts to promote voter participation, Minnesota adopted motor voter in 1987. In the previous chapter, I employed South Dakota and Iowa as control states for the investigation of EDR in Minnesota and Wisconsin. When most think of a state similar to Minnesota, they think of Wisconsin and vice versa. These two states are so alike that they both adopted EDR around the same time; thus, for the analysis of EDR, comparing Minnesota and Wisconsin to one another was not possible. Because Wisconsin never adopted motor voter provisions, to estimate the effect of motor voter in Minnesota, Wisconsin can serve as a control state. To avoid the possibility that the effect of EDR creeps into the coefficient for the effect of motor voter, for this analysis, Iowa and South Dakota are not used as control states.[9]

Figure 4.2 shows turnout in Minnesota (represented with a dark solid line and markers) and Wisconsin (represented with light dashed line and open markers) for presidential elections from 1960 to 2000. As is readily seen, both before and after Minnesota adopted motor voter in 1987, Wisconsin's turnout was lower, but tracked Minnesota's closely. In 1988,

---

[9] Including Iowa and South Dakota in the analysis does not change the substantive conclusions.

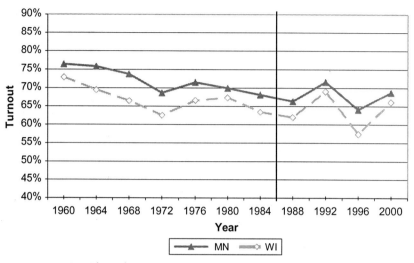

FIGURE 4.2. Presidential year turnout and motor voter in Minnesota (compared to Wisconsin) 1960–2000 (Source: FEC).

the first election for which motor voter registration was available, turnout dropped from its 1984 level in both states at about the same rate. By 1992, a full driver's license renewal cycle had been completed but the increase in turnout was greater in Wisconsin. Overall, the patterns displayed in Figure 4.2 point toward the conclusion that motor voter, when added to a state that already had EDR, did not have any effect.

Further evidence in support of this conclusion is found when the difference in difference model is run on data from the CPS. Table 4.2 shows results from analyses of presidential year turnout using data from the CPS.[10] The first two columns of Table 4.2 display the results from an examination of the short-term effect of motor voter on turnout. In keeping with Piven and Cloward's argument that the full effect of motor voter would not be apparent until at least a four-year driver's license cycle was completed, the analysis of the short-term effect includes data through 1992. The third and fourth columns present the results from analysis extended to include 1996 and 2000. For both sets of results, motor voter is specified as an indicator variable equal to 1 for individuals in Minnesota from 1988 and later, and 0 otherwise. Whether looking at the short- or longer-term effects, the results indicate that motor voter did not have

[10] For simplicity, 1972 is excluded because neither state had EDR or motor voter. Data from 1976 are excluded; as noted earlier, a variable indicating the state in which respondents lived is not included in the 1976 CPS.

TABLE 4.2. *Difference in Difference Probit Estimates of the Effect of Motor Voter on Turnout (MN compared to WI)*

Variable	Short Term Effect (1980–1992)		Longer Term Effect (1980–2000)	
	Coefficient	Standard Error	Coefficient	Standard Error
Motor Voter Effect in MN	0.0028	0.0555	−0.0124	0.0483
MN	0.1096	0.2060	−0.0165	0.1751
Education * MN	−0.0653	0.0269	−0.0690	0.0231
Age * MN	0.0031	0.0083	0.0095	0.0071
Age Squared * MN	−0.00004	0.0001	−0.0001	0.0001
Income * MN	0.0838	0.0280	0.0784	0.0239
Education	0.3323	0.0184	0.3541	0.0160
Age	0.0497	0.0056	0.0405	0.0049
Age Squared	−0.0003	0.0001	−0.0002	0.0001
Income Quartile	0.1769	0.0193	0.1862	0.0166
1984	−0.0614	0.0361	−0.0638	0.0361
1988	−0.1988	0.0460	−0.1983	0.0445
1992	−0.0758	0.0468	−0.0770	0.0454
1996	−	−	−0.4702	0.0466
2000	−	−	−0.3199	0.0488
Constant	−2.4083	0.1416	−2.3721	0.1228
N =	11,830		16,013	
Log likelihood =	−5617.59		−7646.87	

Source: Presidential Year CPS 1980–2000.

an effect on turnout in Minnesota. Both the coefficient for the immediate effect of fully implemented motor voter, reported in column 1 of Table 4.2, and the coefficient from column 3, representing the long-term effect, are very small and statistically indistinguishable from zero ($p = 0.96$ and $p = 0.797$, respectively).[11] Though Minnesotans have

[11] The conclusion of no effect is robust to changes in the way motor voter is specified. The coefficients remain small and are often the wrong sign. Coding motor voter to 1 for those in Minnesota in 1992 and beyond, and 0 otherwise, thus waiting for full implementation to set in, produces a coefficient on motor voter = −0.09 with a p value = 0.188 through 1992, and −0.06 with $p = 0.194$ through 2000. Allowing separate coefficients for the first year of motor voter in 1988 and fully implemented motor voter in 1992 and beyond results in the following: for the analysis through 1992, a coefficient of 0.07 for motor voter in 1988 with $p = 0.322$, and a coefficient of −0.07 for motor voter in 1992 with $p = 0.325$; and for the analysis through 2000, a coefficient of 0.06 for motor voter in 1988 with $p = 0.355$, and a coefficient of −0.04 for motor voter from 1992 to 2000 with $p = 0.399$.

more options, when one has the opportunity to make just one trip to register and vote on election day, arguably the easiest way to register, additional options via motor voter do not fuel turnout further.

Nevada (Betting on Higher Turnout)

State-initiated registration reform moved southwest and to a low turnout state when Nevada adopted motor voter in 1987. In order to estimate the effect of motor voter in Nevada, Arizona serves as the basis of comparison.[12] Strictly speaking, when comparing Nevada to Arizona, an identification assumption of the difference in difference approach is violated. As noted in Chapter 3, one of the identification assumptions is that "apart from the control variables included (X), there are no other forces affecting the treatment and control groups pre- and post-treatment" (Besley and Case 2000, p. F686). Prior to the full implementation of motor voter in Nevada, in 1990, Arizona reduced its especially early registration closing date of fifty days to thirty days prior to the election.[13] Although the analysis can still be performed, the way the results are interpreted must change. Rather than estimating the pure effect of motor voter, the effect of motor voter is judged in comparison to Arizona's relatively large reduction in the amount of time that registration closes before election day, though the closing date remains rather far from election day.

Figure 4.3 reveals that the similarities in terms of demographics in Nevada (represented with the dark solid line and markers) and Arizona (represented with light dashed line and open markers) translated into comparable rates of turnout over the 1960-to-1984 period, the time prior to the adoption of motor voter in Nevada. Turnout was always below 60 percent in both states and the state with the higher rate of turnout changed a number of times. Relative to the rest of the nation, prior to 1987, the best turnout ranking for Nevada was thirty-fourth in 1960, the worst was fiftieth in 1984, and Nevada's average rank was forty-first. Nevada's turnout and turnout rank improved in 1988 and 1992, but turnout in Arizona increased by more in 1992. Overall, it looks as if there was no discernable effect of motor voter above that obtained in Arizona from the reduction in the closing date for registration.

[12] Arizona adopted motor voter provisions via a ballot initiative in 1982 but it was passively implemented. See Appendix D for a comparison of Nevada and Arizona on factors that influence turnout.

[13] In addition, both states adopted unrestricted absentee voting in 1991. Assuming that the effect of unrestricted absentee voting was the same in both states, this does not violate the identification assumptions.

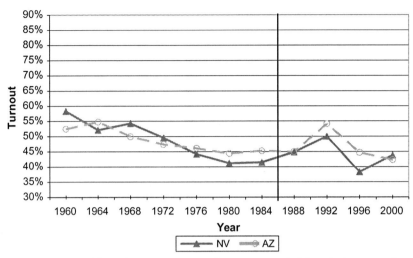

FIGURE 4.3. Presidential year turnout and motor voter in Nevada (compared to Arizona) 1960–2000 (Source: FEC).

This finding holds true when the difference in difference model is applied. Table 4.3 shows the short-term effect of motor voter in Nevada compared with a large reduction in the closing date from fifty to thirty days in Arizona. The coefficient on motor voter is small, negative, and statistically indistinguishable from zero, indicating that motor voter did not have an effect larger than the reduction in the closing date in Arizona.[14] Due to the implementation of the NVRA in both states in 1995, the longer-term effect cannot be estimated with the difference in difference method.

Although Nevada opted for motor voter without prompting from the federal government and the room for improvement in turnout was substantial, the citizenry did not respond. In an environment of low turnout, where, from 1972 to 2000, the turnout rate failed to break 50 percent of the voting age population, more than the good intentions of elected officials to remove barriers to registration is needed to engage those on the outside.

---

[14] The conclusion that motor voter did not have an effect in this context is robust to changes in the way motor voter is specified. Coding motor voter to 1 for those in Nevada in 1992 and beyond, and 0 otherwise, thus waiting for full implementation to set in, produces a coefficient on motor voter = 0.03 with a p value = 0.72. Allowing separate coefficients for the first year of motor voter in 1988 and fully implemented motor voter in 1992 results in a coefficient of −0.08 for motor voter in 1988 with $p = 0.257$, and a coefficient of 0.005 for motor voter in 1992 with $p = 0.945$.

TABLE 4.3. *Difference in Difference Probit Estimates of the Effect of Motor Voter on Turnout (NV compared to AZ, 1972–1992)*

Variable	Coefficient	Standard Error	z	p Value
Motor Voter Effect in NV	−0.0409	0.0569	−0.72	0.472
NV	−0.1466	0.2073	−0.71	0.479
Education * NV	−0.0127	0.0248	−0.51	0.610
Age * NV	−0.0018	0.0088	−0.20	0.839
Age Squared * NV	0.00002	0.0001	0.21	0.834
Income * NV	0.0515	0.0266	1.93	0.053
Education	0.2980	0.0162	18.35	0.000
Age	0.0333	0.0058	5.70	0.000
Age Squared	−0.0001	0.0001	−2.04	0.041
Income Quartile	0.1527	0.0181	8.42	0.000
1980	−0.1157	0.0525	−2.20	0.028
1984	−0.1106	0.0550	−2.01	0.044
1988	−0.1438	0.0586	−2.45	0.014
1992	0.1386	0.0607	2.28	0.023
Constant	−2.4434	0.1415	−17.27	0.000

$N = 9,934$.
Log likelihood $= -5867.91$.
Source: Presidential Year CPS, excluding 1976.

North Carolina (Motor Voter Meets Tobacco Road)

North Carolina was the first state in the South to adopt motor voter through state law, doing so in 1984. However, from 1985 to 1988, under a Republican governor, the program became inactive. Motor voter in North Carolina reemerged in time for the race for president among Bush, Clinton, and Perot, a race that improved turnout rates across the nation. With this stimulating race in progress, it would be expected that there would be an increased likelihood of agreeing to register during driver's license transactions, and then of remembering that one was registered (or perhaps taking the time to check one's registration status). Moreover, once registered, in a competitive electoral climate, the chances of being contacted by a political party or candidate should become greater as well (Rosenstone and Hansen 1993). Thus, the circumstances for motor voter to drive up turnout in North Carolina were quite favorable (see Tolbert et al. 2008 for additional discussion of the interaction between reforms and the competitiveness of the election).

Several states might serve as appropriate controls for North Carolina. The states of South Carolina, Tennessee, and Virginia border North Carolina and are similar on a number of dimensions (see Appendix D).

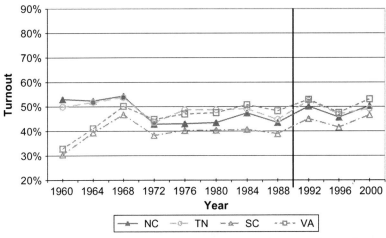

FIGURE 4.4. Presidential year turnout and motor voter in North Carolina (compared to Tennessee, South Carolina, and Virginia) 1960–2000 (Source: FEC).

However, variations in the degree to which restrictions on voting were in force prior to the Voting Rights Act of 1965 led to substantially different turnout rates prior to the 1968 election in South Carolina and Virginia. As Figure 4.4 shows, from 1968 on, turnout in South Carolina and Virginia (represented with lightly shaded short dashed lines and open markers, a triangle and square, respectively) was more in line with turnout in North Carolina (represented with a dark solid line and dark triangular markers), than it was in 1960 and 1964. Nevertheless, given the historical differences in their voting regulations prior to 1965, the effects of which might alter the response to registration reforms, I believe it is appropriate to treat Tennessee as the appropriate comparison state, thus excluding South Carolina and Virginia.

Turning to the comparison of North Carolina and Tennessee (represented with a long light dash and open circular markers) in Figure 4.4, North Carolina saw a jump in turnout in 1984 and again after the restoration of motor voter for the 1992 election. However, Tennessee's turnout rate grew in 1992 as well, and the rise in turnout in 1984 might have just been a return to the resemblance of turnout in the two states that existed from 1960 to 1972.

Once controls are added and the difference in difference model is run using Tennessee as the comparison state, motor voter in North Carolina had a positive and statistically significant effect on turnout after motor voter was fully implemented in 1992. Table 4.4 presents the results. Using

TABLE 4.4. *Difference in Difference Probit Estimates of the Effect of Motor Voter on Turnout (NC compared to TN, 1972–1992)*

Variable	Coefficient	Standard Error	z	p Value
Motor Voter Effect in NC (1984)	−0.0299	0.0526	−0.57	0.570
Motor Voter Effect in NC (1992)	0.1625	0.0513	3.17	0.002
NC	−0.2536	0.1538	−1.65	0.099
Education * NC	0.0027	0.0175	0.15	0.877
Age * NC	0.0045	0.0061	0.73	0.465
Age Squared * NC	0.0000	0.0001	−0.57	0.567
Income * NC	0.0219	0.0217	1.01	0.312
Education	0.3504	0.0144	24.26	0.000
Age	0.0562	0.0050	11.17	0.000
Age Squared	−0.0004	0.0001	−7.17	0.000
Income Quartile	0.1579	0.0179	8.83	0.000
1980	−0.0594	0.0320	−1.86	0.063
1984	0.0154	0.0448	0.34	0.732
1988	−0.2069	0.0298	−6.95	0.000
1992	−0.2455	0.0466	−5.26	0.000
Constant	−2.9703	0.1263	−23.52	0.000

$N = 21,205$.
Log likelihood $= -12284.44$.
Note: NC's motor voter program became inactive between 1985 and 1989.
Source: Presidential Year CPS, excluding 1976.

the information in Table 4.4 and the procedure described earlier, the predicted probability of voting under motor voter in 1992 was 5.3 percentage points higher than in the absence of motor voter. As would be expected, prior to going through a full four year driver's license cycle, motor voter did not have an effect in 1984; the coefficient is the wrong sign but is not statistically significant. In sum, the return to active implementation of motor voter combined with a competitive race led to an increase in turnout comparable to the increase found in Michigan, even in a relatively low turnout state.

Overall, the results from state-level motor voter programs are mixed. Whereas motor voter led to higher turnout in Michigan and North Carolina, it did little in Minnesota and Nevada. The increases in turnout found in Michigan and North Carolina were modest relative to the expectations of those who promoted motor voter as a way to register 90 percent or more of the eligible population, which would then be translated into a cure for low levels of turnout.

THE NATIONAL VOTER REGISTRATION ACT OF 1993 (NVRA)

With the NVRA, motor voter programs were launched or expanded in all but a handful of states.[15] This had the effect of changing some of the details and the menu of registration options in the states that had versions of motor voter in place, and imposing an overhaul of registration procedures in the states that did not have any motor voter provisions in place; in some cases, registration reform was forced where it likely would not have been adopted without federal intervention. A summary of the NVRA's major provisions appears below:

(1) Combining driver's license application and renewal forms with voter registration applications.
(2) Implementation of the Federal Election Commission's mail registration application.
(3) Designation of all state public assistance offices, state-funded agencies serving those with disabilities, and other state offices as voter registration agencies.
(4) Rules for the purging of voter registration lists, preventing the removal of names due to nonvoting.
(5) Procedures to protect against violations of the Act, including criminal penalties for those in violation and a civil right of action for aggrieved parties.

According to estimates from the Federal Election Commission (FEC), 72.77 percent of the voting age population was registered to vote in 1996, and 72.63 percent was registered in 2000 (FEC 2001). The 1996 figure "is the highest percentage of voter registration since reliable records were first available in 1960" (FEC 1997, p. 1). In the states that implemented the NVRA, the percentages were slightly higher, 73.45 in 1996 and 73.8 percent in 2000. These were both up from the 71.63 percent registration rate for the 1992 election.[16] Although registration increased some,

---

[15] As discussed in Chapter 2, states with EDR at polling places and North Dakota, which does not require registration, were exempt.
[16] Estimating the voting age population and the number of registrants are both subject to a variety of errors. For example, Alaska from 1996 to 2002 and Maine from 1992 to 1996 and again in 2000 are recorded as having registration rates of more than 100 percent (FEC, 2002, Table 1). Survey-based estimates from the CPS reveal a different pattern. In the states subject to the NVRA registration rates were 76.9 percent in 1992, 76.21 percent in 1996, and 77.68 percent in 2000. Of course, these, too, are subject to errors.

unarguably, the NVRA did not bring "near universal" voter registration to the United States, contrary to the hopes of its proponents.

To estimate the effect of the NVRA on turnout, I grouped the states in which it was implemented into three categories: 1) those that either did not have active or "model" motor voter programs prior to the NVRA; 2) those with "model programs" but that had not gone through an entire license renewal cycle by 1992 (referred to later as "immature" motor voter states); and 3) those that had fully implemented motor voter prior to the NVRA (referred to as "mature" motor voter states). On the whole, I expect the effect of motor voter in states that adopted or actively implemented it only after mandated to do so to be lower than in states that willingly adopted motor voter via state law and enthusiastically implemented it. However, because the NVRA made only small changes to registration procedures in the states in group 3, in these states the NVRA should have no effect on turnout. The effect in the states in group 2 is more difficult to predict, as countervailing forces were at work on these states. Most of these states initiated motor voter at the state level in the early 1990s and thus reached the full set of potential registrants by the 1996 election. These two factors, along with the additional registration measures added by the NVRA, give rise to the prospect of an increase in turnout greater than that found in states that did not have motor voter in place prior to the NVRA. However, with full implementation occurring around a humdrum election, the likelihood that motor voter registrants would forget that they were registered increases, and the likelihood that such registrants would be contacted by political parties decreases, both of which diminish the outlook for greater turnout as a result of motor voter.

Table 4.5 provides estimates of the effect of the NVRA across these three classifications.[17] A model with state and year fixed effects is used in an attempt to reduce bias that might be introduced by endogeneity. The coefficients and their standard errors for the state variables are reported in Appendix E. To limit the complications associated with endogeneity further, I constrain the sample to the 1992-to-2000 period.

For the first group of states, those that did not previously have motor voter laws, the effect of the NVRA is positive (0.0573) and statistically

[17] A slight modification is made in Table 4.5. North Carolina, although in group 3 along with Michigan and Nevada, was identified as an outlier and was found to be driving the coefficient on Mature Motor Voter*NVRA. To take this into account, I included a separate variable for the NVRA in North Carolina. The substantive results are robust to specifications that allow for separate effects of the NVRA in 1996 and 2000.

TABLE 4.5. *The Effect of the NVRA, State and Year Fixed Effects Model Estimated via Probit (1992–2000)*

Variable	Coefficient	Standard Error	z	p Value
NVRA Motor Voter Only	0.0573	0.0235	2.44	0.015
Immature Motor Voter * NVRA	0.0234	0.0282	0.83	0.408
Mature Motor Voter * NVRA	0.0054	0.0353	0.15	0.879
NVRA * NC	0.1232	0.0419	2.94	0.003
Closing Date	−0.0022	0.0011	−1.96	0.050
Education	0.3301	0.0029	115.43	0.000
Age	0.0385	0.0009	41.57	0.000
Age Squared	−0.0002	0.00001	−21.59	0.000
Mobility	0.1549	0.0030	51.78	0.000
Income Quartile	0.1529	0.0031	48.88	0.000
1996	−0.2943	0.0227	−12.97	0.000
2000	−0.2246	0.0234	−9.60	0.000
Constant	−3.1487	0.0397	−79.27	0.000

$N = 219,173$.

Log likelihood $= -117173.41$.

Notes: State dummies are included in the model but excluded from the table. Utah is excluded from the analysis due to its extensive purging of voter registration lists prior to its implementation of the NVRA.

Source: 1992, 1996, 2000 CPS.

significant ($p = 0.015$), but small. Calculation of the predicted probability of voting in these states suggests an effective increase of 1.7 percentage points. Not only is this smaller than the effect of state-level motor voter laws in Michigan and North Carolina, an increase of 1.7 percentage points falls well short of the dreams of those who saw the NVRA as a means to rescue America from its bottom-of-the-barrel turnout status.

For the second group of states, which had immature motor voter laws, the effect of the NVRA was small (0.0234) and statistically insignificant ($p = 0.408$). This serves as evidence that the forces pushing the probability of voting higher were insufficient to overcome the opposing forces pulling the probability of voting downward.[18]

As for the third group of states, which had state-level motor voter laws that had reached full implementation, the results were mixed. As expected, the NVRA in Michigan and Nevada did not lead to an increase in turnout in these states; the coefficient for Mature Motor Voter * NVRA is small (0.0054) and statistically insignificant ($p = 0.879$). Although

[18] A test that the NVRA Motor Voter Only and Immature Motor Voter * NVRA coefficients are equal can be rejected at the $p = 0.071$ level.

the effect in North Carolina was expected to be similarly negligible, the predicted increase in the probability of voting after implementation of the NVRA was 3.8 percentage points. It is not entirely clear what might explain this. Perhaps the timing of the full implementation of the state-level version of motor voter contributed to an increase in the retention of voters for the 1996 and 2000 elections.[19] Other races on the ballot might also provide a partial explanation.

CONCLUSION

Although the effects of motor voter in Michigan and North Carolina were higher than I anticipated, the effects even under the most auspicious conditions did not live up to the hopes of motor voter's advocates. In a statement of protest against motor voter, Michigan State Senator John A. Welborn,[20] remarked, you can "lead a horse to water but you can't make that horse drink" (*Journal of the Senate*, February 13, 1975, p. 193). This analogy is useful, but to be picky, it misses the distinctiveness of motor voter in terms of the timing of registration and voting. Because registering and voting through motor voter is a two-step process, the horse in Senator Welborn's analogy is not done after taking a drink (registering), it then has to show up for the race. Only those willing to expend additional effort will return on election day.

Consistent with the argument I laid out in Chapter 1, when the federal government stepped in and required the states that would not have otherwise altered the status quo to remove barriers to registration, the effects of motor voter were generally smaller than in states that adopted the policy on their own. Rather than a stampede to the polls by the masses who were previously thwarted by confusing and burdensome registration procedures, only a few stumbled in. Given that motor voter registration takes place around the driver's license renewal cycle it is not entirely surprising that the effect in Michigan eventually died out. For those who either did not register or registered but did not vote during the first cycle, something would have had to have changed during the time between cycles to inspire them to participate. With the completion of the bulk of the cycle at least one year prior to the election, most get asked to register

---

[19] This is consistent with the work by Donald Green and his colleagues, suggesting that voting is habitual (see Green and Shachar 2000; and Gerber, Green, and Shachar 2003). See also Plutzer (2002) and Franklin (2004).

[20] Senator Welborn was a member of the Republican party.

during a time in which the campaign is not particularly visible, thus making it unlikely that those who failed to participate previously will decide to do so. This scenario applies most straightforwardly to those who did not register as they remain off the registration lists used by the candidates and parties for mobilization purposes. Though there is evidence that voting is habitual (Green and Shachar 2000; Plutzer 2002; and Gerber, Green, and Shachar 2003), not enough new voters were brought in to sustain the effect against other forces. However, for North Carolina, the effect did not die out as quickly. The timing of motor voter's implementation seems to have played a role. That is, the relatively interesting 1992 election might have brought more people to the polls, many of whom sat out the 1996 election but who then returned in 2000 when the result again (as we now know all too well) was anything but a foregone conclusion. Overall, these analyses provide another call for caution against the extrapolation of effects across contexts.

Although overall turnout did not increase substantially as a result of either EDR or motor voter programs, the effects might differ across individual level characteristics. Before exploring this avenue of research, in Chapter 5, I examine reported usage of EDR and motor voter registration based on new survey questions incorporated into the CPS since the implementation of the NVRA.

5

Registration and Voting in the Post-NVRA Era

Previous chapters have shown that the selection of election laws is purposeful, that the overall effects of the two registration reforms projected to have the largest impact on turnout have resulted in much smaller than anticipated (and smaller than previously estimated) increases in turnout, and that the magnitude of the effects varies based on the social and political contexts into which the reforms are placed. That is, lowering the costs of participation does nothing directly, and apparently very little indirectly (I take this up in Chapter 7) to engage those who do not want to vote. Having estimated the overall effects of election day registration (EDR) and motor voter laws, as implemented by the states on their own and via impetus from the federal government, the present chapter provides a bridge to the analysis of how the effects vary across individual characteristics. In this chapter, I explore what can be learned from self-reports of registration behavior when individuals are asked about the timing and method they used to register.

Beginning in 1996, Current Population Survey (CPS) Voter Supplement respondents who voted or were registered but did not vote were asked a series of questions regarding when, relative to the implementation of the National Voter Registration Act (NVRA), and by what means (at a government office, by mail, and so on) they registered. The first new question asked whether or not the individual registered after January 1, 1995, the implementation date of the NVRA. Unfortunately, the CPS did not probe whether the registration transaction involved registering for the first time, making a change to an existing registration, or registering again after having been purged from the registration lists. Respondents who registered after the implementation of the NVRA were then asked whether they registered through the department of motor vehicles (DMV) or some other way. Those who registered some other way received another question: they were asked how they registered to vote with the following choices: at a public assistance agency; through the mail; at a school, hospital, or on campus; at a county or government voter registration office; at a registration drive; some other way; or at the polls on election day.[1]

These new questions represent a significant contribution to the availability of data to estimate directly two important indicators of political behavior in the post-NVRA era. First, the data allow us to determine the extent to which citizens utilize various registration methods. That is, these data allow us to come to a deeper understanding of which registration methods citizens choose in the environment of greater options. In states with motor voter: To what extent do citizens take advantage of the various motor voter provisions? In states with EDR: What percentage of new registrants opts to register on election day? Do the patterns differ based on the length of time the provisions have been in effect and/or the simultaneous availability of motor voter and EDR (as is the case in Maine and Minnesota)? Second, these data allow for the direct examination of turnout across the menu of registration options, and thus an assessment of the claim that most registrants vote (see Erikson 1981; Glass, Squire, and Wolfinger 1984; Squire, Wolfinger, and Glass 1987; and Piven and Cloward 1988). Does this result hold when registration becomes easier and in some cases can be achieved as a byproduct of nonpolitical activity?

The chapter is organized around the questions discussed in the previous paragraph. Using the questions on when and how one registered from the 1996 and 2000 CPS Voter Supplement Files, I first report the percentage of registrants in the post-NVRA era and their turnout rates across classifications of state implementation of motor voter and/or EDR. Next, I examine the extent to which those registering after January 1, 1995 used the various registration methods available in their state. I then report turnout rates across the available registration methods as a way to test the claim that most registrants vote. The hope, expressed primarily by Piven and Cloward but also by Raymond Wolfinger and colleagues (see Glass, Squire, and Wolfinger 1984; and Squire, Wolfinger, and Glass 1987), that those registering under easier provisions would vote at rates similar to

---

[1] The categories are listed in the order they were given in 1996. In 2000, "other," rather than "at the polls on election day" was the last choice in the list of responses, a much more sensible ordering. In addition, the CPS 2000 wording of the answer choice for EDR was changed to "registered at polling place (on election or primary day)." I collapse the school/hospital/campus, registration drive, and other categories into one category.

those already registered partially motivated the campaign for the NVRA. Divergent from these expectations, the results show that NVRA registrants tend to vote at lower rates than others, but not by as much as critics assumed they would. Finally, I examine registration rates by registration method across the individual characteristics of education and age.

To the best of my knowledge, only one published source contains analysis using portions of these data. Wolfinger and Hoffman (2001) studied the 1996 data but treated all states subject to the NVRA together, and ignored mail and EDR.[2] I include all of the registration methods in my analysis, and hypothesize that the variations in the number of years the registration methods have been available – that is, their maturity – will result in different patterns of usage. Accordingly, I group states based on the registration options available as well as the length of time EDR or motor voter has been allowed. Another difference between the work here and Wolfinger and Hoffman's (2001) is that I utilize the data for descriptive purposes only. The logit estimates reported in Wolfinger and Hoffman (2001) require one to make assumptions I am not willing to maintain; in my view, the application of statistical models to these data is ill advised.[3] Although the new CPS questions are a step in the right direction, as I now discuss, there are additional limitations that narrow the degree to which they can contribute to our understanding of the effects of EDR and motor voter programs.

LIMITATIONS OF THE DATA

For the states recently adopting either EDR or the NVRA, the CPS questions capture the types of individuals who responded in the initial stages of implementation. With respect to EDR, because those who registered at previous elections cannot be identified as having done so, these data

[2] Separate papers using the 1996 data were presented by Wolfinger and Hoffman (2000) and myself (Hanmer 2000) on separate panels at the 2000 Annual Meeting of the American Political Science Association, in Washington DC.
[3] Wolfinger and Hoffman (2001) fail to acknowledge that new registrants are not a random subsample of the eligible population, and treat DMV and public assistance agency registration as separate binary choices, thus failing to account for how the choices available affect the decision. As one can tell from the descriptive analyses (theirs and mine) the assumptions necessary to run simple logit models do not hold up. Techniques are available to account for each of these issues independently, though not simultaneously. What is more, they introduce additional assumptions and thus raise other concerns.

fall short of providing a complete picture. Similarly, in the states that had these programs (or similar versions) in place prior to 1996, the picture is less complete, given that the rate of usage generally and across individual characteristics is obtained only for 1996 and 2000, which, in some cases, is as much as twenty-six years after implementation.

Before jumping into the analysis, a few more words of caution are necessary. It is widely known that misreporting is a problem in studies of voting (see, for example, Duff, Hanmer, Park, and White 2007). Given that registering to vote is not a widely celebrated event, one would expect the retrieval of information about when and how one registered to be an arduous task for respondents. Thus, some respondents likely did not remember when they registered, how they registered, or even if they registered at all. Although I was not able to uncover all misreports, I was able to discover certain types of misreporting. That is, those who reported they had registered at the DMV, public assistance agencies, or at the polls on election day, but did not live in a state that allowed registration via these means, respectively, were easily discovered. In addition, those who reported registering at the polls on election day and who either did not vote, reported voting early or absentee, or did not know whether they voted at the polls on election day, early, or by absentee ballot, were also assumed to be misreporting their registration method.[4] I treated the responses of these known misreporters as missing values. This removes fewer than 1 percent of the respondents who were asked how they were registered in 1996 and just under 4 percent in 2000.[5] The higher rate of misreporting in 2000 is, no doubt, a reflection of the longer time span between January 1, 1995 and the 2000 election. Whereas the 1996 respondents had to recall how they registered at most one year and ten months prior to their participation in the survey, those in 2000 might have had to recall their behavior from as far back as five years and ten months prior to being surveyed. Even with these shortcomings, these data

---

[4] It is possible, especially in 2000, due to that year's wording change in the EDR answer choice, that some registered at the polls in a previous election and either did not vote in the 2000 general election, or voted absentee. Keeping these cases requires stronger assumptions than does dropping them. That is, it is more likely that the individuals in this category simply misreported.

[5] Because North Dakota does not require registration, respondents from North Dakota were excluded from this analysis. The question asking registration status seems to cause some confusion for North Dakotans. Most (93 percent in 1996 and 95 percent in 2000) seem to consider themselves registered to vote, whereas 7 percent in 1996 and 5 percent in 2000 reported that they were not registered to vote.

supply information about individual-level behavior that was previously unknown.

REGISTRATION AND TURNOUT AMONG NEW REGISTRANTS IN 1996 AND 2000

In 1996, 16 percent of registrants said they registered after the implementation of the NVRA, whereas 29 percent did so in 2000. In light of the longer period of time between the NVRA's implementation and the 2000 election, this increase is not surprising. Of those registering after January 1, 1995, 77 percent voted in 1996 and 80 percent voted in 2000. These turnout rates are lower than the rates for those who registered prior to January 1, 1995. Turnout among those registering prior to the NVRA's implementation was 84 percent for the 1996 CPS sample and 89 percent for the 2000 CPS sample. That is, these new registrants were less likely to vote than previous registrants, thus pulling down the overall turnout rate among registrants. Though inconsistent with the predictions derived from previous research on turnout among registrants, to the extent that voting is a habitual act (Green and Shachar 2000; Gerber, Green, and Shachar 2003) it is not entirely unexpected that new registrants would be less likely to vote than those who have been registered longer. That is, citizens who have been registered for a longer period of time are more likely to have developed a greater attachment to electoral politics, which, in turn, makes them more likely to vote.

Given variations across states in the methods of registration available and the length of time the provisions have been in place, I partitioned the states to examine whether, as I hypothesized, these distinctions translated into differences in rates of registration and turnout among the new registrants. They did. Table 5.1 reports the percentage who registered after January 1, 1995 and the percent who voted among these new registrants by state law classification for 1996 and 2000. In the first row, I group together the states that adopted EDR in response to the NVRA (New EDR). Because Maine and Minnesota allow both EDR and motor voter, I group these two states together. Although Minnesota did not implement the NVRA, its motor voter provisions are implemented effectively, meaning that the range of registration options across these two states is comparable. Wisconsin is in its own row because it is the only state that had a longstanding EDR program, but did not have motor voter provisions. Vermont is also separated as it had neither EDR nor motor voter in 1996, but did implement the NVRA for 2000. As was done in

TABLE 5.1. *Percentage Registering after January 1, 1995 and Percent Voting among Those Registering after January 1, 1995 (weighted)*

State Category	1996		2000	
	% Who Registered	% Voted among Newly Registered	% Who Registered	% Voted among Newly Registered
New EDR	18	92	37	89
ME and MN	17	88	33	89
WI	16	87	29	95
New NVRA	15	78	27	81
Immature Pre-NVRA	19	72	32	75
Mature Pre-NVRA	14	76	30	78
VT	11	83	25	84

EDR = Election day registration; NVRA = National Voter Registration Act.
Source: 1996 and 2000 CPS.

Chapter 4, I divide the NVRA states into three groups: 1) states that first implemented motor voter after the NVRA (New NVRA); 2) states that had immature motor voter programs prior to the NVRA (Immature Pre-NVRA); and 3) states that had mature motor voter programs prior to the NVRA (Mature Pre-NVRA).

The patterns of registration and voting across states in both years were quite similar. A notable exception was the sizable increase in Wisconsin's turnout rate, relative to the other states, from 1996 to 2000. Overall, the differences across states tended to be small. The higher turnout rates in states allowing EDR reflects, in part, the lack of slippage between registration and voting for those who register on election day. Whereas those registering prior to election day have to make a separate trip to vote, by assumption, although one that is easily defended, those who register on election day vote. In both years, Vermont had the lowest percentage of new registrants, and the new EDR states had among the most, especially in 2000. The larger percentage of new registrants in new EDR states is likely a function of the relatively high rates of population growth there, chiefly in Idaho, the population of which grew nearly 30 percent between 1990 and 2000.[6] Although the percentage of registrants in immature pre-NVRA states was quite high in both years, 19 percent and 32 percent respectively, the turnout rate among those registrants was the lowest (72 percent in 1996 and 75 percent in 2000). Meanwhile, in new NVRA states, although the rates of new registrations were relatively low

---

[6] This growth rate was calculated using data from the Census; see Appendix B.

(15 percent in 1996 and 27 percent in 2000), the turnout rates among those registrants of 78 percent in 1996 and 81 percent in 2000, were slightly higher than in states that previously had either mature or immature motor voter laws.

The values reported in Table 5.1 average over all of the registration methods available, and thus do not supply enough information to determine whether registration rates were driven by EDR or motor voter, respectively, or something else. The distribution of new registrants across registration methods by state classification, shown in Table 5.2, provides greater insight.[7]

Taking the states that allow EDR first, it is clear that both in 1996 and 2000, EDR was the most popular in Wisconsin. In 1996, 52 percent of all new registrants in Wisconsin registered on election day, compared with 36 percent in Maine and Minnesota, and 22 percent in the new EDR states. For the 2000 election, an even larger percentage of Wisconsin citizens registered on election day relative to the other registration methods available to them. Increases in the relative use of EDR were larger in 2000 than in 1996 in the other EDR states as well. It appears that by 2000, more eligible citizens in new EDR states were cognizant of their ability to make a single trip to register and vote, and rather than making registering and voting a two-stop process, they took advantage of their one-stop option. However, 39 percent registered at a government office, a much higher percentage than in the other states allowing EDR, suggesting that even after more than five years with the policy, a fair number of citizens either were not aware of the availability of EDR or were not comfortable waiting until election day to register to vote.

In both years, the percentage of new registrants who registered when obtaining or renewing a driver's license was the highest in the states that had mature motor voter programs prior to the NVRA, followed by the immature pre-NVRA states, then the new NVRA states, with Maine and Minnesota coming in last. The variation across the states that do not allow EDR too, is likely a reflection of the greater familiarity with motor voter among citizens and administrators in the places that had the program in place for a longer period of time. That motor voter registration is not as common in Maine and Minnesota is not surprising; the option

---

[7] When we report on the same items, my results correspond with Wolfinger and Hoffman's (2001); the slight differences in a few cases are likely the result of different decision rules regarding known misreporters. Wolfinger and Hoffman (2001) do not indicate that any of the observations were dropped or recoded due to failed matches between reported registration methods and state laws.

TABLE 5.2. *Percentage Registering by Registration Method among Those Registering after January 1, 1995 (weighted)*

Registration Method	New EDR	ME and MN	WI	New NVRA	Immature Pre-NVRA	Mature Pre-NVRA	VT[a]	Total
1996								
Driver's License	NA	22	NA	27	43	48	NA	30
Public Agency	NA	0	NA	3	3	5	NA	3
Mail	8	4	3	21	24	11	NA	20
Government Office	50	19	27	22	13	19	65	24
Election Day	22	36	52	NA	NA	NA	NA	21
Other	20	18	18	27	16	16	35	3
TOTAL	100	100	100	100	100	100	100	100
2000								
Driver's License	NA	24	NA	36	56	68	17	40
Public Agency	NA	1	NA	2	2	1	4	2
Mail	3	2	2	14	13	4	1	12
Government Office	39	16	21	19	11	14	67	18
Election Day	50	50	72	NA	NA	NA	NA	4
Other	9	7	5	29	19	13	12	25
TOTAL	100	100	100	100	100	100	100	100

EDR = Election day registration; NVRA = National Voter Registration Act.
a In 1996, the number of cases for Vermont is fewer than 20.
Source: 1996 and 2000 CPS.

of registering on election day would be expected to depress the percentage of registrants who register via motor voter. Registration through the other NVRA provisions was less frequent across the board, but especially in 2000. This was particularly true with respect to registration at public assistance agencies, the places where Piven and Cloward held out hope for sizable gains among the least-well off; only 3 percent of all new registrants in 1996 and 2 percent in 2000 registered while at an office that provided Medicaid, food stamps, unemployment services, or services for the disabled. The final item of note is that after Vermont implemented the NVRA, only 22 percent of those who registered did so through NVRA provisions (17 percent at the DMV, 4 percent at public agencies, and 1 percent through the mail). With the exception of the percentage registering at public assistance agencies, the NVRA options in Vermont were much less popular there than they were in 1996 among those in states first adopting this menu of registration methods in 1995 (that is, compare with new NVRA in 1996).

Although patterns of registration are interesting in themselves, voting in the motor voter states is a two-stop process, and a complete evaluation requires an analysis of the extent to which new registrants made the additional stop and voted. Turnout rates across state registration provisions and registration method are presented in Table 5.3. Because all those who register on election day are assumed to vote, the election day row is not included. In a number of cells, labeled NR, the results are not reported because the sample size was too small to obtain reliable estimates.

The results in Table 5.3 of greatest interest are those for the NVRA provisions. Overall, turnout among those registering at the time when they obtained or renewed their driver's license was 70 percent in 1996 and 75 percent in 2000. The average turnout rate among DMV registrants is consistent with Wolfinger and Hoffman's (2001) analysis of the 1996 CPS data. However, a more nuanced understanding is obtained through my examination of a wider variety of registration provisions and across classifications of the states based on the registration options available and the maturity of the motor voter laws. The turnout rate of those using this method was the highest in Maine and Minnesota (dramatically so in 2000). Given the well-known commitment to participation in these states, this result is not startling. Turnout among DMV registrants was the lowest (66 percent in 1996 and 70 percent in 2000) in the immature pre-NVRA states, and was comparable in the new NVRA and mature pre-NVRA states, differing only slightly in both years. As expected, those who took the more costly and directly political route of registering at

TABLE 5.3. *Turnout by Registration Method among Those Registering after January 1, 1995 (weighted)*

Registration Method	New EDR	ME and MN	WI	New NVRA	Immature Pre-NVRA	Mature Pre-NVRA	VT[a]	Total
				1996				
Driver's License	NA	75	NA	72	66	70	NA	70
Public Agency	NA	NR	NA	53	42	45	NA	50
Mail	NR	NR	NR	83	79	89	NA	82
Government Office	94	89	82	84	79	79	84	84
Other	87	91	86	78	77	87	81	79
				2000				
Driver's License	NA	91	NA	76	70	77	NR	75
Public Agency	NA	NR	NA	58	60	NR	NR	58
Mail	NR	NR	NR	87	82	84	NR	86
Government Office	91	83	87	86	87	88	90	86
Other[b]	71	84	91	81	79	77	NR	81

EDR = Election day registration; NVRA = National Voter Registration Act.

[a] In 1996, the number of cases for Vermont is fewer than 20.

[b] The number of cases for New EDR and Wisconsin is fewer than 20.

Notes: NR indicates not reported due to small sample size.

Source: 1996 and 2000 CPS.

government offices turned out at higher rates than DMV registrants; the difference in turnout between DMV registrants and government office registrants was fourteen points in 1996 but declined to eleven points in 2000. When broken down by pre-NVRA status, a larger gap between DMV and government office registrants emerged in 2000 for those in immature pre-NVRA states and mature pre-NVRA states, while it was reduced slightly in new NVRA states. Unexpectedly, year 2000 turnout among DMV registrants in Maine and Minnesota was higher than turnout in any other registration category.

As noted, at least two things might distinguish those using motor voter from those registering at government offices or some other way – intention and the costs incurred. For the individuals who are aware of motor voter provisions, registering to vote while obtaining or renewing a driver's license provides an efficient way to accomplish two tasks. But the DMV is not a place most like to visit, so to describe motor voter registration as "costless" (Wolfinger and Hoffman 2001) is perhaps going too far. The hours tend to be inconvenient (unfortunately for them, most do not have the flexibility afforded by the academic lifestyle), the lines are long, the driving and eye tests can be stressful, and so on. With all the commotion, for those who decide to register, it is perhaps easy to lose sight of the fact that a registration transaction also took place, especially for citizens who had no intention of registering in the first place.[8] Registering in more traditional ways – say, at a government office – though more burdensome, is something individuals set out to do. Having the desire to register in the first place and having expended extra effort, it is logical that these citizens are more likely to exercise their right to vote on election day.

The other registration methods implemented under the NVRA were public agency and mail registration. Public agency registrants were the least likely to turn out; only 50 percent of them voted in 1996. Although the turnout rate improved, it was still only 58 percent in 2000, 28 percentage points lower than citizens who registered at government offices. Mail registration differs from DMV and public agency registration in that those registering by mail are likely doing so because it was their initial

---

[8] The experience of my sister-in-law provides an example of this. After graduating from law school, she moved to the New York City area and, as required by law, changed her driver's license. After the 2000 election, when I asked if she voted, she responded that she did not have time to register. I probed further, asking why she did not do so when getting her new license; she was not aware that motor voter registration was available but noted she very well might have registered and forgot. When she moved again, this time more cognizant of motor voter, she decided to register at the DMV.

intention, rather than being a byproduct of another activity – say, meeting with a case worker. Although mail registration might involve fewer costs than going to a government office, one must figure out how to obtain a card, fill it out, and then return it before the deadline, making it more costly than simply filling out a few lines while getting a driver's license. Given this, it is not surprising that those who registered by mail voted at rates comparable to the rates achieved by the highest turnout group – those who registered at government offices.

The results regarding turnout among DMV registrants from the afore-mentioned tables fall between the predictions from research conducted by Knack (1995) and Franklin and Grier (1997). Both sets of authors used state-level data and wrote prior to the availability of the data described here. They agreed that motor voter would have a positive and statistically significant impact on turnout; however, they diverged on the percentage of motor voter registrants who would turn out. Knack predicted that only 50 percent of motor voter registrants would vote, but Franklin and Grier concluded that motor voter registrants would vote at the same rate as other registrants. Some skeptics, myself included, thought even Knack's prediction would be on the high side. We were all wrong; the 70 per-cent to 75 percent turnout rate among motor voter registrants is not on par with those choosing more costly methods, whether registering before or after the first day of January 1995, but is considerably better than a turnout rate of 50 percent. Because they use state-level data that do not provide information about individual-level registration behavior, let alone information about the mechanisms individuals used to register, it is not shocking that the predictions made by Knack (1995) and Franklin and Grier (1997) were off the mark. Of course, the larger issue is what turnout would have been without motor voter. As noted at the beginning of the chapter, the data do not allow one to separate those who would not have registered in the absence of the NVRA from those who would have registered anyway. The presence of those who would have registered anyway almost surely inflates the turnout rate among NVRA registrants, but the amount by which the rate is inflated is not known.

I conclude this chapter with an analysis of election day registrants and motor voter registrants across categories of education and age. Two sets of analyses are presented. First, I examine registration across individual level characteristics using new registrants as the base. This allows for a comparison of EDR and DMV registration rates, respectively, based on the individual attributes of education and age. However, it does not take into account disparities in the rate of registration across groups. The

TABLE 5.4. *Percentage Registering on Election Day among Those Registering after January 1, 1995 by Education and Age (weighted)*

Category	New EDR[a]	ME and MN	WI
	Education		
	1996		
No HS Degree	24.5	28.2	38.7
HS Degree	18.7	34.4	54.6
1–3 Years College	23.7	30.5	55.9
College Degree	25.5	47.9	50.8
College +[b]	16.9	33.8	53.3
	2000		
No HS Degree	39.5	66.1	66.9
HS Degree	50.7	40.5	73.5
1–3 Years College	53.0	53.7	69.1
College Degree	47.9	54.6	76.1
College +[b]	42.7	42.3	72.7
	Age		
	1996		
18–25	21.2	34.9	49.6
26–29	31.0	42.4	41.8
30–39	23.9	37.4	52.0
40–65	18.6	30.9	52.6
66 and older[b]	13.4	33.0	80.4
	2000		
18–25	61.0	48.3	76.3
26–29[c]	64.1	44.4	74.3
30–39	47.3	58.6	77.2
40–65	43.7	44.1	65.3
66 and older[c]	28.7	65.6	62.0

EDR = Election Day Registration; HS = high school.
[a] Sample sizes for 1996 and 2000 No HS Degree, 1996 College Degree, 2000 College +, 1996, 26 to 29 are less than 20.
[b] Sample size for each state category is less than 20.
[c] Sample sizes for New EDR and Wisconsin are fewer than 20.
Source: 1996 and 2000 CPS.

second set of analyses takes this into account by adding nonregistrants to the base.

Table 5.4 presents the percentage who registered on election day among those who registered after January 1, 1995 by age and education. Unfortunately, in a number of cells, especially in the New EDR column, the number of cases is quite small.

The top portion of Table 5.4 presents election day registration rates among recent registrants across levels of educational attainment. In 1996, those with the lowest levels of education tended to be the least likely to register via EDR. In Maine and Minnesota, college graduates utilized EDR at the highest rate, whereas in Wisconsin, those with a high school degree or some college experience had the highest rates. A notable change in 2000 was that, although those who did not have a high school degree, relative to those in the other education categories, were the least likely to register on election day in the new EDR states (roughly 40 percent) and Wisconsin (67 percent), they had the highest proportion (66 percent) of election day registrants among those in Maine and Minnesota.

Overall, the patterns varied across both states and years. Only in one case did the least educated take advantage of EDR more so than others who registered after January 1, 1995. High school graduates were never the most likely to register on election day, but in 1996 and 2000, they were among the most likely in Wisconsin.

Variations across state registration system classifications and year are also evident in the bottom half of Table 5.4, which displays EDR rates by age. Again, in some cases, interpretation is hindered by small sample sizes. Overall, few clear patterns are evident. However, the youngest age group had relatively high rates of EDR usage in Wisconsin in both years, as did the youngest in the new EDR states for the year 2000 election.

Table 5.5 contains analogous information for those who registered through driver's license transactions, the primary component of the NVRA. In three of the four state categories in both 1996 and 2000, college graduates who registered after the implementation of the NVRA were among the most likely to register through a DMV transaction. The popularity of EDR among college graduates in Maine and Minnesota, as shown in Table 5.4, translated into lower rates of motor voter registration for this group. Across both elections, in all but one of the state classifications, those without high school degrees were the least likely to register when obtaining or renewing a driver's license. The only exception occurred in 1996 for immature pre-NVRA states, but even there, the least educated had the second lowest motor voter registration rate.

Rates of motor voter registration across age categories can be found in the bottom portion of Table 5.5.[9] Two things stand out. First, for the most part, the percentage choosing to register through the DMV was the

---

[9] Here, the sample size is sufficient to allow the eighteen- to twenty-five-year-old age group to be disaggregated into two groups.

TABLE 5.5. *Percent Registering Via Driver's License Transactions among Those Registering after January 1, 1995 by Education and Age (weighted)*

Category	ME and MN[a]	New NVRA	Immature Pre-NVRA	Mature Pre-NVRA
		Education		
		1996		
No HS Degree	16.1	17.8	41.2	29.5
HS Degree	20.2	29.0	45.4	48.7
1–3 Years College	22.9	25.1	43.0	51.5
College Degree	20.3	31.2	44.3	57.2
College +	47.2	30.8	35.8	43.6
		2000		
No HS Degree	11.8	24.3	46.4	52.2
HS Degree	24.4	37.2	57.7	69.3
1–3 Years College	20.9	35.7	54.1	68.5
College Degree	28.4	39.1	62.8	72.1
College +	38.3	36.6	53.2	70.0
		Age		
		1996		
18–21	25.1	22.6	44.4	38.1
22–25	22.9	31.3	49.2	52.0
26–29	22.5	28.1	47.6	57.7
30–39	31.5	29.6	42.8	53.7
40–65	11.4	27.2	41.3	51.2
66 and older	4.9	18.0	32.1	26.3
		2000		
18–21	10.1	32.1	56.9	51.1
22–25	21.5	39.2	69.7	69.0
26–29	47.2	40.9	55.5	78.8
30–39	21.8	39.0	55.9	78.1
40–65	29.2	34.7	53.1	66.4
66 and older	7.8	24.2	30.9	54.2

NVRA = National Voter Registration Act; HS = high school.
[a] Sample sizes for 1996 College +, and 1996 age 66 and up are fewer than 20.
Source: 1996 and 2000 CPS.

lowest among citizens in either the forty to sixty-five or sixty-six or older age group. The only case where this was not true was in the 2000 data for states that had mature motor voter prior to implementing the NVRA, where eighteen- to twenty-one-year-olds had the lowest percentage of motor voter registrants, followed by those who were sixty-six or older. Second, the age group with the highest rate of DMV registration varies across state classifications and years but the eighteen- to twenty-one-year-old group never earns this distinction.

The least educated and the young are widely known for having low rates of registration. That is, as both education and age increase, so, too, does the rate of registration. Given that individuals in these groups did not register via EDR or motor voter, respectively, at rates wildly higher than their more educated and senior counterparts suggests that when nonregistrants are added to the base, the overall conclusions will be reinforced. Tables 5.6 and 5.7 demonstrate this is the case. Table 5.6 presents information similar to that in Table 5.4, and Table 5.7 corresponds with Table 5.5, with one modification, the addition of nonregistrants to the base.

The message from Tables 5.6 and 5.7 is quite straightforward. For the 1996 and 2000 elections, EDR and motor voter served primarily as a convenience for those who are thought of as having the skills necessary to overcome the burden of registration. Relative to the overall rate of registration within groups, those with the most to gain, the least educated and the young, barely put a dent in their registration disadvantage. Not only were those who were young or had little educational experience never the group with the largest percentage of EDR or motor voter registration, respectively, they tended to be among the worst, especially with respect to education, sometimes by a large margin.

CONCLUSION

Taken as a whole, the citizens who registered after the implementation of the NVRA were less likely to vote than those who were previously registered. With the exception of people who registered by mail, those who registered through the NVRA's provisions were even less likely to turn out than those who registered after January 1, 1995 but registered through other procedures. However, a sizable proportion of NVRA registrants turned out on election day.

Variations in the usage of EDR across contexts were also evident. Even twenty-five years after the implementation of EDR, a higher proportion of eligible citizens registered on election day in Wisconsin than they did in the states that adopted EDR as a way to escape the NVRA. That many in the new EDR states chose to register prior to election day might suggest a lack of awareness of the new option. In the two states with both EDR and motor voter, EDR was the most popular means of registering,

TABLE 5.6. *Percentage Registering on Election Day among Those Registering after January 1, 1995 and Those Not Registered by Education and Age (weighted)*

Category	New EDR[b]	ME and MN	WI
	Education		
	1996		
No HS Degree	4.5	8.8	11.3
HS Degree	4.5	12.8	17.4
1–3 Years College	9.8	18.6	30.2
College Degree	15.0	36.4	37.8
College +[a]	12.6	28.9	48.1
	2000		
No HS Degree	9.1	21.9	21.1
HS Degree	19.8	21.9	36.1
1–3 Years College	29.2	39.5	49.6
College Degree	35.7	49.4	56.6
College +	36.7	36.9	61.3
	Age		
	1996		
18–21	7.8	17.8	17.3
22–25	5.8	16.5	28.0
26–29	9.8	26.3	21.7
30–39	8.0	20.6	22.2
40–65	7.1	14.4	22.4
66 and older	2.0	9.6	38.5
	2000		
18–21	22.9	30.7	39.8
22–25	29.4	26.9	46.7
26–29	32.1	30.6	29.8
30–39	24.4	41.3	49.8
40–65	21.5	31.8	37.8
66 and older	13.3	40.3	31.3

EDR = Election Day Registration; HS = high school.
[a] Sample sizes for 1996 College + are fewer than 20.
[b] Sample size for 2000 College + is fewer than 20.
Source: 1996 and 2000 CPS.

followed by DMV registration. This implies that some of those who went to the DMV primarily to conduct business relating to their driver's licenses preferred to complete their transactions with the DMV more quickly and chose not to register. These citizens, if they became motivated to vote, had the luxury of waiting until election day to register.

TABLE 5.7. *Percentage Registering Via Driver's License Transactions among Those Registering after January 1, 1995 and Those Not Registered by Education and Age (weighted)*

Category	ME & MN[a]	New NVRA	Immature Pre-NVRA	Mature Pre-NVRA
		Education		
		1996		
No HS Degree	5.0	3.0	7.2	5.0
HS Degree	7.5	7.2	13.6	13.7
1–3 Years College	14.0	9.9	20.8	22.4
College Degree	15.4	16.2	25.6	36.0
College +	40.4	19.1	23.0	26.8
		2000		
No HS Degree	3.9	5.6	11.9	13.0
HS Degree	13.2	12.8	25.3	28.9
1–3 Years College	15.4	19.4	32.1	40.8
College Degree	25.7	27.0	45.7	57.8
College +	33.5	27.7	43.1	53.3
		Age		
		1996		
18–21	12.8	8.4	17.9	14.7
22–25	10.8	9.2	18.6	17.8
26–29	13.9	9.1	17.9	21.9
30–39	17.4	9.1	15.8	18.2
40–65	5.3	8.0	14.5	14.5
66 and older	1.4	4.1	10.2	7.5
		2000		
18–21	5.9	14.4	30.8	21.2
22–25	13.1	20.0	38.7	39.7
26–29	32.6	19.8	29.0	42.3
30–39	15.4	18.2	28.5	40.7
40–65	21.0	14.6	25.7	32.4
66 and older	4.8	8.4	11.3	22.1

NVRA = National Voter Registration Act; HS = high school.
[a] Sample sizes for 1996 and 2000 College + are fewer than 20.
Source: 1996 and 2000 CPS.

Overall, the investigation of who used the EDR and motor voter registration options across the individual characteristics of education and age failed to turn up much in the way of easily discernable patterns. However, those who tend to have the highest rates of turnout, and who likely would have registered anyway, took advantage of the added convenience afforded by EDR and motor voter at relatively high rates. With respect to motor voter, this might explain the higher than expected turnout rate among DMV registrants. In Chapter 6, I address the question of which types of individuals benefit the most, in terms of turnout, from EDR and motor voter laws, respectively.

6

Election Reform and the Composition of the Electorate

The essence of Arend Lijphart's (1997) Presidential Address to the American Political Science Association was that who votes matters – for the types of candidates that get elected to office, the policies they enact (see Hill and Leighley 1992), and as an indicator of the health of our democratic society. Lijphart began his address by stating: "Political equality and political participation are both basic democratic ideals" (1997, p. 1). The results offered in Chapters 3 and 4 reveal that relaxed registration laws will not take us as far as reformers might like toward increased participation, the second of these ideals. Motivation, not costs, represent the most significant barrier to higher turnout in the United States. But what have registration laws done to address political equality? Even though the increases in turnout resulting from EDR and motor voter failed to reach the heights imagined by some, previous scholarship has not come to a firm conclusion regarding whether the turnout rates of some types of individuals are more likely to grow than others and, if there is variation, which types of individuals are expected to gain the most ground.

The answer has important implications. If the effects are concentrated among those who tend to be left out of politics, then the conclusion that EDR and motor voter have a limited effect might require revision. On the other hand, if these registration procedures lead to an exacerbation of the gap in turnout between the haves and the have-nots, then the argument that these policies are simply an added convenience for those who would have registered and voted anyway gains strength.[1] Smolka (1977), for

---

[1] With respect to policies aimed at increasing turnout among the registered (early voting, unrestricted absentee voting, and voting by mail) Berinsky (2005) finds that these policies

example, found that many using EDR in 1976 would have registered or updated their registration information prior to election day if EDR were not an option. Without any data on which individuals would not have registered in the absence of the respective registration options and which would have registered differently, if they had to, the best way to get a handle on this is to examine the effects across various demographic categories. Thus, an investigation of where the effects are the largest contributes to the evaluation of the policies themselves, as well as the prospects for the future of our democracy. Moreover, obtaining this information is a prerequisite to the development of additional strategies to improve turnout.

Given our previous uncertainty with respect to the overall effects of election reforms, it is not surprising that there is debate regarding which types of individuals are the most responsive to these reforms. In earlier chapters, I contended that the choice of assumptions and statistical methods play a key role in the evaluation of registration reform; that argument continues here. So, in addition to making a substantive contribution, this chapter aims to highlight the strengths and weaknesses of several methodological approaches. Drawing on the difference in difference method, and in one case, a state and year fixed effects model, in combination with the bounds approach, a method that allows for a test of the assumptions imposed by traditional models, I develop a more complete and accurate assessment of where the effects are the largest.[2]

This chapter is structured as follows. The first section provides a review of the debate over which individuals are most responsive to registration reform and discusses methodological concerns that cast suspicion on previous results. Next, I return to the methods used in Chapter 3 to estimate how the effects of election day registration (EDR) differ across individual characteristics. I conclude by performing similar analyses for motor voter laws.

THE DEBATE OVER WHERE THE EFFECTS ARE THE LARGEST

As I discussed in Chapter 1, along with the assumption that individual responses to election laws are uniform across contexts – that is, the

---

increase the turnout gap between those with the most resources and those with least resources.

[2] As has been the case throughout, I rely primarily on the difference in difference method, but when evaluating the NVRA, I use a state and year fixed effect model. The bounds estimates, used for testing purposes, are reported in Appendix G.

exogenous selection assumption – most of the previous attempts to understand who will see the largest gains in turnout due to EDR or motor voter
have used probit or logit models exclusively. A basic assumption of these
models is that the effect of a change in one of the independent variables
will be at its maximum for those whose initial probability of voting is
equal to 50 percent. That is, the results are driven by the assumptions
built into the method. Thus, our ability to uncover who is most likely to
respond to changes in registration laws is severely hindered.

Nagler (1994) introduced the scobit (skewed-logit) model to the political science literature as a possible alternative to logit and probit. Although
scobit maintains the assumption that the distribution is unimodal (a
potentially problematic assumption), the model is intuitively appealing as
it relaxes the assumption that the largest impact of a change in an independent variable occurs where the initial probability of success (defined
here as voting) is equal to 50 percent. Thus, if one has a theory about
where the effect is the largest, scobit should allow one to test that theory. However, elsewhere I have shown that scobit is unreliable in small
samples (Hanmer 2002; see also Achen 2002) and is especially sensitive
to specification errors (Hanmer 2002, 2006).[3] Because the scobit estimator fails to live up to its task (estimating which types of individuals are
most sensitive to changes in stimuli), it is still unclear whether the effects
of the registration laws vary across individuals and, if so, which types
of individuals will be the most responsive to these changes. Moreover,
the extent to which any variations across subgroups are meaningful also
remains murky.

---

[3] Using data from the 1984 CPS, Hanmer (2002) shows that even with nearly 100,000
observations, changes in the variables included in the model result in substantively different conclusions regarding where the largest impact occurs. Monte Carlo simulations
corroborate the finding that scobit estimates are especially sensitive to model specification. Skeptical readers hesitant to cast aside scobit based on my yet to be published
work should be assuaged by the fact that, in the more than 10 years since Nagler's
article appeared in the *American Journal of Political Science*, the only other empirical article using scobit published in political science is one co-authored by Nagler (see
Leighley and Nagler 2007). Interestingly, the authors note that scobit does not con-
verge when they run their turnout models for midterm elections. Unfortunately, they do
not provide any discussion of this problem and simply report logit results for midterm
elections. To the best of my ability, I cannot construct a theoretical argument that
would suggest that scobit would be problematic in midterm elections. Given they had
hoped to use scobit for midterm elections, it seems that Leighley and Nagler would
agree.

Previous Results[4]

The work in this area centers around Wolfinger and Rosenstone (1980), who argue that education provides individuals with skills and experience that should make registering to vote easier.[5] Thus, one might expect the effect of EDR to vary by education level. Motivated by this expectation, the debate regarding who is most sensitive to changes in registration laws has concentrated on the effect across education categories. Using a probit model and data from the 1972 CPS, Wolfinger and Rosenstone (1980) note that "[t]he most striking variations in the effects of registration reform would be among people at different levels of education," with the largest effects for those with the least amount of education (p. 79). Although Wolfinger and Rosenstone used data from 1972, a year in which only North Dakota had a closing date coded to 0 and motor voter was not yet available anywhere, Highton (1997) draws a similar conclusion based on CPS data from 1980 and 1992.

Nagler (1991) calls these findings into question, citing methodological flaws in the specification of the model used by Wolfinger and Rosenstone. Also using a probit model but interacting closing date with education, he concludes that there is not a special link between easing barriers to registration and those with low levels of education. Rather, Nagler's (1991) results suggest that "individuals with higher levels of education will be more affected by the closing date than will individuals with low levels

[4] Because the theoretical relationship of interest exists at the individual level (that is, individuals make the decision to vote or abstain) and the data are readily available at the individual level, the literature I address here uses individual-level estimates of voter turnout. Several scholars utilize aggregate data and work from a slightly different perspective than those analyzing survey data. Calvert and Gilchrist (1993) use county-level data in 1990 from Minnesota and do not detect a reduction in class bias as a result of EDR. In their investigation of the representativeness of state electorates, Jackson, Brown, and Wright (1998) aggregate CPS data from 1984 and 1986 to the state level. The estimates they obtain suggest that the least educated and poor are the most sensitive to easier registration requirements. Martinez and Hill (1999) employ aggregated polling data from fourteen states to study changes in education bias as a result of the NVRA and data from the fifty states and Washington, DC to study racial bias. According to their results, there was no reduction in the educational bias of the electorate and the advantage in turnout among whites was exacerbated by the NVRA in 1996. Using CPS data aggregated to the state level, Knack and White (2000) examine whether or not inequality between various demographic groups is reduced as a result of EDR in ID, NH, and WY. They find that inequality among the young and mobile was reduced in new EDR states from 1990 to 1994.

[5] Some earlier studies using survey data (see, e.g., Campbell et al. 1960; and Kim, Petrocik, and Enokson 1975) also addressed legal requirements and turnout.

of education" (p. 1400). Unfortunately, Nagler does not provide any explanation to aid our understanding of his admittedly counterintuitive results.

The points raised in Nagler (1991) resonated with others (see Teixeira 1992; Mitchell and Wlezien 1995; Huang and Shields 2000; and Knack and White 2000). For example, cognizant of the assumptions built into logit and probit models, Teixeira (1992) is careful to note that the appearance of larger effects among those least likely to participate is, in part, a byproduct of their low initial probabilities of voting and the model's assumptions.[6] However, Nagler himself was not so easily convinced by the totality of the results from his 1991 work. The last few paragraphs of the 1991 article hint at his next attempt to discover where the impact of registration reform would be the largest. Using the scobit model on data from the 1984 CPS, Nagler (1994) determined that the least educated were the most responsive to registration reform. This conclusion derives from his finding that those whose initial probability of voting was 40 percent, not 50 percent, as probit and logit would require, are the most likely to see increases in their turnout rates. Nagler (1994) interprets his more recent results in light of Wolfinger and Rosenstone's, remarking that his conclusion:

is *not* because a particular link between education and registering early [exists]; it is because individuals with less education are more sensitive to any changes likely to increase turnout. In fact, Wolfinger and Rosenstone were even "more" correct than they realized, since the scobit estimates indicated that logit and probit will underestimate the sensitivity to stimulus of persons with extremely low initial probabilities of voting (p. 252, emphasis in original).

Thus, although Nagler (1994) comes to the same substantive conclusion as Wolfinger and Rosenstone, these scholars differ in their assessment of the mechanism underlying the results.

More recent studies provide yet another answer to the question of who is most affected by relaxed registration laws. Huang and Shields (2000) focus on the interaction between education and registration laws and replicate Nagler (1991) using 1972 and 1992 CPS data. They find that those with moderate levels of education, specifically those with high school degrees but no further education, stand the most to gain from registration reform. Brians and Grofman (1999, 2001) classify individuals

---

[6] Mitchell and Wlezien (1995) examine turnout among the registered, and find that the effect of reducing the closing date is relatively uniform across education categories. Huang and Shields (2000) is discussed in the text that follows.

differently than others but come to a conclusion similar to that of Huang and Shields. By combining educational attainment and income quartiles, they create categories of socioeconomic status (SES) and compare predicted changes in turnout across these groups. Their results suggest that the largest gains in turnout are found among those in the middle SES group, which they define as high school graduates with middle income.[7]

The work of Brians and Grofman (1999) is especially important in that they contribute a formal model to help predict where the effect should be largest by explicitly taking motivation into account. As I hope I have made clear by now, I am sympathetic to the notion that the effect of removing barriers to registration is conditional on motivational factors. However, their classification of individuals by SES acts only as a proxy for variations in motivation across educational and income categories.

At present, it seems favor has swung toward the more recent conclusion that the effects are largest among those with moderate levels of education (Highton 2004). The results presented here suggest a revision.

Three hypotheses emerge from previous work. First, Wolfinger and Rosenstone (1980) contend that the least educated are the most likely to benefit from registration reform because they are less able to overcome more difficult hurdles. Though they do not bring data to bear on the issue, Piven and Cloward (1988, 1989, 2000) also hold firm to the belief that the least well off stand the most to gain when barriers to registration are reduced. Second, Brians and Grofman (1999, 2001) maintain that the largest impact should be found among those in the middle of the pack – that is, those who have moderate levels of interest and skills and need just a small reduction in costs to get them involved. It is crucial to note that their model does not necessarily predict that the largest effect will be on those who initially have a fifty–fifty chance of voting (that is, $p = 0.5$). When summing up the predictions generated from their model, Brians and Grofman (1999) hypothesize that "groups that are 'in the middle' with respect to [socioeconomic status] variables... should be obtaining the greatest turnout gains when registration barriers are lowered by the adoption of election day registration" (p. 165). That is, the model makes predictions about where one lies within the distribution of demographic characteristics and *not* the distribution of voting probabilities. Of course,

---

[7] Gronke, Galanes-Rosenbaum, Miller, and Toffey (2008) describe convenience voting reforms as those having to do with "mode[s] of voting other than precinct-place voting" (for example, voting by mail, early voting) (p. 438). However, the conclusions drawn by Huang and Shields (2000) and Brians and Grofman (1999, 2001) fit well with the notion that reforms make it more convenient for those who are already inclined to vote to do so.

these may be related (though this is an empirical question) but the fact remains that a theory that directly links the largest impact of registration reform to an initial voting probability of 50 percent is absent from the literature. Moreover, to test properly a theory that suggests the greatest impact is at the point where voting is a fifty–fifty proposition, as I discuss subsequently, one must use a method that does not assume that this is the case and test it against methods that rely on this very assumption. The final hypothesis is that registration laws do not differentially affect some types of citizens more than others.

The only thing that is clear is that after more than twenty-five years of research, political scientists have failed to produce a definitive answer. This is true even though most of the researchers in this area analyzed similar data from the CPS.[8] In addition, those using individual-level data, with the exception of Nagler (1994), used either logit or probit models. By employing multiple methods and testing the assumptions implicit in probit and logit models, I hope to remove the fog that hangs over this question. My primary interest is in variations in effects across levels of educational attainment – the individual attribute for which there are the strongest theoretical expectations regarding which types of individuals should be most likely to take advantage of the registration reforms under study and, accordingly the characteristic to which the literature has given the greatest amount of attention. Given the growing concern with youth voting (see, for example, Wattenberg 2007), I also examine the effects across age groups. Given that Brians and Grofman (1999, 2001) examine the effect of EDR by combining categories of education and income, I follow this approach to show that any differences in my results and theirs are not an artifact of the way the comparisons between the resource rich and resource poor are made.

THE EFFECTS OF REGISTRATION REFORM BY INDIVIDUAL CHARACTERISTICS

In Chapters 3 and 4, I estimated the overall effects of EDR and motor voter, respectively. Here, using the results from the models in those chapters I estimate the effects according to the respondents' educational

---

[8] The number of elections incorporated into the analysis of individual-level data varies: a single cross-section was used by Wolfinger and Rosenstone (1980), and Nagler (1994); multiple years individually were employed by Nagler (1991) and Huang and Shields (2000); and pooled cross-sections were examined by Teixeira (1992), Mitchell and Wlezien (1995), Highton (1997), and Brians and Grofman (1999, 2001).

attainment, age, and combinations of education and income.[9] The difference in difference method was used to account for endogeneity, but the model was run using probit, meaning that the effect will be largest among those with a fifty–fifty initial probability of voting. I discuss the results of tests designed to examine this assumption subsequently and report them in Appendix G (see also Hanmer 2007).

Election Day Registration

As a reminder, when I compared the effect of EDR in Minnesota and Wisconsin versus the comparable states of Iowa and South Dakota, the estimated effect was about 4.5 percentage points. In the new EDR states, the effect could not be distinguished from zero. That is, when Idaho and Wyoming were compared to Montana, and New Hampshire to Vermont, EDR did not appear to be responsible for an increase in the probability of voting.

Table 6.1 displays the effects from the difference in difference models run using probit by education and age. These results were derived from Table 3.1, from Appendix E, Table E.3, and Table E.5 respectively. The difference in difference models use states that adopted EDR and states that were deemed comparable. Included in the model, in addition to the variable representing the effect of EDR, were a set of demographic variables (a linear and quadratic specification of age, and linear specifications of education, income quartile, and, when available, mobility), along with dummy variables for the years included in the analysis, a dummy for living in a treatment state or not, and interactions between the demographic variables and the treatment state variable. After obtaining the overall effects (calculated by generating predicted probabilities for each individual under a scenario in which all received the EDR treatment, then a scenario in which EDR was not allowed anywhere, taking the difference, and averaging), I simply generated the average effect for the various subpopulations of interest.[10] Due to the small number individuals in the zero to four years of education categories in the new EDR state

---

[9] The effect of motor voter in MN and NV across individual characteristics is not reported. Not only was the effect of motor voter statistically insignificant in these states, more importantly, it was substantively insignificant.

[10] That is, I used the same procedure as described in Wolfinger and Rosenstone (1980). Alternatively, the sample could be subdivided based on values for the demographic characteristics of interest; due to small sample sizes in some of the cases, this method is not used.

TABLE 6.1. *Difference in Difference Probit Estimates of the Short Term Effect of EDR by Education and Age*

Category	MN and WI versus IA and SD (1972 and 1980)	ID and WY versus MT (1992 and 1996)	NH versus VT (1992 and 1996)
All	4.5	2.8	3.6
Education			
0–4 Years	6.3	NA	NA
5–8 Years	5.9	NA	NA
0–8 Years	6.0	3.8	4.6
9–11 Years	5.4	3.5	4.2
High School Degree	4.7	3.3	4.3
1–3 Years of College	3.9	2.8	3.6
College Degree	2.4	1.7	2.5
College +	1.2	0.7	0.9
Age			
18–21	6.0	3.6	4.1
22–25	5.4	3.7	4.3
26–29	5.0	3.6	4.4
30–39	4.2	3.2	3.9
40–65	3.7	2.4	3.0
66 and older	4.8	2.4	3.4

Note: The Difference in Difference approach compares states with EDR to comparable states.
Source: 1972, 1980, 1992, and 1996 CPS.

columns, I collapsed the categories for zero to four and five to eight years of education into one category.

For the most part, across both education and age classifications, as the values increase, the effect of EDR decreases. That is, in the three sets of state comparisons, the least educated and the young appear to have experienced the largest increases in turnout as a result of EDR. The largest increases, on the order of 6 percentage points, were found in Minnesota and Wisconsin for those with zero to eight years of education as well as those who were eighteen to twenty-one years old. The size of the effect shrinks with each level of education. For example, the effect in Minnesota and Wisconsin was estimated to be 4.7 percentage points among those with a high school degree, but only 2.4 percentage points for those who graduated from college. Comparing across the columns reveals that the least educated in Minnesota and Wisconsin gained more from EDR than did those in either of the other sets of comparisons. This gap begins to vanish among citizens with higher levels of education.

Overall, the disparity between those predicted to gain the most and those predicted to gain the least was relatively small. For the Minnesota and Wisconsin analysis, the gap between those with zero to eight years of education and those with schooling beyond college was 4.8 percentage points. The same calculation in the other two columns produced a 3.1 and 3.7 point difference, respectively. These increases are modest relative to the more than thirty-point turnout gap[11] that existed between the most and least educated prior to the adoption of EDR.[12] That is, setting the size of these effects into the context of the preexisting tendency for the highly educated to exceed the turnout rates among those with less formal education, reinforces the conclusion that registration reform is not a panacea for the unequal turnout rates between those with high levels of education and those with minimal or moderate levels of education.

Although the effect of EDR generally decreased with age, the degree to which it did so was slight. The largest difference was between eighteen to twenty-one year olds and forty to sixty-five year olds in the analysis of Minnesota, Wisconsin, Iowa, and South Dakota, but was a mere 2.4 percentage points. In the other comparisons, the largest such disparity was just over 1 percentage point. Again, these minor increases barely put a dent in the degree of turnout inequality by age. The pre-EDR difference in turnout rates among the least sensitive and the most sensitive groups was between 19 and 31 percentage points.[13]

Before moving on, it is important to note that the effects are not influenced by combining groups into SES categories as did Brians and Grofman (1999, 2001). When one compares the effects for the least

---

[11] The gap, calculated using only the states included in the respective difference in difference models varied: in MN, WI, IA, and SD in 1972 the gap was thirty-three points; in ID, WY and MT in 1992 the gap was forty-one points; and in NH and VT in 1992, the gap was thirty-nine points.

[12] Wolfinger and Rosenstone (1980), Teixeira (1992), and Mitchell Wlezien (1995) provide convincing evidence that when registration laws are relaxed, subsequent changes in the overall composition of the electorate are small. With even smaller effects, as estimated here, there is little reason to call this result into question.

[13] In all three comparisons, forty- to sixty-five-year-olds were the least sensitive to the switch to EDR. Although one of the subgroups under thirty years old was always the most sensitive group, the particular group with the most sensitivity varied across the comparisons (of course, as noted in the text, the differences across groups were rather small). The degree of turnout inequality in the presidential election just prior to the adoption of EDR by comparison set was as follows: nineteen points in MN, WI, IA, and SD; twenty-five points in ID, WY, and MT; and thirty-one points in NH and VT.

TABLE 6.2. *Difference in Difference Probit Estimates of the Effect of EDR by Socioeconomic Status (Combined Education and Income Categories)*

Category	MN and WI versus IA and SD (1972 and 1980)	ID and WY versus MT (1992 and 1996)	NH versus VT (1992 and 1996)
No High School Degree and Lowest Income Quartile	6.0	4.4	3.5
High School Degree and 2nd or 3rd Income Quartile	4.8	4.3	3.3
College Degree and Highest Income Quartile	1.8	1.1	1.9

Note: The Difference in Difference approach compares states with EDR to comparable states.
Source: 1972, 1980, 1992, and 1996 CPS.

educated (no high school degree), who also have the lowest income; those with high school degrees and medium levels of income; and those with at least a college degree and the highest levels of income, the effects remain the largest for the least educated. The differences are small, particularly in the new EDR states, but EDR never has the largest effect on those with high school degrees. Table 6.2 displays the results.[14]

The conclusions based on the evidence presented here stand in contrast to those found in Brians and Grofman (1999, 2001) and Huang and Shields (2000), who suggest that those with a high school degree will benefit the most from EDR. What accounts for these conflicting results?

Modeling issues may play some role, but each set of authors comes to similar conclusions using different models. Whereas Brians and Grofman (1999, 2001) use pooled cross-sections and estimate a state and year fixed effects model in which they do not interact education with election law variables, Huang and Shields (2000) use two cross-sectional data sets and interact education with the closing date for registration.

This leads to a consideration of the approach to calculating predicted probabilities. Whereas (à la Wolfinger and Rosenstone) I study the effect of EDR by calculating a set of predicted probabilities for each individual, Brians and Grofman (1999, 2001) and Huang and Shields (2000) examine the effect of EDR based on predicted probabilities for a so-called "typical" individual by setting values of the variables to their respective means, medians, or modes, a practice that is common in the literature. As Hanmer

---

[14] This analysis was repeated for the motor voter states, with similar results. The effects were not the largest among those in the middle category.

TABLE 6.2. *Predicted Turnout from EDR by Socioeconomic Status and Sex Using Logit Coefficients from Brians and Grofman (1999)*

		EDR		
Education Level	Income Quartile	Yes (%)	No (%)	Difference (%)
Panel a. Men: largest effect is for high school and second income				
Grade School	Lowest	29.8	21.8	8.0
High School	Second	71.3	61.9	9.4
Some College	Third	88.8	83.9	4.9
Four-Year Degree	Highest	94.7	92.1	2.6
Panel b. Women: largest effect is for grade school and lowest income (though difference with high school and second income is small)				
Grade School	Lowest	34.7	25.8	8.9
High School	Second	75.6	67.0	8.6
Some College	Third	90.9	86.7	4.2
Four-Year Degree	Highest	95.7	93.6	2.1

Notes: Predictions are calculated for employed, married, white citizens, in the base state (with active motor voter set to 0), closing date set to 30 for the No EDR treatment, in 1992.

Brians and Grofman's (1999) results for men could not be exactly replicated but the same substantive conclusion is obtained – that is, the largest effect occurs for those with a high school degree and second lowest income.

and Kalkan (2008) argue, by its very nature, this breaks the link between the research design and the results, thus limiting the ability to generalize the results. With the CPS data, not only is this unnecessary, it represents an inefficient use of the available information. As noted earlier, one of the chief benefits of the CPS is that it provides a sample that is representative of the nation and the individual states. As a result, calculating predicted probabilities for each individual has a clear theoretical advantage over procedures that limit their attention to just a subset of the sample – usually white, males, in their forties, who we know are not a particularly representative group.

As a test of this idea, I attempted to replicate the results from Brians and Grofman (1999) using their results table and definition of the typical individual.[15] Table 6.2 shows that the estimates can be quite sensitive to changes in the values chosen to represent the typical individual. Comparing panel a to panel b from Table 6.2 demonstrates that by changing just one attribute of the "typical" individual, making this individual female rather than male, the conclusion about where the effect is the largest

[15] Brians and Grofman's (1999) results for men could not be exactly replicated but the same substantive conclusion is obtained; that is, the largest effect occurs for those with a high school degree and second lowest income.

changes from those in the second SES category (among males) to a virtual tie between those in the lowest category and those in the second category (among females). Thus, although the conclusions reached by Brians and Grofman (1999) about their "typical" individual remain valid, their approach limits the extent to which we can learn about the effect of EDR more generally.[16]

Like the results presented in Wolfinger and Rosenstone (1980), Nagler (1994), Mitchell and Wlezein (1995), and Highton (1997) – although Nagler's assessment of the underlying reasons for this differ – my results, which take into account the roles of social and political context, suggest that those with the least amount of resources will see the largest turnout gains under EDR. I performed tests of the probit model using the bounds approach to discern how well the functional form and distributional assumptions hold up and to gain insight into whether the evidence points to a relationship (albeit a weak one) between registration barriers and the ability of the least educated and young to surmount them, or whether those with little formal education and the young are just more sensitive (though only mildly so at best) to stimuli than are others. The details are contained in Hanmer (2007) and Appendix G, but the conclusion can be stated succinctly. Tests of probit against a method that relaxes the assumption that the largest effect is found among those with an initial probability of voting equal to 50 percent do not allow for the rejection of this assumption. Though this is an important methodological issue, a substantive point of great consequence holds regardless of one's faith in probit models. That is, whether one believes that strict registration laws are especially problematic for the least well off (Wolfinger and Rosenstone 1980) or that those with low probabilities of voting are simply more sensitive to stimuli (Nagler 1994), the small estimated differences across categories reveal that EDR did little to boost turnout among the lowest turnout groups. I now turn to an exploration of the effects of motor voter.

Motor Voter

As I predicted, the effect of state-implemented versions of motor voter in Michigan and North Carolina, even though they were not as far reaching

---

[16] I do not mean to suggest that taking the approach that calculates predicted probabilities for "typical" observations is always problematic. However, consistent with Hanmer and Kalkan (2008), my analysis suggests that researchers who calculate predicted probabilities for "typical" observations consider the nature of their sample and provide results for more than one "typical" observation, as well as the average effect across all individuals in the sample.

TABLE 6.3. *Probit Estimates of the Short-Term Effect of Motor Voter by Education and Age*

Category	MI versus OH[a] (1972 and 1980)	NC versus TN[a] (1972–1992)	New NVRA[b] (1992–2000)
All	5.4	5.3	1.7
	Education		
0–4 Years	6.7	5.6	2.0
5–8 Years	6.7	6.1	2.1
0–8 Years	6.7	6.0	2.1
9–11 Years	6.2	5.9	2.0
High School Degree	5.7	5.8	2.0
1–3 Years of College	4.8	5.1	1.8
College Degree	3.1	3.6	1.3
College +	1.6	2.0	0.7
	Age		
18–21	6.6	5.6	2.0
22–25	6.3	5.8	2.0
26–29	6.0	5.7	2.0
30–39	5.4	5.4	1.9
40–65	4.7	5.0	1.6
66 and older	5.6	5.4	1.6

[a] Estimated using the difference in difference method.
[b] Estimated using a state and year fixed effects model.
Source: Presidential Year CPS, Excluding 1976.

as the NVRA in terms of the options made available to eligible citizens, still played a larger role in improving the probability of voting than did the NVRA. The arguments put forth by the advocates of motor voter registration procedures centered around the notion that if registration were made easier or nearly automatic, those with the fewest resources would then be able to overcome the hurdle of registration and complete the race by casting a ballot on election day. Given the inability of EDR, the least restrictive of all registration requirements, to produce substantially larger increases in turnout among the have-nots compared with the haves, there is little reason to suspect motor voter would do better. With a mere 2–percentage-point increase in the overall probability of voting due to the NVRA, it is especially unlikely that the effects will vary enough for the expectations of motor voter's proponents to be met.

Based on the experiences in the three cases in which motor voter had success, I now compute the predicted increase in the probability of voting if motor voter were universally available. The estimates in Table 6.3

were computed from the models in Tables 4.1, 4.4, and 4.5 in Chapter 4. For Michigan and North Carolina, I obtained the estimates using probit and the difference in difference approach. The variable specifications correspond to those described in the previous section on EDR. For the NVRA, I ran probit on a state and year fixed effects model (that is, dummy variables for the states and years were included), using the same demographic variables and specifications as used for the other analyses, a variable for registration closing date, and dummy variables to represent states' experience with motor voter laws prior to the NVRA. As I did for EDR, after calculating the overall effect of motor voter, by averaging over the predicted probabilities estimated for each individual, I then summarized the results across categories of education and age. Table 6.3 shows again that the overall effect of the NVRA in the states upon which it was imposed was smaller than the effect of motor voter in Michigan and North Carolina. Consistent with the theoretical framework developed in Chapter 1, this results from the lack of demand for registration reform in the states that were obligated by federal legislation to implement the NVRA.

The first pattern of note from Table 6.3 is that the largest effects tend to be concentrated among the least educated and the young. The predicted increase of 5.6 percentage points in turnout for citizens in North Carolina with zero to four years of education is slightly lower than the predicted increase for those up through the high school degree category, but the substantive difference is negligible. In the first two columns, representing the effects of mature motor voter as implemented by state law, variations in the size of the effects do not begin to emerge until the college degree category is reached. That is, the decline in the size of the effects is rather gradual. The difference in the size of the effects among citizens with fewer than eight years of education and citizens with one to three years of college education is roughly two points in the analysis of Michigan and Ohio and about one point in the analysis of North Carolina and Tennessee. As expected, in states that previously did not have motor voter provisions, the NVRA failed to produce distinguishable effects across individual levels of educational attainment. At best, the least educated saw their turnout rise by two points, whereas the most educated gained around one point. As I did when studying EDR, for each set of models, I calculated the inequality in turnout rates in the year prior to the adoption of motor voter. The turnout rate for those with zero to eight years of education fell short of turnout among those with the highest levels of education by at least forty-two points. As a result, these small gains do little to improve the turnout rates of the least educated relative to the more highly educated.[17]

The lack of differentiation across age categories is remarkable. The largest difference in the projected increase in turnout across age groups occurred in the analysis of motor voter in Michigan compared with Ohio. It was just under 2 percentage points; in that analysis, the smallest increase was 4.7 points for forty- to sixty-five-year-olds, whereas the largest was 6.6 points for eighteen- to twenty-one-year-olds. In both of the other two columns, the largest discrepancy is a mere 0.4 percentage points. The insignificance of any gains by the youngest group of citizens is clear when set against the overall disparity in turnout between younger and older citizens. For each of the cases presented in Table 6.3, in the respective elections before the adoption of motor voter, the difference in turnout between forty- to sixty-five-year-olds and the age group for which the largest gains were predicted was in the neighborhood of 30 percentage points.[18] In sum, there is no escape from the conclusion that the effects of registration reform are not only smaller than expected, but those who were thought to benefit the most did so only at the margins.

CONCLUSION

This chapter has shown that the least educated appear to gain the most from easier registration procedures. Although the estimates were derived using probit models that make distributional assumptions that shape the results, tests of the probit assumptions did not lead to their rejection (Hanmer 2007; Appendix G). The effects are not uniform across contexts, but the overall differences across categories are quite small. In fact, they do little to reduce the inequality in turnout, contrary to expectations of proponents of registration reform. With respect to the turnout disadvantage of the young, there is even less reason to celebrate registration reform as a means to increase the equality of participation.

[17] Across the columns, the difference in turnout is forty-two points, forty-three points, and forty-eight points respectively.
[18] For the 1972 election, in MI and OH, there was a thirty-four point difference in turnout between forty- to sixty-five-year-olds and eighteen- to twenty-one-year-olds. In 1992, the election prior to the implementation of the NVRA, the gap between the same age groups considered in MI and OH was twenty-nine points. The inequality in turnout rates in NC and TN, when comparing forty- to sixty-five-year-olds to twenty-two- to twenty-five-year-olds in the 1988 election was twenty-seven points.

Thus, for those hopeful that registration reform would be a driving force in the march toward the democratic ideals of participation and political equality, this chapter has provided more bad news. That is, in addition to the failure of registration reforms to generate substantial increases in turnout, the young and least educated gained little ground on those who are older and more educated, respectively. Even after a substantial decrease in the costs of participating, the least advantaged remain the least motivated, and thus the least likely to participate. After discussing challenges to the results presented thus far and providing an account of how the parties operate under EDR, I take up the task of describing what might be done to improve turnout in the United States.

7

EDR on the Ground and Prospects for the Future

The results presented thus far demonstrate that recent registration reforms have not led to substantial increases in turnout, nor have they amplified the voices of those who are the least likely to vote beyond a blip on the volume meter. In order to address concerns that variations in the effect of election day registration (EDR) across contexts could be the result of poor implementation in the states that adopted it in response to the National Voter Registration Act (NVRA) and/or differences in the strategies political parties have used to mobilize unregistered but eligible citizens, this chapter reports on interviews I conducted with state election officials and state Democratic and Republican party leaders across the EDR states.[1] Systematic data on EDR implementation and party responses, to the best of my knowledge, are simply not available from existing sources. Although the National Election Studies (NES) provides information regarding party mobilization efforts, asking respondents whether or not they were contacted by the political parties, the NES was designed to provide a representative sample of the nation, not individual states. Moreover, the sample size for the EDR states, which have small populations, is insufficient to allow one to draw inferences; in fact, in some study years, individuals in the less populous EDR states are not even sampled. As a result, interviews with both election officials and party leaders are used to provide insight into the implementation of EDR and how the

---

[1] After a change in the administration, the Maine Democratic party refused my request for an interview on the grounds that they do not engage in such activities, even for educational purposes. Piven and Cloward (2000) address NVRA implementation and speculate about how the parties responded to the NVRA.

parties' strategies are shaped by its availability. The survey instruments can be found in Appendix H.

Most of my interviews took place in early 2003, after the respondents' work on the 2002 election had settled down. It quickly became clear to me that scheduling time with the respondents before the election was impossible, even during the early summer months. As a result, I was able to experience a great range of temperatures, from −11°F in Concord, New Hampshire, to 64°F in Boise, Idaho.[2] Whenever possible, the interviews were conducted face-to-face in the office of the interview subjects. Due to schedule conflicts, however, some of the interviews were conducted over the phone and one took place as late as September 2003.[3] Given the nature of the questions and the fact that the interview subjects are experts in their field, I do not believe that variations in the mode of interview nor the timing of the interview altered the quality of the responses. I do not conceal the names of the representatives from the state elections divisions because, as public officials, they could be easily identified anyway.[4] However, given the sensitivity of the information provided by party leaders who are in competition with one another, and as a means to improve the response rate, I agreed not to release the names of those interview subjects, nor discuss their answers in a manner that could lead to their identification.

In the following section, I evaluate my findings from interviews with party leaders in EDR states in light of expectations derived from Rosenstone and Hansen's (1993) study of mobilization. Next, I discuss the

---

[2] I was in Boise just before a storm turned the unseasonably warm temperatures in the other direction. It was 5°F in Augusta, ME, 20°F in Madison, WI, −2°F in St. Paul, MN, and 47°F in Cheyenne, WY.

[3] I owe a debt of gratitude to Chris Thomas, the director of elections in Michigan, for helping me secure an interview with his colleagues in one of the states. After the 2004 election, I conducted follow-up interviews over the phone with party officials, finding that the conclusions reported subsequently were not specific to the 2002 elections.

[4] The list of state elections officials that I interviewed, their positions, and the date of the interview follows: Idaho (3/13/03), Penny Ysursa (Administrative Secretary Elections Division); Maine (9/18/03), Julie Flynn (Deputy Secretary of State) and Deborah Cabana (Director of Elections); Minnesota (2/26/03), Michael McCarthy (Assistant Director Elections Division), Michele McNulty (Election Administrator), Lisa Kramer Rodacker (Program Administrator); New Hampshire (1/16/03), William Gardner (Secretary of State); Wisconsin (2/27/03), Kevin J. Kennedy (Executive Director, State of Wisconsin Elections Board); Wyoming (3/11/03), Peggy Nighswonger (Elections Director), and Lori Klassen (Elections Officer). In all cases in which more than one individual participated, the interview was conducted as a single session with each of the participants present.

results of my interviews with election officials in EDR states. I conclude by discussing the prospects for the future of voter turnout in the United States and avenues of research in need of further exploration based on the results of this study.

EDR AND PARTY MOBILIZATION

Reflecting on the low level of voter turnout in 1996, the first election after the NVRA went into effect, Piven and Cloward (2000) placed blame on the Democratic party and its candidates for passing up the opportunity to make an appeal to new registrants, especially members of minority groups and the poor. Interestingly, the reports produced by Human SERVE said nothing of party responsiveness as the mechanism that would drive the results. That is, higher turnout rates were reported but were not attributed to mobilization efforts by the Democrats. Given their leaning toward the Democratic party, the omission of their belief that the Democrats would benefit could have been strategic. Had they announced that the benefits would be expected to accrue to the Democrats, even when Republicans tended toward this view (see Calvert and Gilchrist 1993), fuel would have been added to the Republican party's fire. Piven and Cloward do not directly examine the behavior of the Democratic party. However, their conclusion seems sensible given the results of the 1996 and 2000 elections. Were their expectations reasonable?

A brief review of Rosenstone and Hansen (1993) suggests their hopes should have been tempered. Rosenstone and Hansen (1993) explain the logic of party mobilization strategies in the following fashion:

> The goal of political parties is to win enough votes to elect their candidates to office. Mobilizing efforts are designed to make that happen, by inducing people to vote, persuade, contribute, and volunteer. Given their limited resources, however, parties must decide on whom they will target their efforts. Resources they devote to people who are unlikely to turn out or unlikely to support them are resources wasted (p. 163).

The crucial component of this argument has to do with the recognition that parties have limited resources. That is, resource constraints limit the extent to which parties can reach out for support. They cannot contact everyone, nor do they want to. That some citizens do not come into play is not necessarily pernicious. If the Democratic party knocks on doors in a heavily Republican precinct, it might increase turnout but likely is reminding the opposition to vote. Obviously, for them, this would be a bad move; regardless of the Democratic party's overall interest in participation, it surely does not want to use its resources to increase turnout among supporters of its competition.

The problem Piven and Cloward would raise has little to do with the failure of the parties to mobilize in opposition districts, however. Rather, their complaint derives from the decision of the parties to ignore some districts and therefore certain types of people entirely. Again, one should keep in mind the role of resource constraints. That is, time and energy spent on individuals not likely to vote, in a world of scarce resources, is time and energy that is diverted away from making sure the most loyal supporters make it to the polls. This is not to discount Piven and Cloward's (2000) stance that the parties have historically played a role in shaping who the players are in the game, but clearly, there are additional considerations.

Rosenstone and Hansen (1993) also point out that those whom the parties contact are those who are easy to identify. Drivers are a heterogeneous group, and if they do not have a voting history, deciding which ones to mobilize is costly and contacting them entails greater risk. Although public agency registrants can be identified more easily, history would suggest that these registrants, who tend to be poor, would be unlikely to turn out. As was shown in Chapter 5, turnout rates among public agency registrants were about twenty points lower than turnout rates even for Department of Motor Vehicle registrants, which were already relatively low. As a result, it is not surprising that new and unproven NVRA registrants were not sought after to the extent that Piven and Cloward had expected they would be.

What happens when the parties are given more time to seek out unregistered but eligible citizens? As I discussed in Chapter 1, the ability of citizens moved to vote late in the campaign is an important feature that distinguishes EDR from systems that close registration days or weeks before the election. The extra time does permit the campaign to reach more eligible citizens, but identifying the individuals who become interested is not a straightforward task. Although the parties have an opportunity to mobilize those who have not previously exercised their right to vote or have not taken the time to register, these individuals are not only costly to identify, they are less dependable in terms of the likelihood that they will show up to vote, and are less predictable with respect to their choices on the ballot.

The chief purpose of my interviews with party officials was to discover how the major parties tend to allocate their scarce resources – that is, how they distribute resources between the mobilization of the base and the less reliable pool of unregistered but eligible citizens. I also obtained information regarding how high-ranking officials in the state party administration feel about EDR as implemented in their state.

Overall, the evidence pointed to the conclusion that party mobilization under EDR does not diverge from the description provided by Rosenstone and Hansen (1993). Generally, party leaders reported that the bulk of their resources were directed toward reminding their strongest supporters to vote (for them of course). Only one Democratic and one Republican party leader described the distribution of resources among the registered and unregistered as similar; in all other cases the disparity was considerable.

The parties use myriad methods to identify and mobilize supporters. To identify supporters, they employ aggregate and individual information. At the aggregate level, the parties classify precincts[5] based on their previous support for the party and target those with high performance (usually defined as at least 60 percent to 65 percent of the vote going to their party). Census tract data sometimes are used as well. Specific individuals are identified through registration and vote history lists, internal polling, the purchase of marketing data, lists of recent movers, group memberships, and lists of those with hunting and fishing licenses. It should not be surprising that hunting and fishing license lists are used given that all of the EDR states are outdoors-person friendly, with deer, moose, bears, and so on roaming around and a variety of fish swimming in their streams, rivers, and lakes.

Calls are then generated from phone banks or through automated systems (sometimes using celebrities), literature is delivered, and mail (often regarding how one can vote by absentee ballot) is sent directly to the targeted individuals. On election day, the calls continue and "flushers" are sent to "knock and pull/drag" people to the polls. That is, party volunteers visit high-performance precincts to knock on doors, remind the individuals who answer to vote and sometimes offer rides to the polling places. One party official reported that the organization staffs the polls with individuals who, using a list of likely supporters, keep track of who has voted and who has not. At specified times, they call those who have

---

[5] Technically speaking, not all of the states use the term precinct; for example, in Wisconsin, local election jurisdictions are referred to as wards. For the sake of simplicity, throughout the discussion, I refer to local election jurisdictions as precincts.

not yet voted to remind them to do so. Mass appeals through television, radio, and newspaper ads also are used, as are rallies and other efforts aimed at increasing visibility, but all to a lesser degree than direct contacts.

For the most part, even with EDR, mobilizing the unregistered is a lower priority than is mobilizing those who are already registered. As a result, the list of mechanisms used for EDR is less extensive, especially for the Republican party. A Democrat in one of the new EDR states remarked that the state party does not place much weight on the distinction between the registered and unregistered and provided one of only two reports that resources devoted to mobilization were distributed about equally across these two types of citizens. However, this party official maintained that registering people to vote on election day "is a very difficult thing to do" and described the usual methods of doing so as "a wish and a prayer."

Another Democratic party official, but in a state that adopted EDR in the 1970s, expressed similar views regarding the task of registering people to vote but made clear distinctions between the registered and unregistered. This party leader reported that the state party is not concerned with targeting individuals who do not vote. He noted that cost-per-voter calculations come into play and that it is less costly (by a factor of about 12) to persuade a former voter to vote again than to get someone to register and vote for the first time. Obviously, getting the most supporters out as possible is the goal and, with limited resources, it is simply easier and less expensive to motivate habitual and intermittent voters. According to this respondent, a campaign to get people registered can be a winning strategy; however, registering to vote is viewed as a personal decision, and getting people to vote for the first time is extremely difficult. In this state, the responsibility for getting people registered falls on the candidates and their campaigns. That is, according to this party official, the candidates "need to start rallying the troops and go into the bars and the cafés, wherever it is and talk to people and say listen are you registered to vote, or on the campuses or even into high schools and do what they can." He went on to say that, with EDR, "there really isn't a big drive from us ... you hope that you motivate them ... and [that] they show up." The campaigns might also mobilize the unregistered to register and vote on election day through the knock and pull strategy, but these efforts are concentrated in the high-performance precincts. Again, this official reinforced the challenge, saying "it's a hard thing to do, to motivate somebody to vote is a really hard thing to do." He

summed up the state party's position arguing that registering people to
vote:

is so candidate driven, there's not really a message that's going to come from us.
It is not going to be us that says something that motivates [individuals] for the
first time-it is either going to be something that makes [them] really mad ... or it
is going to be candidate driven.[6]

Together with the remarks from the official in one of the new EDR states,
these comments highlight the complexity of the task in places where EDR
is long established as well as in its infancy.

A Democratic official in another state that has allowed EDR for more
than 25 years explained most of the party's resources are allocated to
promoting turnout among registrants. In that state, the Democrats do not
focus much on EDR and gear most registration efforts toward pushing
people to register before election day. The reason cited for this was that
getting individuals registered early facilitates contacts from the candidates
and makes voting easier on election day. However, in this state, the party
utilizes knock and pull strategies in high Democratic performance areas,
literature drops, and rallies in the last few days before the election and on
election day itself with the hope of mobilizing college students, members
of minority groups, and labor union members.

The most extensive lists of mechanisms used to get people registered
on election day were generated by the Democratic party in two of the
new EDR states.[7] As part of the party's efforts to increase the number of
EDR transactions for the 2002 election, the Democrats in one state used
paid television commercials and direct mail specifically geared to providing information about EDR, along with a variety of methods to mobilize
college students, including print ads, phone calls from a phone bank with
recorded messages from celebrities, organizers on college campuses, vans
on college campuses to transport students to the polls, and e-mails to college students with flash movies attached. Also for the 2002 election, the
Democrats in another new EDR state, in addition to running radio and
television ads, made a number of direct contacts with unregistered but

---

[6] The election of former professional wrestler Jesse Ventura to the office of Governor in
Minnesota provides additional support for the importance of candidate's abilities to spark
interest in voting among nonregistrants (see Lentz 2002).

[7] A caveat is in order. It might be the case that party strategies in the early days of EDR
in Minnesota, Wisconsin, and Maine placed more weight on registering eligible citizens
on election day than the parties in these states do today. Unfortunately, records of party
behavior from nearly thirty years ago were not maintained by the parties and, to the best
of my knowledge, were not collected by researchers; thus, we will never know for sure.

eligible citizens. They contacted individuals in high Democratic performance but low turnout precincts as well as unregistered citizens who were identified through matching information against the voter file via phone, mail, and door knocking. Additionally, the state party worked with nonprofit organizations concerned with turnout among Native Americans and Hispanics. Although it seems that much was done in these two states, more than double the amount of money was spent on mobilizing those who were already registered; in the state I discuss second, four times as much money was spent on mobilizing the registered than was spent on registration campaigns.

Republicans in several states lamented their performance with respect to mobilizing unregistered citizens to take advantage of EDR, recognizing that the Democrats do a much better job. The Republican party in one of the mature EDR states is an exception to this. There, resources are not separately allocated toward mobilization of the registered and unregistered. The focus is on getting supporters, identified primarily by previous performance of the precinct, to the polls regardless of their registration status. They used direct mail and phone call campaigns with information about EDR along with door knocking in targeted areas as part of their overall strategy for the 2002 election. Overall, the Republicans in this state tend to rely on direct mail and phone calls to get people registered on election day.

The situation just described stands in contrast to a general lack of concern with unregistered citizens on the part of Republican party organizations in EDR states. Few, if any, resources were employed in two states – one a new EDR state and the other a mature EDR state. In these states, the Republicans did not have any concentrated efforts targeted at registering people on election day. One of the Republican party officials working in a new EDR state reported that the state party ceases efforts to seek out new voters after the primaries, citing a lack of resources to attract new voters once the campaign is in full swing. However, in this state, some work is done at the county level and by college-based Republican organizations. College Republican organizations also bore the primary responsibility for EDR efforts in one of the states that has allowed EDR since the 1970s.

Another Republican party leader in a new EDR state remarked that EDR was put into place to save money and many believed the unregistered would remain unregistered. This official also admitted that, in the initial days of EDR, the state party did not change its mobilization strategies at all. The Republican party in this state got "left behind" and, due to the

Democratic party's quicker adaptation – especially its mobilization efforts in college towns – this official remarked that Republican candidates lost some district-level elections. This example makes clear that, although the parties do not do much, relative to energy spent on getting out the base of registrants, party efforts that are narrowly targeted appear to make some difference.

College students emerged as a group that was mobilized to register and vote on election day.[8] When examined against the criteria set out by Rosenstone and Hansen (1993), this does not stand out as a big surprise. The environments in which college campuses spring up are diverse, but anyone who has walked or driven through a college community stands a good chance of picking out the students. That is, because college students are generally of the same age, tend to be dressed casually, and are concentrated in small geographic areas (on or around college campuses) they are easy to identify. Furthermore, the unique intellectual and social environment on college campuses facilitates thinking and talking about political issues. One should expect a sizable portion of students to discuss politics in their classes and also through formal and informal activities that abound on campuses. Thus, despite their age, which alone might predict a lack of interest, one can reasonably expect college students to be interested in the election and susceptible to messages designed to encourage voting. Therefore, in states with EDR, the parties often view college students as valuable allies in their fight for victory on election day. However, when college students are more supportive of one party over the other, they are regarded as foes by the party that comes up short on support. Generally, the Democrats were more enthusiastic about mobilizing college students, with the Republicans noting that they do their best to minimize the Democratic advantage.

Some respondents also listed recent movers, mainly those buying homes, as targets. With recent home buyers, the Republicans feel they tend to have an advantage, except when homes are bought in the Democratic high-performance precincts. Other populations that were listed as targets in some states were those who are not registered but reside in the same household as known supporters, people identified as being concerned with issues at stake in the election (usually issues to be voted on through the ballot initiative process), members of labor unions, and minorities.

---

[8] College students are not examined in the earlier chapters because the CPS, like most other surveys of its type, fails to sample students who are the most likely targets of party mobilization, those living on campus. Insights from the results reported here informed one of the first studies focused on college student turnout (see Niemi and Hanmer 2008).

It was not universally true that all of the state party organizations feared wasting resources on mobilizing the opposition. For example, the Republican party in a new EDR state revealed that it has used direct mail to reach all postal addresses in targeted state legislature elections.

Unfortunately, it was not possible to study party behavior before and after EDR, and none of the party officials was in their present position prior to the implementation of EDR in their state. Thus, in order to learn how party behavior might be different if EDR were not allowed, I asked the respondents to consider how they would operate in the absence of EDR. Most party officials reported that their strategies would take a different shape. For example, one of the Democratic officials in a mature EDR state noted that if EDR were not available, a more elaborate registration program would have to be developed. He "would give [registration] a lot more thought," and "it would be very bad for us." Others in the mature EDR states – both Democrats and Republicans – agreed that more effort would have to be put into registration but also commented that more would fall through the cracks and would never be contacted. One of the Republican leaders in a new EDR state also mentioned that, without EDR, unregistered citizens would not be targeted, because the party would rather mobilize those likely to vote. In a new EDR state, the Democratic official suggested that an unintentional consequence of EDR is that it places less urgency on registering people to vote. A Republican in a mature EDR state that has done little to take advantage of EDR provided a similar response; he reported that without EDR, his party would have a "huge push for voter registration." In sum, EDR does seem to alter party strategies but it does not do so uniformly or to the extent to which critics of the two major parties in the United States might like.

Party officials' feelings about EDR tend to correspond with views about participation and the perceived effect EDR has had on the success of their party. Table 7.1 summarizes the responses to my question

TABLE 7.1. *Statements by Party Leaders about EDR in Their State*

Democrats	Republicans
It is fantastic.	It stinks.
It is great.	It works pretty well.
It is good.	Not real fond of it.
EDR is all right.	It is adequate.
It is good.	It is appropriate.

asking how the officials feel about EDR as implemented in their respective states. The responses from Democratic party leaders appear on the left and responses by Republican party leaders from the same state, on the right. Overwhelmingly, EDR is preferred by the Democrats, with responses ranging from "It is all right" to "It is fantastic." The most favorable response provided by Republicans was that EDR "works pretty well." And the most unflattering comment was that EDR "stinks."

The Democratic official who declared that EDR is fantastic, works in a new EDR state and supports the concept that individuals who make up their minds late in the campaign should be allowed to participate. The Republican counterpart in this state argued that Republicans are generally more politically engaged and are therefore more likely to be registered, leaving fewer opportunities for the Republican party to take advantage of EDR. Furthermore, according to this official, the requirements to register on election day should be more strict. This is the same individual who reported that Republican candidates lost district-level elections due to efforts by the Democrats to mobilize college students.

It was a Democrat in a mature EDR state who claimed that EDR "is great." He went on to argue that all Americans should vote, it should be as easy as possible to do so, and "anything that we can do to do that, I think, makes this a better place." In this state, the Republican official's response that EDR "works pretty well" was couched in an explanation that, in his state, the people on the ground who implement the program are fair and competent and that fraud is not a problem.

In one of the new EDR states, both party officials brought up the NVRA as part of their answers. Although fraud has not been a problem, the Republican party leader who said that EDR is "adequate" expressed concern with the potential for fraud. However, this official was glad to have avoided the NVRA and the logistical "nightmare" it has posed for others, declaring "if we are required to have EDR or motor voter then I am definitely in favor of same day registration [aka EDR]." Voter apathy was described as unfortunate by this official, who then compared motor voter and election day registrants, asserting that, at least when individuals register on election day, they do so consciously. The Democratic party official in this state was among the least enthusiastic about EDR, describing EDR as just "all right." This respondent went on to say that motor voter would be beneficial to citizens. That is, this party leader maintained that if people are offered a right, they will be inclined to take it. In other words, motor voter, because individuals are asked if they would like to register, so goes the argument, should improve the state's registration rate.[9]

The official who was not "fond" of EDR represents the Republican party in one of the mature EDR states. He was not opposed to the concept of EDR, but voiced concern with the identification requirements in his state, arguing that more stringent requirements should be in place to curtail fraud. Support for the ability of citizens to register on election day, but a criticism of the way EDR is implemented, was also noted by the Republican, who answered that EDR is "appropriate." This individual, who works in one of the states that adopted EDR to avoid the NVRA, worried that the training of poll workers was inadequate, thus leading some eligible voters to be turned away mistakenly.

The evidence from my interviews with party leaders leads to a number of clear-cut conclusions. Similar to the general situation outlined by Rosenstone and Hansen (1993), in states with EDR, resources are limited and tend to be channeled toward activities that reach individuals thought to be the most responsive – that is, those who are registered. In the short term at least, this is more a reflection of scarce resources than disdain for those who do not take the initiative to register prior to election day. It seems party leaders agree with Green and Gerber (2004), who conclude their study of Get Out the Vote (GOTV) activities by speculating that "[a]lthough by no means cheap or easy, mobilizing supporters may turn out to be the most cost-effective way to influence elections" (p. 111). Although EDR does not lead to drastic changes in party behavior, party leaders reported that if EDR were removed, they would modify their approach to voter registration, with the likely result being that more of the unregistered would fail to make it onto the parties' radar screens. When the parties endeavor to utilize EDR, the targets are those who are easy to identify and likely to have an interest in the election. College students fit this description well and were the most frequently mentioned group targeted for EDR. On the whole, the Democratic party is more enthusiastic about EDR, and more actively seeks out unregistered citizens as part of their mobilization strategies. Finally, the two major political parties in the new EDR states tended to place greater emphasis on taking advantage of EDR than did the parties in Minnesota and Wisconsin. Thus, the hypothesis that party behavior explains the smaller effect of EDR in the

[9] Recall that earlier, I provided an argument to dispel the notion that citizens view motor voter as an invitation from the government to join the electorate.

states that adopted EDR as a way around the NVRA is not supported by the data. Even with slightly more emphasis in the new EDR states, the turnout gains found in the mature EDR states have not been replicated.

Of course, one might wonder what would happen in a more diverse state – that is, one with a larger proportion of racial minorities or other groups besides college students that might be easily located. It is certainly possible that EDR, say, in Mississippi, might lead to greater mobilization of blacks. However, if motor voter, which reduces the cost of identifying individuals by placing more names on the registration lists, has not stimulated a major shift in party mobilization patterns there is little reason to suggest EDR would do so.

LESSONS FROM ELECTION OFFICIALS

My goal in talking with state election officials was simple – to learn how EDR is implemented in their state. The interview focused on ascertaining information regarding: the processing of EDR transactions (how it is done, how long it takes, and the challenge process); administrative difficulties; costs; fraud; the dissemination of information about EDR; outcomes; their overall assessment of EDR; and advice for officials in other states thinking about incorporating EDR into their electoral processes. My primary interest was in comparing the experiences in the new EDR states to the experiences in the states that pioneered EDR.

Owing to the reason that prompted the adoption of EDR in Wyoming, New Hampshire, and Idaho – that is, avoiding the NVRA – one might worry that implementation in these states would be half-hearted and fraught with difficulties. Based on a comparison of survey responses as well as the overall sense I was able to gain from the interviews, I found that this was not the case. Certainly, in the states of Wyoming, Idaho, and New Hampshire, the officials responsible for the administration of a program that was part of a maneuver to maintain state control over elections would have an incentive to paint a positive picture of EDR implementation. Who is going to report that they put the table for EDR in a dark basement no one could find? Any concerns along these lines can be alleviated as the interviews with party leaders serve as a check, and overall, the party leaders never took issue with the way the election officials implemented the law. As noted earlier, some were not particularly fond of EDR, but with the exception of an official worried about poll worker training, the issues had to do with the party officials' beliefs about features of the law and not about administration.

In order for EDR to have any effect, the eligible citizenry must be made aware of its availability. According to the officials with whom I spoke, press releases and information on official Web sites are the primary methods used to notify the public about EDR. In general, however, the states did not stop there. Each of the new EDR states also made use of radio and print ads and, in Idaho, television ads were used when the law first went into effect. New Hampshire also used television ads to inform citizens of their ability to register on the day of the 2000 election. Of the mature EDR states, Minnesota stood out as continually investing a great deal of resources toward the dissemination of information about EDR. There, television, radio, and newspaper ads, as well as outreach efforts to new citizens, associations, and ethnic organizations, are still used. Wisconsin has also long embraced EDR, but due to resource constraints, the state relies on press releases, information on its Web site, and coordination with GOTV groups. In sum, although there was variation across the states, none stood out as having failed to make an effort to inform citizens about their option to register on election day.

One of the most serious concerns with EDR is its vulnerability to fraud. The states varied in terms of their fraud protection mechanisms. In addition to identification requirements and procedures whereby the eligibility of election day registrants can be challenged by poll watchers on the spot, both Minnesota and Wisconsin send nonforwardable postal verification cards to election day registrants and investigate those that are returned. Wisconsin sends the verification cards to all election day registrants, whereas Minnesota sends the cards to a random sample of election day registrants. Minnesota also has a statewide registration system that is used to discover people who voted in more than one location. Wyoming deals with the potential of fraud by setting aside EDR cards for follow-up verification by the county clerks; the clerks have discretion over the method of verification that is used.

The other EDR states do not use verification after the election and rely exclusively on measures taken at the time of registration. Idaho and New Hampshire place additional requirements on election day registrants that do not apply to those who register prior to election day. Election day registrants must provide a photo ID in Idaho[10] and they must sign an affidavit in New Hampshire. Officials in Maine listed several fraud prevention mechanisms. In addition to their provisions for proof of identity

[10] This was in place prior to the Help America Vote Act of 2002 (HAVA).

and residency,[11] the parties can have a poll watcher at each polling place, and registration monitors can challenge one's right to vote after the registration transaction has been completed.

In all of the EDR states, cases of EDR fraud were rare. Records on fraud are not usually kept, but some of the state officials were able to provide fraud statistics and others had examples. The Deputy Secretary of State in Maine was not aware of any recently proven cases of fraud. Debate in the 1977 legislature suggests that, in the early days of EDR in Maine, there was at least one case. According to State Senator Danton:

> there was one screwball that decided he wanted to vote two times. Most usually, we cannot get people to the polls one time. This guy wanted to prove a point.... He voted two times and then he went and bragged about it, and I guess he got convicted for breaking the law. That is the only known fraud. Maybe there are others, I do not know it, and I am sure none of you in here can prove that there were (*Legislative Record – Senate*, June 17, 1977, p. 1779).

Minnesota's Assistant Director of Elections, Michael McCarthy, noted that "[t]he [Minnesota] system is designed to err on the side of providing extra access, relying on effective deterrent after the fact." Although systematic data on fraud are not kept, problems do occur. One example of fraud was relayed by Michele McNulty, an election administrator in the Minnesota Secretary of State's Office. While in a position with Washington County, she discovered that an individual who lived in Washington County on the border with Chisago County registered and voted in both counties for roughly four years. Given the odd address, he was able to get away with this for some time because when one of the counties removed him from the records, he could register there again on the next election day. In a memorandum sent to "Persons Interested in Election Day Voter Registration" dated June 19, 1995, Kevin Kennedy, Executive Director of the Wisconsin State Elections Board, stated the following:

> I am not aware of any prosecutions under these provisions. There have been a small number, less than six, anecdotal references, which I have picked up from local election officials relating to violations or prosecutions, which involved election day registration.

During the interview, Mr. Kennedy added that there are anecdotal stories about fraud by college students in Wisconsin, but he was not aware of

---

[11] Prior to HAVA, the local registrars had discretion over what constituted satisfactory proof.

any convictions. There was no reported case of fraud in Idaho and only five investigations in New Hampshire, resulting in two prosecutions. In Wyoming, six people have been charged with EDR fraud, two people voted in both Utah and Wyoming and four voted both in Colorado and Wyoming. A Republican party representative in one of the newly minted EDR states noted suspicions about college students and union members registering fraudulently, suggesting some crossed state lines; however, this representative was quick to note the lack of hard evidence to substantiate these claims. The history of clean elections and rural character of the present EDR states likely plays a role in the prevention of fraud. In some cases, it is difficult to get from one polling place to the next and, given the small size of the precincts, it is more likely that local officials will notice when residents of another jurisdiction attempt to register fraudulently. As an extreme example, election officials in Maine told me about a jurisdiction in the northern part of the state with just two people; clearly, anyone attempting to register fraudulently there would be caught.

Another way I assessed the implementation of EDR was to investigate the degree to which local officials or the public reported administrative difficulties. During each interview I asked what the most common administrative difficulties were and then asked the officials to rank them from most problematic to least problematic. The number reported and the type of problems listed varied across the six states. Some officials did not perceive any difficulties beyond those that exist with pre-election day registration and others listed as many as four issues.

Officials in the new EDR states were less likely to report administrative difficulties. For the first two elections for which EDR was allowed in New Hampshire, there was some difficulty with gauging how many people would register at the polls, thus leading to long lines in some instances. Long lines have not been a problem in Wyoming, where the State Elections Director did not report any difficulties. Penny Ysursa, from the Idaho Secretary of State's office, noted that recent movers who register on election day inflate the number of registrants until the clerks can clean the lists, but followed up saying that this is an issue with regular registrants, too. She later noted that there were perceived problems with a former provision that allowed registered voters to vouch for election day registrants as a means to satisfy identification requirements, and that a few who had not brought proper identification with them to the polls logged complaints. Part of the reason for the lack of difficulty with implementing EDR, according to Ms. Ysursa, is the overwhelming support it received from the Governor, the Secretary of State, the Legislature, and local clerks, which resulted in a great deal of cooperation.

Although EDR runs smoothly in the states that adopted it in the 1970s, the systems are not free from administrative difficulties. In Minnesota, registrants' lack of knowledge of rules, specifically rules related to identification requirements, was cited as the most problematic issue. This was followed by lack of knowledge of the rules among election judges, and then extra labor requirements for the election judges. Data entry to get new registrants on the lists, management of people attempting to register, management of the postcard verification system, and the attitude of some local clerks who believe that election day registrants are lazy and should not be catered to were listed (in order from most problematic to least problematic) as administrative difficulties in Wisconsin. Election officials in Maine reported two issues: 1) making sure staffing is adequate in larger communities and those that have more transient populations and 2) the logistics of processing people in line at 8 P.M., when the polls close.

State election officials agreed that EDR was not costly to the voter or to the state.[12] For voters, the process tends to be quick, usually taking under five minutes to register.[13] Of course, the time to register increases with the number of other citizens seeking to register on election day. Having one's eligibility called into question by election workers or poll watchers through challenge processes is a fraud prevention mechanism but can increase the costs to eligible citizens. On the whole, the election officials I interviewed reported that challenges to election day registrants at the polls by either election workers or poll watchers were not at all frequent.[14] However, challenges are more common in some states and with respect to certain types of citizens. For example, one of the Democratic party officials I interviewed accused the Republican party of "political foulness and intimidation." This official claimed that the Republican party challenged heavily during peak voting times in order to hold up the process. Moreover, this party leader noted that challenges were more likely to occur in college towns. It was alleged that in precincts with large numbers of college students, the Republican party strategically placed poll watchers who were charged with the task of using the challenge

---

[12] Officials in Wyoming were not able to determine whether costs changed under EDR.

[13] Recording requirements (including a driver's license number or the last four digits of the social security number) that are part of HAVA will increase the time it takes to register.

[14] The answer choices were as follows: Very frequent, Somewhat frequent, or Not at all frequent.

process to harass and intimidate potential registrants in the hopes of slowing down the process, getting the people in line to leave, or getting those coming in to register and vote to turn around. Election officials in Maine also reported that challenges by poll watchers were "somewhat frequent" in college towns. Given the ambiguity of registration rules across the nation as they relate to college students (see Niemi and Hanmer 2008 and Niemi, Hanmer, and Jackson 2008), it is not surprising that challenges are more frequent in college communities. Although records of challenges are not kept, Minnesota officials also noted that, for the 2002 elections, the parties broke from their usual patterns and organized a large number of challengers.

The administrative costs of EDR include additional staff at the polling places (but only in some areas), additional training and labor by election workers, extra registration forms, and, in Minnesota and Wisconsin, the printing and mailing of verification cards. Nowhere was it reported that EDR led to more than a small increase in costs, however. In Idaho, long-time election official Penny Ysursa reported that EDR led to a small *decrease* in costs as the need for precinct registrars was eliminated. Minnesota officials remarked that some of the added costs were offset by a savings in the form of less time addressing complaints from people claiming to have been disenfranchised. Moreover, during our meeting, the chief election official in Wisconsin, Kevin Kennedy, put the costs of EDR into perspective, noting that:

the value to the voter is immeasurable... The idea of having to be registered 30 days before the election or be frozen out of participating, it's hard to put a price on the fact that you can decide on election day I'm going to vote, as long as you have met the 10 day residency requirement. It is clearly very frustrating to people in other states sometimes, that they don't have that benefit.

Across the board, the officials I interviewed looked upon EDR favorably. For the most part, state officials believed that EDR had at least some effect on registration and turnout but several were careful about recommending it be adopted elsewhere. Those taking this stance argued that although EDR works in their state, they were not confident it would work everywhere. For example, the Maine Deputy Secretary of State noted that "it has worked for us," but remarked that it would be hard to say whether it should be adopted elsewhere "because... every state is a little bit different" and must face different challenges so they would have to see how EDR would fit into their election process. A similar sentiment was expressed by the New Hampshire Secretary of State and the

Executive Director of the State of Wisconsin Board of Elections. The Wyoming Elections Director took a middle ground, supporting the concept, but suggesting that EDR not be expanded until a real-time voter registration system is available. Minnesota officials provided the strongest support for expanding EDR, arguing that all states should have EDR and they should use Minnesota as the model. That is, registration should be made as easy as possible, but to ensure that citizens can be confident that the system has integrity, there must be a commitment to intensive poll worker training and fraud prevention mechanisms. In Minnesota, a minimum of two hours of training is required for all poll workers. The state election officials with whom I spoke expressed confidence in their system's ability to catch those who commit fraud.

None of the questions I asked dealt directly with the NVRA; however, several state election officials brought it up as part of their responses. In each case, the spirit of the comment was that they were glad to have avoided it. For example, according to Penny Ysursa of Idaho, EDR is perceived as superior to the NVRA because EDR does not involve the "paper shuffling required by the NVRA." Rather, EDR provides:

a cleaner, more current listing of eligible voters . . . and also, in my opinion, gives the individual the opportunity to register and vote [on election day] where[as] in a state where election day registration is not offered they would be disenfranchised.

The exemption from the NVRA was also viewed positively by state election officials in New Hampshire (as previously noted), Wyoming, and Wisconsin. Peggy Nighswonger, the Wyoming Elections Director, expressed appreciation for Wyoming's exemption from the NVRA. She also drew attention to list maintenance, noting that the NVRA purging rules make it tough to keep the lists clean. Wisconsin's Executive Director of Elections believes the exemption from the NVRA was beneficial for Wisconsin's local election officials. That is, EDR saves local election officials from administrative record-keeping tasks that would tie them up if the NVRA were in effect. Thus, it was not just those who were induced to adopt EDR who favor EDR over the NVRA.

In sum, EDR works well in all six states, and fraud is not a systematic problem, a few "screwballs" notwithstanding. The evidence did not support concerns that the new EDR states would fail to enthusiastically implement EDR, leaving voters to encounter significant obstacles. Thus, the results from Chapter 3 regarding the larger effect of turnout in Minnesota and Wisconsin cannot be explained by differences in implementation.

PROSPECTS FOR THE FUTURE

Registration laws are not the answer to solving the democratic dilemma of low and unequal turnout, either directly or indirectly through changes in the incentives of the political parties. After a review of my argument, I turn to a discussion of other approaches to increasing turnout, concluding that creative ways to connect citizens to the political process are needed. Given the difficulty of the task, and the lack of research on ways to increase motivation, my discussion involves a good deal of speculation. My hope is that by facing the root of the problem head on, both the research and reform communities will begin to grapple with new ideas and put them to the test.

There are three general categories into which attempts to increase turnout can be placed. The focus of the present project has been on the extent to which local and federal laws can facilitate voter turnout, mainly by lowering the costs of voting but also by expanding the opportunities for political parties to mobilize eligible citizens. When voting is made easy, so the argument goes, turnout will increase. I have shown that there is more to the story. Mobilization by candidates, political parties, and other elite groups represents another way through which turnout can be increased. Though mobilization surely influences turnout (Rosenstone and Hansen 1993), as indicated in my interviews with party leaders, the targets of these efforts are likely to remain those who are already at least somewhat interested in voting and have developed an attachment to either the candidates or parties. This leaves increasing levels of motivation as the most likely path to increased voter turnout. Later, I discuss how this might be done.

My interest in the ways institutional factors influence the decision of eligible citizens to vote motivated this project. By taking the selective nature of the adoption of registration laws into account, I have shown that the factors that influence both the adoption of the laws and subsequent outcomes do, in some instances, revise the conclusions that have been drawn regarding the effect of registration reform on turnout. I have argued that care must be taken when extrapolating results across contexts, and have demonstrated that the same set of rules does not bring about identical outcomes in every context. The results are consistent with my hypothesis that the effect of registration reforms differ based on the degree to which the reforms fit within the existing social and political contexts. Evidence from interviews with election officials and party leaders has shown that the alternative hypotheses that patterns of implementation or party behaviors are responsible for the estimated variations in outcomes are not supported. As the conduct of registration and voting continues to evolve, through the Help America Vote Act of 2002, state initiative, or future federal legislation, greater attention must be paid to the reasons for change and how they condition subsequent effects.

Most will view the news presented in this book as rather bad. The two recently implemented registration reforms that do the most to lower the costs of voting and facilitate party mobilization efforts have come up short on the promise of delivering higher rates of turnout and have done little to reduce the inequality of turnout among the best and least well off. The view presented by legendary political boss Frank Hague, the mayor of Jersey City from 1917 – 1947, though harsh, appears to be close to the mark. Dayton David McKean (1940) quotes Mayor Hague as saying:

According to reformers, the average American can hardly wait for election day so he can exercise the sovereign right that the forefathers bought with their blood. That's [a] laugh. A full fifty per cent [sic] of the voters have got to be coaxed or dragged to the polls (p. 269).

Opening the door to participation by reducing or removing registration hurdles has not changed the degree to which average Americans have to be "coaxed or dragged" to the polls.

Consistent with my argument, when registration reforms were forced on places where demand for participation was low, the effect of the reforms was quite small, at best a few percentage points. Even when EDR was established for the explicit purpose of increasing turnout, as it was in Minnesota and Wisconsin, turnout increased by about 4.5 percentage points, an effect smaller than previously thought. However, the turnout advantage resulting from EDR has been durable there. Motor voter in Michigan and North Carolina boosted turnout at a similar rate, but in Michigan, the birthplace of motor voter, the effect faded away after the third presidential election for which motor voter was available. The timing of full and active implementation in North Carolina during a stimulating presidential race seems to have influenced the size of the effect.

In Chapter 1, I drew comparisons between an individual growing up in Minnesota and a similar individual in Mississippi. Having reviewed the effects of EDR and motor voter, I continue that analogy, with a small alteration, here. Hockey has been transplanted to the U.S. South and Southwest but it has required time to take hold. Although the

Dallas Stars (who relocated from Minnesota), Tampa Bay Lightning, Carolina Hurricanes (who relocated from Connecticut), and the Anaheim Ducks (formerly Mighty Ducks) have recently won the Stanley Cup (the National Hockey League's championship trophy), it will be some time, if ever, before Dallas, Tampa Bay, Raleigh, or southern California produce hockey players in large numbers.[15] Most people in these areas simply do not care enough to learn the game; its presence is not enough. Texas is known for producing football players, and no matter how successful the Dallas Stars or the Houston Aeros are, Texas will continue to produce more football players than hockey players. Do not expect many future pro hockey players to list Tampa Bay, the winner of the 2004 Stanley Cup, as their hometown, either. The Bay still does not freeze in the winter; and football still dominates in Florida – by the time football season started, the seven-game series against Calgary was likely a distant memory. And after the confetti from the parade had been cleared away, rather than playing street hockey games commemorating the 2006 Carolina Hurricanes victory over the Edmonton Oilers, most kids in North Carolina likely returned to the courts to simulate Duke and North Carolina basketball games. Despite the active support of rapper and reality show star Snoop Dogg, excitement over several powerhouse football and basketball programs in southern California surely reigns supreme over the once mighty Ducks as they strive to prove their might again in pursuit of another championship.[16] The current structure of individual interests, infrastructure, and institutional incentives (hockey rinks are not abundant; frozen ponds and backyard ice rinks are nonexistent) and the fact that hockey scholarships are not offered by the state university systems in Texas, Florida, North Carolina, California, and so on, developed together and are mutually reinforcing.

The same is true when transplanting registration rules to places where they are not in high demand. Although new rules that make voting easier are in place, they have failed to produce many new voters. That is, the barriers have been broken down and the government has taken a more active role, but for those lacking the motivation to vote, these efforts are insufficient. The argument and evidence provided in this book point clearly toward a change in the approach used to boost turnout; yet, some remain focused on tinkering with the rules.

---

[15] Some, rather, all fans of the Buffalo Sabres, the team Dallas "beat," due to a failure to implement properly one of the rules, question the legitimacy of the Dallas win.

[16] Snoop Dogg was interviewed during the telecast of the Stanley Cup playoffs and got on-ice lessons from the Ducks as part of his reality show.

Whom to Target

Even among those who promote legal changes to generate higher levels of turnout, not all agree on where to target their efforts. Wattenberg (2002), for example, claims that "one basic aspect of U.S. politics explains much of why so few Americans vote as the twenty-first century begins: American elections are complex and anything but user friendly" (p. 2). On the surface, it might appear that the complexity of registration requirements fits well with Watterberg's concern. However, according to Wattenberg, the problem is not with encouraging people to register but getting the registered to vote. Using state-level registration and turnout data from the Federal Election Commission, he explains that the decline in turnout is the result of falling rates of turnout among the registered, dropping from a high of 88.1 percent in 1960 to 65.6 percent in 2000. The solution Wattenberg (2002) promotes as the best, conditional on feasibility concerns – making election day a holiday – targets the registered and would have little effect on the unregistered (except those in EDR states).

As part of their fight for the NVRA, Piven and Cloward (1989),[17] took up the issue of whether getting people registered was a more serious problem than promoting turnout among the registered. They argued (mainly with Curtis Gans, the Director of the Committee for the Study the American Electorate) that state-level data "are so inflated as to be useless for the specific purpose of estimating either registration or voting by registrants" (p. 582). The source of the inflation, known as "deadwood," consists of those who have died or moved, yet remain on the rolls.

Using more recent data, consistent with the conclusions drawn by Piven and Cloward (1989), my calculations reveal that the downward trend in turnout among the registered is less severe when using data from the CPS. Specifically, the drop in turnout from 1972 to 2000 among registrants was about nine points using the Federal Election Commission (FEC) data and just over one point using the Current Population Survey (CPS) data.[18] Even if the difference between the highest and lowest rates over the 1972-to-2000 period are used, the difference between the two estimates is not as sizable, but the gap remains smaller in the CPS data.

[17] See also Piven and Cloward (2000) chapter 9.
[18] In order to make comparisons using the same base of eligible citizens, I believe it most appropriate to start the analysis in 1972. Severe barriers, mainly in the South, and the inability of eighteen- to twenty-year-olds to vote prior to 1972 complicate comparisons using data prior to 1972.

Across both data sources, 1992 marks the highest rate of turnout among the registered and 1996 the lowest; the difference between the two years based on the FEC data is 11.5 points but when using the CPS data, is 8 points.

Although Wattenberg is right to note that adding millions of registrants who are not interested in voting is sure to bring down the overall rate of turnout among registrants,[19] flaws in the data he uses explain away some of the decline he observes. An examination of the FEC data reveals that the rate of registration is overstated in several states, sometimes exceeding 100 percent of the voting age population. Piven and Cloward (1989) illustrate the problem using Mississippi as an example. They explain that the reason for Mississippi's 90 percent registration rate in 1984, up from 68 percent in 1968, is that "many county election officials fear[ed] being charged with racially biased purging practices, so they simply let the deadwood accumulate" (p. 584). The problem of inflated registration estimates is not limited to places with histories of racial injustices; registration rates reported by the FEC for Alaska, Maine, and Montana have exceeded 100 percent of the voting age population. Part of the decline in turnout among the registered is also likely to be the result of stricter rules for purging. More people registered with the implementation of the NVRA and fewer people got dropped from the rolls because purging for nonvoting is no longer permitted. This inflates the denominator and brings the turnout rate down.

Overall, I am inclined to put more stock in the survey data, which show there has been a decline, but it is not as severe as the state-level data would lead one to believe. The survey data suffer from overreporting, but for the state-level measures, there are errors in the estimates of registration as well as voting age population. Moreover, the problem with getting people registered seems more severe than getting registrants to vote. Though this applies less well since the implementation of the NVRA, those who have registered have taken at least some step toward the expression of interest in politics.

More Structural Reforms?

The larger point is that, whether dealing with registration or turnout among the registered, institutional changes are not the right medicines. Significant effort has been expended to get from the Jim Crow South to

---

[19] My analysis in Chapter 5 shows this is the case.

the era of the NVRA, expanded EDR, early voting, unrestricted absentee voting, and vote by mail (VBM). Policies such as early voting (see, for example, Stein 1998), unrestricted absentee voting (see, for example, Oliver 1996), and voting by mail (see, for example, Berinsky, Burns, and Traugott 2001), aimed at making voting easier for the registered, also have had limited effects. Furthermore, Berinsky (2005), in his review of the literature on reforms designed to make voting among registrants easier, shows that these policies have made voters less representative of the eligible population. The evidence is unmistakable; reforms aimed at reducing costs, on their own, are not capable of producing substantially larger rates of turnout.[20] Oregon provides an excellent example.

In Oregon, there is a tradition of relatively high rates of participation, voting is quite easy, and there has been a sustained commitment by the government to make it so. Presently, the government reaches out to eligible citizens at both the registration and voting stages. Provided one has a driver's license, all it takes to register is a minute or so to fill out the form as part of the license transaction. One need not remember the election is coming up because a ballot and voter pamphlet containing information about the candidates and issues will be sent automatically. All it takes is the time to complete the ballot (though in Oregon the ballot tends to contain a number of initiatives, so this might take longer than in most other states)[21] and a stamp. Yet turnout is not much higher than it was before motor voter and VBM. The missing piece is motivation. Like the free samples of the latest shampoo that go to those happy with their current brand, or buy-one-donut–get-one-free coupons for people on a low carbohydrate diet (and the willpower to stay on it) that arrive in the mail, a ballot for those who do not want to vote ends up in the trash. VBM serves mainly to retain those who have voted previously and less to mobilize new voters (Berinsky et al. 2001).

The door is open wider than ever, but even in this period of lower costs, between 20 percent and 30 percent of the eligible population have not bothered to register and about 50 percent of the eligible population failed to cast a vote in 2000. The problem did not emerge overnight, nor will the solutions. Moreover, even with the additional opportunities

---

[20] Although they treat costs as exogenous, through innovative modeling techniques, Bendor, Diermeier, and Ting (2003) reach a similar conclusion: "a substantial [increase] in cost leads only to a fairly moderate decrease in turnout" (p. 273).

[21] Rolloff in Oregon is quite low, and turnout on referenda is not a function of placement on the ballot (Hanmer and Traugott 2004). Thus, the length of the ballot is not responsible for depressing turnout in Oregon.

afforded under EDR and motor voter, the parties have done little to draw unregistered citizens to the polls.

Few would argue against the notion that voting is more difficult in the United States than it is in most other Western democracies. As a result, reform groups and scholars continue to promote easier voting procedures as tools to improve turnout. For example, DEMOS and the Boston Foundation, along with members of the Caltech/MIT Voting Technology Project (see Alvarez and Ansolabehere 2002 and Caltech/MIT Voting Technology Project 2003) continue to advocate the expansion of EDR. As previously noted, Wattenberg (2002) supports making election day a holiday that coincides with Veterans' Day. The National Commission on Federal Election Reform (2001), as part of its list of policy recommendations, also makes this recommendation. A June 16, 2004 article by Norman Ornstein of the American Enterprise Institute appearing in *Roll Call* contends that election day should be "a major civic event." According to Ornstein, one way to make voting easier is to keep the polls open for a 24-hour period over the weekend. Further expansion of EDR, making election day a holiday, and so on might be worthwhile goals but reformers should consider the possibility that the time and energy devoted to modifying structural costs might impede progress on the development of strategies aimed at reconnecting the citizenry to politics. If the movements to make voting easier persist, the results of this book make it clear that the argument cannot be won on empirical grounds. Instead, normative concerns, such as those outlined in Chapter 1 (see James 1987; and Piven and Cloward 1988, 2000) will have to be relied upon.

Of course, compulsory voting is an institutional change that would target those who are registered or unregistered. Although one might dismiss compulsory voting as implausible, the fact that Lijphart (1997), in his Presidential Address to the American Political Science Association, and Wattenberg (2007), in his study of voting among young people, promoted compulsory voting as a solution to low and unequal turnout requires that it not be dismissed simply because it is politically infeasible.[22] Both authors champion this solution based primarily on evidence that it has worked in the countries that have employed it. They also agree that political scientists have been too shy about endorsing compulsory voting. Wattenberg (2007) gives credit to safety engineers who promoted seat belt usage and health scholars who advocated for smoking bans in

[22] Wattenberg (2007) notes that he still favors holding election day on a holiday and promotes compulsory voting because it is the only "proven solution" (p. 161).

public places despite arguments against policies that might be seen to limit individual freedom. But even for those who see low and unequal turnout as harmful to democracy, the negative spillovers from the failure to vote differ markedly from the more immediate and severe negative spillovers associated with the failure to wear a seat belt (which has the potential to cause physical injury or death to others) or secondhand smoke (which has the potential to cause serious illness or death to others).

Although the problems associated with low and unequal turnout do not rise to the severity of car crashes and smoking, those who think it is the best fix should be more willing to make the case. I am simply not convinced that compulsory voting is the right answer. Surely, it raises the turnout rate and closes the gap in turnout between the so-called "haves" and "have-nots." I am sympathetic to Pateman's (1970) argument that participation has educative effects (see Hanmer 2008), and thus concede that by requiring participation citizens might begin to pay more attention. However, like my argument regarding the smaller effects of reform when the federal government mandates a change, the educative effects of participation might not take hold among those who are voting primarily to avoid being subjected to some penalty. Yet, this concern could be mitigated if compulsory voting were to alter the strategic nature of campaigns, leading the candidates and parties to pay more attention to the issues not currently on the agenda, which later in the process could translate into policies that are favorable toward those who are currently on the sidelines.

Even in the rosiest scenario, I oppose compulsory voting because I simply do not think that citizens in a free democratic society should be forced to go to the polls or send a ballot through the mail. Lijphart (1997) and Wattenberg (2007) are careful to point out that compulsory voting does not require that one actually vote, as one can simply submit a blank ballot. Yet, one's freedom is still infringed upon by the requirement to participate in the electoral process by showing up to the polls (which, at a minimum, requires standing in line and submitting a blank ballot) or by requesting and sending in a blank absentee ballot.[23] Regardless of how easy or burdensome it is to cast a blank ballot, in my view, citizens in a free democratic society should have the freedom to participate or not participate in the process. When combined with the minuscule chance that compulsory voting will be adopted in the United States, it is

---

[23] In a vote by mail system, one would not need to request ballots because election officials send them to registrants.

evident that there is a need to look beyond overnight changes in election laws and toward strategies that might connect citizens to the electoral process.

Implementing a voting system based on proportional representation is another avenue that might increase turnout. However, some of the best evidence (Bowler, Donovan, and Brockington 2003) suggests that the effects are modest. The small effects combined with the low likelihood that such a large change in the U.S. voting system would be adopted, and possibility of "political disruption" (Teixeira 1992, p. 154) suggest that proportional representation is not the answer. In addition, although proportional representation might provide incentives for mobilization, we should strive for an approach that can work with any voting system, including our current system.

Increasing Motivation

The call for greater focus on voter motivation is not new, although the conclusions drawn here regarding the small effects of registration reform give greater weight to the role motivation plays. Setting the task of increasing turnout in the context of Blais' (2000) argument exposes its difficulty. For Blais, "the major motivation that leads most people to vote is the feeling that if one truly believes in democracy one has a moral obligation to vote" (2000, p. 140). Getting those who have been marginalized by the political system (Piven and Cloward 1988, 2000) to first form a strong attachment to democracy and then feel a moral compulsion to vote is a Herculean task. Making it easier to register will not do the trick. Even if the Democratic party had responded as Piven and Cloward suggest they should have, reaching out once or even a few times to those who are worst off is surely insufficient to instill this type of deep-seated belief in democracy. Until those who are presently on the outside demonstrate that they want their voice to be heard, they will not find their way in. That is, if citizens do not step up to the plate, the candidates and parties are not likely to make the pitch. So, how can more citizens be brought into the system? I now turn to a review of a variety of proposals aimed at increasing turnout by increasing motivation.

In addition to recommending registration reform, both Teixeira (1992) and Patterson (2003) examine a variety of ways in which motivation might be increased and thus provide a useful starting point for discussion. I evaluate their proposals based primarily on their ability to connect citizens to electoral politics, but also in terms of their feasibility.

Part of Teixeira's plan involves campaign finance reform. The guidelines he provides are directed toward legislation to make campaigns more competitive by leveling the playing field between challengers and incumbents. I agree that more competitive campaigns could help "[enhance] the perception that the government is responsive to ordinary citizens" (Teixeira 1992, p. 164). Nonetheless, absent changes to the two party system, most viable challengers will be constrained by the structure imposed by their party, thus doing little to change fundamentally the status quo. For example, under this system it is doubtful that the types of issues that get on the agenda will change, leaving the segments of the population who are least involved on the outside. Furthermore, one must wonder how likely incumbents will be to enact legislation that poses a threat to their re-election.

Patterson (2003) also expresses concern with leveling the playing field. Changes in the presidential nomination process are at the heart of his reform proposal that seeks to balance the influence of voters in all states and the influence of well and poorly funded candidates. To boost interest and give citizens in all of the states a meaningful voice in the process, Patterson advocates a shorter campaign with a series of single-state primaries followed by a day upon which the voters in the remaining states would vote, with the nomination conventions occurring shortly thereafter. I agree that giving citizens in all of the states a chance to vote before the outcome has been decided will increase interest, and that some who would not have otherwise paid much attention will be mobilized; however, the effects are likely to be felt most strongly among those who have already formed some allegiance to one of the parties. In other words, the base of each party is likely to become more interested and engaged but there are generally few incentives in the primary process for the parties to educate and attract those who are on the sidelines. Thus, although this proposal has a great deal of merit, it does not do enough to instill within citizens a belief in democracy and democratic processes. Moreover, Wattenberg (2007) provides evidence that a shorter campaign has done little to increase turnout in other countries.[24]

---

[24] Whereas the 2008 nominating process, which included a "Super Duper Tuesday," on which a record number of states held primaries or caucuses, saw increases in participation, the combination of an unpopular president, unpopular war, shaky economy, and set of candidates that the best fiction writers probably could not have dreamed up suggests caution when generalizing to the future. Moreover, the evidence suggests that turnout on Super Duper Tuesday fell short of turnout in the early races in Iowa and New Hampshire, leading one scholar to call Super Tuesday a "Super Flop" (McDonald 2008).

Both Teixeira (1992) and Patterson (2003) argue that the media must change their practices. Free or lower cost ads and more informative coverage might be preferable to the present situation, but to work, these proposals require people to tune in. With respect to Teixeira's proposal, there is a missing piece: How do we get people to pay attention in the first place? This, in itself, is a difficult dilemma. If there is a solution, it will surely require a great deal of time to take hold. Moreover, even if the candidates and parties could reallocate their resources from media ads to direct mobilization efforts, it is not clear (see earlier discussion) how much more would go into mobilizing those least likely to turn out.

Patterson fills in some of the gap. His plan calls for more and better television coverage of the primary debates and conventions. With respect to debate coverage, again, it is unlikely that more and better coverage of the primaries and conventions will generate interest among those who are not connected to the parties or the larger system. Candidate interviews on popular talk shows and interviews with news anchors have the potential to reach those outside the system. The problem here, as Patterson notes, is that unless the television executives think this is profitable, they are not likely to implement this plan.

Based on evidence from an experiment sponsored by the Republican National Committee, Teixeira contends that a volunteer-driven campaign to promote registration and turnout can change the degree to which the parties and the public connect. The information I obtained from party leaders in states with EDR, who view getting people registered as an arduous task, suggests that most would question the efficacy of such a program. Additionally, as argued in my critique of Teixeira's plan for the media, if a larger pool of volunteers could be generated, these new resources might simply serve to supplement the main component of the party strategy – getting out the base.

The only hope, in my opinion, is to inject politics into the lives of citizens as early as possible; such attitudes might be cultivated through formal education. Teixeira includes engaging children in politics while they are in school as part of his reform package and more recent work by Niemi and Junn (1998) provides reason to believe that school curriculums might be the key to a more engaged and participatory citizenry. Campbell (2006) is also optimistic that schools can be a mechanism for boosting turnout. His research provides powerful evidence that the civic environment of a high school can have lasting effects on participation.

The approach Teixeira focuses on is Kids Voting, a program that teaches students about the political system and encourages students to get involved by discussing politics with their parents, going to the polls with their parents on election day, and participating in simulated elections. Since the time Teixeira wrote, Kids Voting USA has expanded beyond a pilot program in Arizona and is now implemented in thirty states (Meirick and Wackman 2004). Though their measure of exposure to the Kids Voting curriculum is not ideal (as the authors admit), Meirick and Wackman (2004) find that exposure to the Kids Voting curriculum was associated with increases in political knowledge, a key prerequisite to informed participation, as well as interest in the campaign, campaign discussion, and attention to news about the campaign. Although knowledge gaps were not closed based on the individual's sex, or grades, those who initially had the lowest levels of knowledge tended to gain the most, with larger gains for blacks than whites. Surely, much more research is necessary, but these results provide hope that civics education might fuel a more informed and participatory citizenry.

To me, the best plan of action to foster belief in democracy, an understanding of how it works, the role of the parties and other major institutions, and one's role as a citizen, and thus increase and equalize turnout, starts by looking to the educational system. Working through the education system makes sense for a variety of reasons. One appeal is that this approach has the greatest potential to reach a large and diverse set of citizens. The timing is also conducive to long-term success. School curricula reach citizens at a time in their lives when they are expected to take in the information and can do so without the outside pressures of work or other obligations faced by adults. Getting adults who are not connected to the system to believe in democracy or become attached to a party is a difficult task. Simply put, there is not a single mechanism through which all adults could be educated about the political system. Even if such a system existed, getting the message across can be more challenging because some portion will have already decided politics is not for them or that they do not have the time necessary to devote to becoming informed. Moreover, using the education system provides a stable mechanism to expose generation after generation with the information and skills necessary to create and then sustain a high level of engagement. Although more research needs to be done, especially with respect to the long-term influence of civic education programs, recent empirical work has shown signs of success.

The development of a detailed plan of action is beyond the scope of the present project. That said, at the core of any plan must be a commitment to active learning aimed at providing students with not just the knowledge but also the skills and experience relevant to involvement in the political process. For example, rather than just learning about Supreme Court decisions from a textbook, students might become involved in a series of role-playing exercises in which they wrestle with and decide issues as if they were members of the Supreme Court and the lawyers presenting the cases. The ability to understand textbook treatments of how the court operates and some of the major decisions certainly has value, but more valuable is an ability to engage in the debates as a justice or lawyer presenting the case. After a short time, the facts learned from the textbook will fade but the skills learned in the practice of politics will remain and will facilitate learning in other areas.

Once they are at the point at which they can reasonably do so, students should be given the opportunity to make decisions that will govern some set of their classroom activities. To the extent that the activities simulate political processes, as students encounter politics, they will do so with familiarity, understanding, and confidence. One way to accomplish this is to challenge students through classroom exercises to craft and implement institutions such as decision-making bodies and political parties. This will provide firsthand knowledge of the difficulties involved with the design of institutions, a clear point of comparison with existing institutions, and so on. If boosting turnout is a goal, providing experience with elections is obviously an important component to include. Again, studying elections has some value but conducting campaigns, participating in debates, holding elections, and transferring power peacefully at subsequent elections will impart a deeper appreciation for the democratic process.

It is also important to introduce the reality of political discourse. Niemi and Junn (1998) provide guidance on this front. They contend that a wide variety of topics should be covered and with a focus on issues that resonate with students. Moreover, they suggest doing so in a manner that reflects the heated nature of real political debates. Challenging students to form their own opinions on important issues is an important step but they should also be challenged to take action beyond the classroom by writing their representatives, writing a letter to the editor, or participating in council meetings. Gone should be the "Pollyannaish" treatment of the issues and parties (Niemi and Junn 1998, p. 150). Attachment to a party is less likely when the distinctions between the parties are blurred and the consequences of who wins and who loses are not clear.

Schools and students should also be encouraged to involve their parents as a means to bolster what is learned in the classroom and maximize the potential for positive spillovers into the adult population. This might be encouraged through activities that move beyond the classroom, perhaps in the forms of participation in community service projects, observation of city council meetings, interactions with government officials, and volunteering on a campaign, to name a few possibilities.

When should these programs start? Although Niemi and Junn (1998) suggest that senior year in high school is an appropriate time, this seems far too late to develop the sort of long-term commitment necessary to build toward and sustain a high level of participation. The Kids Voting project serves as an example of success among students much younger than high school seniors. Although I leave it to education scholars to sort out the best curricula and best timing for each component, I am optimistic that basic introductions to and experience with elections, decision-making processes that simulate institutions such as legislative bodies and the courts, and other methods of instruction that focus on gaining relevant experience can be successful even at the elementary school level.

As part of this approach, reformers must stop pointing fingers at those they blame for low levels of voter turnout. We have a system that is not conducive to high rates of turnout. The system developed in a manner that reinforced the advantage of some at the expense of others. The entirety of the blame for the current state of affairs cannot be placed on the citizenry. For certain, the blame is shared between the elites who erected a system that provides limited choices, makes it difficult to participate, selectively mobilizes certain segments of the population, and so on, but also on the citizenry for letting it happen. Moreover, though turnout was higher in the days of machine politics, those who lament the decline of the influence of political parties cannot, in good conscience, support a return to that system.

Although major modifications to the electoral system could strengthen the link between the government and the governed, to think large-scale reform will happen is foolish. To increase participation, the government must surely take on more responsibility. But this unquestionably will not come in the form of large-scale structural changes, such as the institution of a more proportional representation system or compulsory voting. Expecting the parties to take more risks is also misguided; unless they have the incentive to be responsive, they will seek to maintain the status quo. The way to get the government involved is through the education system.

A strategy based on altering the way students learn about politics has some drawbacks, but those serious about reform should focus their attention on ways to leverage the education system as the source of a solution. The measures taken to increase turnout thus far were far from costless. As was shown in Chapter 2, in many places, establishing EDR was a struggle. Getting the NVRA passed was no easy chore either (Piven and Cloward 2000). But if turnout is to be increased, a new approach, and one that is likely to take even more time and effort, is necessary.

Will a plan centered on school curricula work? Parts of the U.S. system of education are a mess (see Kozol 1991), and, unfortunately, adding a new set of requirements will likely exacerbate the current chasm between participation rates of the most advantaged and the least advantaged. Teachers, no matter how dedicated, cannot overcome all of the obstacles on their own, and the supply of parents and community leaders in places that are most needy is too small. Though the hope would be that all would be reached and that all would be receptive,[25] it is unreasonable to believe this would be the case. If social programs, which arguably stand to provide more immediate and tangible benefits, fail to reach all those in need, any realistic view must recognize that the same must be true with regard to plans to promote political engagement. Thus, the likelihood that some are not brought in through this plan is not a sufficient reason to reject trying it. To address the question at the beginning of this paragraph: though I recognize the difficulties, there is no perfect solution and I believe this approach provides the greatest chance for producing and sustaining a high level of turnout in the United States.

---

[25] Wattenberg (2007) expresses concern with the extent to which some types of students would be receptive to a civics education approach.

APPENDICES

Appendix A. Variable Coding

Age: Age in years, 18–90 years.

Age Squared: Age in years squared.

Black: Race of the respondent, 1 = black, 0 = white or other.

Closing Date: Days before the election that registration ends. 1972–1988, 0–50 days; 1992, 0–31 days; 1996–2000, 0–30 days.

Education: 0–4 years = 1; 5–8 years = 2; 9–11 years = 3; high school graduate or GED = 4; 1–3 years of college = 5; four years of college = 6; beyond fifth year of college = 7.

Immature Motor Voter: For 1996, state adopted an active motor voter program prior to implementation of the NVRA, CO, DC, HA, ME, MT, OR, TX, and WA.

Income Quartile: Family income categories coded into quartiles, by year.

Mature EDR: For 1996 and 2000, states that adopted EDR prior to 1980, ME, MN, ND, and WI.

Mature Motor Voter: For the year 2000, all states but ID, NH, ND, VT, WI, and WY. For 1996, MI, MN, NC, and NV.

Mobility: Less than one month at current residence = 1; 1–6 months = 2; 7–11 months = 3; 1–2 years = 4; 3 years or longer = 5.

New EDR: States that adopted EDR in the 1990s, ID, NH, and WY.

NVRA Motor Voter Only: states not in the *Immature Motor Voter*, *Mature EDR*, *Mature Motor Voter*, and *New EDR* classifications.

South: States of the Old Confederacy: AL, AR, FL, GA, LA, MS, NC, SC, TN, TX, VA.

Vote: reported voting = 1; reported did not vote = 0.

All variables are from the Current Population Survey: Voter Supplement File with the exception of closing date and the motor voter variables. The *Book of the States* was used as the initial source of information on closing date with the information confirmed or corrected through an examination of state laws at the University of Michigan Law Library. Coding for the motor voter variables was accomplished using records from Project Human SERVE and verification of state laws at the University of Michigan Law Library.

Appendix B. Census Data Related to Chapter 3

TABLE B.1. *Total Population (in Millions)*

State	1970	1980	1990	2000
MN	3.80	4.08	4.38	4.92
WI	4.42	4.71	4.89	5.36
SD	0.67	0.69	0.70	0.75
IA	2.82	2.91	2.78	2.93
All others	191.50	214.16	235.97	267.46
ID	0.71	0.94	1.01	1.29
WY	0.33	0.47	0.45	0.49
MT	0.69	0.79	0.80	0.90
All others	201.47	224.35	246.45	278.73
NH	0.74	0.92	1.11	1.24
VT	0.44	0.51	0.56	0.61
All others	202.03	225.11	247.04	279.58

TABLE B.2. *Percentage Noncitizens*

State	1970	1980	1990	2000
MN	0.59	1.04	1.42	3.32
WI	0.71	0.86	1.18	2.19
SD	0.15	0.35	0.43	1.07
IA	0.36	0.66	0.84	2.09
All others	1.82	3.21	4.93	6.81
ID	0.67	1.17	1.69	3.31
WY	0.60	0.78	0.81	1.23
MT	0.46	0.60	0.65	0.77
All others	1.75	3.10	4.77	7.24
NH	1.71	1.33	1.65	2.30
VT	1.48	1.39	1.23	1.77
All others	1.74	3.09	4.75	6.63

TABLE B.3. *Percentage High School Degree or More*

State	1970	1980	1990	2000
MN	59.47	73.05	82.36	87.95
WI	56.52	69.61	78.60	85.09
SD	55.03	67.93	77.07	84.57
IA	61.27	71.53	80.09	86.10
All others	54.75	66.21	74.97	80.09
ID	61.87	73.72	79.75	84.72
WY	65.36	77.91	83.04	87.86
MT	61.33	74.42	81.00	87.15
All others	54.90	66.40	75.19	80.34
NH	60.42	72.25	82.15	87.41
VT	59.80	71.02	80.79	86.42
All others	54.93	66.44	75.19	80.35

TABLE B.4. *Percentage Age Sixty-Five or Older*

State	1970	1980	1990	2000
MN	10.34	11.77	12.49	12.06
WI	10.23	11.99	13.31	13.10
SD	11.69	13.18	14.73	14.32
IA	11.87	13.30	15.34	14.91
All others	9.25	11.22	12.49	12.39
ID	9.09	9.92	12.03	11.28
WY	8.74	7.92	10.37	11.64
MT	9.55	10.75	13.32	13.40
All others	9.34	11.29	12.55	13.55
NH	10.05	11.18	11.27	11.98
VT	10.18	11.37	11.76	12.70
All others	9.33	11.28	12.55	12.43

TABLE B.5. *Percentage Black*

State	1970	1980	1990	2000
MN	0.88	1.31	2.17	3.41
WI	2.80	3.88	4.99	5.60
SD	0.27	0.31	0.45	0.60
IA	1.09	1.43	1.70	2.04
All others	11.22	12.24	12.52	12.65
ID	0.27	0.29	0.36	0.41
WY	0.72	0.72	0.73	0.63
MT	0.25	0.23	0.26	0.26
All others	10.75	11.81	12.14	13.43
NH	0.35	0.43	0.65	0.73
VT	0.14	0.22	0.39	0.49
All others	10.72	11.77	12.11	12.29

TABLE B.6. *Median Family Income in 1999 Dollars*

State	1969	1979	1989	1999
MN	39,734	40,761	41,526	47,111
WI	40,842	40,576	39,555	43,791
SD	29,280	30,193	30,233	35,282
IA	35,771	38,554	35,239	39,469
ID	33,965	35,079	33,933	37,572
WY	36,475	45,886	36,403	37,892
MT	33,756	35,389	30,884	33,024
NH	39,276	39,045	48,808	49,467
VT	36,139	33,943	40,026	40,856
All others	35,882	37,919	40,380	40,816

Appendix C. Maine and EDR

As can be seen from Figure C.1, 1972 was an unusual year for turnout in Maine; turnout was at its lowest across the entire 1960–2000 series! The fact that turnout in Maine in the most recent elections is as high as turnout in the 1960s, while turnout nationally has trended downward, provides further evidence of Maine's uniqueness. After 1972, it appears that there is a regression to the mean effect. This, plus the fact that registration on election day did not necessarily occur at the polling places, thus requiring two trips on election day, suggests the effect of EDR obtained for Maine is likely overstated (Figure C.2 and Tables C.1, C.2).

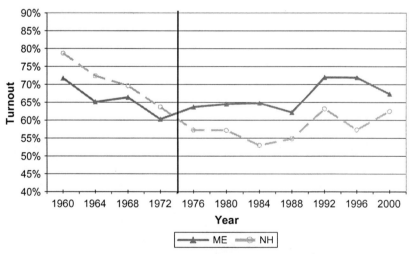

FIGURE C.1. Presidential year turnout in Maine and New Hampshire 1960–2000 (Source: FEC).

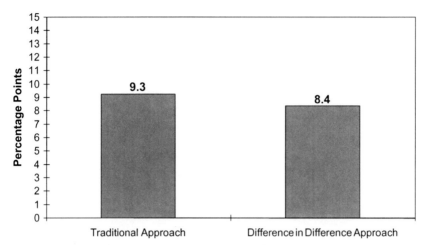

FIGURE C.2. Percentage-point increase in turnout due to EDR in Maine by statistical approach.

TABLE C.1. *Traditional Probit Estimates of the Effect of EDR on Turnout (EDR State is ME, 1972 and 1980)*

Variable	Coefficient	Standard Error	z	p Value
EDR	0.1073	0.0379	2.83	0.005
Closing Date	−0.0073	0.0004	−16.99	0.000
Education	0.2941	0.0029	102.22	0.000
Age	0.0612	0.0010	61.96	0.000
Age Squared	−0.0004	0.0000	−41.78	0.000
Income Quartile	0.1607	0.0033	49.05	0.000
South	−0.1548	0.0075	−20.64	0.000
1980	−0.1521	0.0067	−22.65	0.000
Constant	−2.4618	0.0274	−89.96	0.000

$N = 176,595$.
Log likelihood $= -99366.27$.
Source: 1972 and 1980 CPS.

TABLE C.2. *Difference in Difference Probit Estimates of the Effect of EDR on Turnout (ME compared to NH, 1972 and 1980)*

Variable	Coefficient	Standard Error	z	p Value
EDR Effect	0.2877	0.1173	2.45	0.014
ME	0.4791	0.3784	1.27	0.205
Education * ME	0.0345	0.0442	0.78	0.435
Age * ME	−0.0315	0.0143	−2.20	0.028
Age Squared * ME	0.0003	0.0001	1.77	0.077
Income * ME	0.0695	0.0515	1.35	0.178
Education	0.3240	0.0319	10.14	0.000
Age	0.0865	0.0108	8.02	0.000
Age Squared	−0.0006	0.0001	−5.51	0.000
Income Quartile	0.1336	0.0374	3.57	0.000
1980	−0.0898	0.0919	−0.98	0.328
Constant	−3.4124	0.2825	−12.08	0.000

$N = 3,678$.
Log likelihood $= -1906.378$.
Source: 1972 and 1980 CPS.

Appendix D. Census Data Related to Chapter 4

TABLE D.1. *Total Population (in Millions)*

State	1970	1980	1990	2000
MI	8.88	9.26	9.30	9.94
OH	10.65	10.80	10.85	11.35
All others	183.68	206.49	228.57	260.13
NV	0.49	0.80	1.20	2.00
AZ	1.77	2.72	3.67	5.13
All others	200.95	223.03	243.84	274.29
NC	5.08	5.88	6.63	8.05
TN	3.92	4.59	4.88	5.69
SC	2.59	3.12	3.49	4.01
VA	4.65	5.35	6.19	7.08
All others	186.97	207.60	227.53	256.59

TABLE D.2. *Percentage Noncitizens*

State	1970	1980	1990	2000
MI	1.43	1.67	1.69	2.85
OH	0.84	0.92	0.96	1.50
All others	1.81	3.25	5.04	6.96
NV	1.70	3.44	5.11	10.00
AZ	1.80	2.95	4.62	9.01
All others	1.74	3.08	4.73	6.53
NC	0.28	0.57	0.99	3.94
TN	0.26	0.48	0.67	1.86
SC	0.30	0.58	0.70	1.82
VA	0.75	1.76	3.01	4.77
All others	1.86	3.28	5.04	6.91

TABLE D.3. *Percentage High School Degree or More*

State	1970	1980	1990	2000
MI	55.17	67.99	76.78	83.41
OH	55.59	66.97	75.67	82.97
All others	54.92	66.38	75.15	80.17
NV	71.18	75.48	78.77	80.66
AZ	61.34	72.35	78.66	80.97
All others	54.87	66.37	75.17	80.39
NC	40.55	54.84	69.96	78.14
TN	44.20	56.16	67.06	75.92
SC	40.23	53.71	68.29	76.34
VA	49.97	62.43	75.16	81.47
All others	55.87	67.31	75.67	80.61

TABLE D.4. *Percentage Age Sixty-Five or Older*

State	1970	1980	1990	2000
MI	8.03	9.85	11.91	12.27
OH	8.87	10.83	12.96	13.28
All others	9.42	11.37	12.55	12.40
NV	5.73	8.21	10.58	10.93
AZ	8.56	11.31	13.02	13.01
All others	9.35	11.29	12.55	12.43
NC	7.66	10.26	12.10	12.05
TN	9.19	11.27	12.68	12.35
SC	6.87	9.20	11.36	12.11
VA	7.49	9.45	10.71	11.17
All others	9.46	11.39	12.62	12.48

TABLE D.5. *Percentage Black*

State	1970	1980	1990	2000
MI	10.77	12.95	13.87	14.10
OH	8.80	9.97	10.62	11.35
All others	10.77	11.73	12.03	12.18
NV	5.37	6.37	6.52	6.63
AZ	2.86	2.76	3.00	3.01
All others	10.75	11.82	12.20	12.42
NC	21.19	22.42	21.96	21.54
TN	15.16	15.81	15.93	16.34
SC	28.89	30.39	29.83	29.48
VA	17.84	18.86	18.80	19.55
All others	9.85	10.83	11.21	11.35

TABLE D.6. *Median Family Income in 1999 Dollars*

State	1969	1979	1989	1999
MI	45,381	44,117	41,675	44,667
OH	42,122	40,745	38,567	40,956
NV	43,148	41,794	41,663	44,581
AZ	37,219	37,748	37,000	40,558
NC	31,890	33,234	35,800	39,184
TN	30,101	32,456	33,328	36,360
SC	31,027	33,762	35,275	37,082
VA	37,646	40,105	44,776	46,677
All others	35,882	37,919	40,380	40,816

Appendix E. Models Associated with Results in Chapters 3 and 4

TABLE E.I. *Traditional Probit Estimates of the Effect of EDR on Turnout (EDR States are MN and WI, 1972 and 1980)*

Variable	Coefficient	Standard Error	z	p Value
EDR	0.1675	0.0278	6.02	0.000
Closing Date	−0.0078	0.0004	−18.43	0.000
Education	0.2936	0.0028	103.10	0.000
Age	0.0611	0.0010	62.74	0.000
Age Squared	−0.0004	0.0000	−42.44	0.000
Income Quartile	0.1593	0.0032	49.29	0.000
South	−0.1582	0.0075	−21.16	0.000
1980	−0.1588	0.0066	−24.01	0.000
Constant	−2.4320	0.0268	−90.58	0.000

$N = 181,819$.
Log likelihood $= -101924.04$.
Source: 1972 and 1980 CPS.

TABLE E.2. *Traditional Probit Estimates of the Effect of EDR on Turnout (EDR States are ID and WY, 1992 and 1996)*

Variable	Coefficient	Standard Error	z	p Value
EDR	0.0515	0.0342	1.50	0.133
Closing Date	−0.0058	0.0006	−9.90	0.000
Education	0.3281	0.0034	95.62	0.000
Age	0.0395	0.0011	35.02	0.000
Age Squared	−0.0002	0.0000	−18.93	0.000
Income Quartile	0.1427	0.0037	38.26	0.000
South	−0.0648	0.0084	−7.75	0.000
Mobility	0.1559	0.0036	43.66	0.000
1996	−0.2512	0.0073	−34.19	0.000
Constant	−3.0190	0.0335	−90.23	0.000

$N = 148,056$.
Log likelihood $= -80024.588$.
Source: 1992 and 1996 CPS.

TABLE E.3. *Difference in Difference Probit Estimates of the Effect of EDR on Turnout (ID and WY compared to MT, 1992 and 1996)*

Variable	Coefficient	Standard Error	z	p Value
EDR Effect	0.1037	0.0752	1.38	0.168
ID & WY	0.3711	0.3027	1.23	0.220
Education*ID and WY	0.0128	0.0387	0.33	0.741
Age*ID & WY	−0.0322	0.0113	−2.85	0.004
Age Squared*ID and WY	0.0003	0.0001	2.70	0.007
Income*ID and WY	0.0222	0.0403	0.55	0.582
Mobility*ID and WY	0.0142	0.0348	0.41	0.684
Education	0.3940	0.0307	12.84	0.000
Age	0.0632	0.0089	7.09	0.000
Age Squared	−0.0004	0.0001	−4.48	0.000
Income Quartile	0.1439	0.0326	4.41	0.000
Mobility	0.1638	0.0279	5.86	0.000
1996	−0.2416	0.0603	−4.00	0.000
Constant	−3.8325	0.2435	−15.74	0.000

$N = 6,608$.
Log likelihood $= -3233.9165$.
Source: 1992 and 1996 CPS.

TABLE E.4. *Traditional Probit Estimates of the Effect of EDR on Turnout (EDR State is NH, 1992 and 1996)*

Variable	Coefficient	Standard Error	z	p Value
EDR	−0.1951	0.0506	−3.86	0.000
Closing Date	−0.0052	0.0006	−8.89	0.000
Education	0.3270	0.0035	94.72	0.000
Age	0.0398	0.0011	35.06	0.000
Age Squared	−0.0002	0.0000	−19.20	0.000
Income Quartile	0.1420	0.0038	37.79	0.000
South	−0.0648	0.0084	−7.74	0.000
Mobility	0.1555	0.0036	43.15	0.000
1996	−0.2490	0.0074	−33.77	0.000
Constant	−3.0334	0.0338	−89.75	0.000

$N = 145,459$.
Log likelihood $= -78747.582$.
Source: 1992 and 1996 CPS.

TABLE E.5. *Difference in Difference Probit Estimates of the Effect of EDR on Turnout (NH compared to VT, 1992 and 1996)*

Variable	Coefficient	Standard Error	z	p Value
EDR Effect	0.1299	0.1067	1.22	0.223
NH	0.4102	0.4513	0.91	0.363
Education*NH	−0.1092	0.0521	−2.10	0.036
Age*NH	0.0142	0.0170	0.84	0.402
Age Squared*NH	−0.0002	0.0002	−1.39	0.166
Income*NH	−0.0162	0.0566	−0.29	0.775
Mobility*NH	−0.0518	0.0520	−1.00	0.319
Education	0.4917	0.0382	12.87	0.000
Age	0.0496	0.0126	3.94	0.000
Age Squared	−0.0002	0.0001	−1.84	0.066
Income Quartile	0.1413	0.0423	3.34	0.001
Mobility	0.2353	0.0384	6.13	0.000
1996	−0.4482	0.0777	−5.77	0.000
Constant	−4.3938	0.3383	−12.99	0.000

$N = 3,069$.
Log likelihood $= -1508.4272$.
Source: 1992 and 1996 CPS.

TABLE E.6. *State Dummies from Model in Table 4.5*

Variable	Coefficient	Standard Error
AL	0.0025	0.0313
AK	0.2772	0.0316
AZ	−0.1523	0.0280
AR	−0.0574	0.0269
CO	0.0191	0.0306
CT	0.0181	0.0342
DE	−0.0180	0.0331
DC	0.2248	0.0370
FL	−0.0634	0.0189
GA	−0.1419	0.0270
HA	−0.3637	0.0340
ID	0.1551	0.0369
IL	0.0713	0.0197
IN	−0.0476	0.0279
IA	0.1084	0.0322
KS	0.0608	0.0300
KY	−0.0375	0.0281
LA	0.3101	0.0294
ME	0.3309	0.0433
MD	−0.0427	0.0305
MA	0.0776	0.0218
MI	0.1415	0.0256
MN	0.2916	0.0396
MS	0.1700	0.0285
MO	0.1375	0.0292
MT	0.2636	0.0302
NE	−0.0449	0.0307
NV	−0.1249	0.0349
NH	0.0017	0.0401
NJ	−0.0327	0.0208
NM	−0.0526	0.0276
NY	−0.0474	0.0171
NC	−0.1097	0.0257
ND	0.2090	0.0386
OH	0.0398	0.0195
OK	0.0609	0.0278
OR	0.1855	0.0335
PA	−0.1556	0.0188
RI	0.1134	0.0329
SC	−0.1109	0.0289
SD	0.0825	0.0286
TN	−0.0950	0.0276
TX	−0.0451	0.0225
VT	0.1209	0.0359
VA	−0.0707	0.0267
WA	0.0513	0.0318
WV	−0.1370	0.0265
WI	0.2370	0.0386

Note: Excluded state is California.

Appendix F. Bootstrapped Confidence Intervals

TABLE F.1. *Ninety Percent Confidence Interval on Worst Case Bounds on the Probability of Voting (corresponds to Table 3.3.)*

	Probability of Voting if All States Allowed EDR		Probability of Voting if No States Allowed EDR		Classical Treatment Effect	
	$P(y_1 = 1\|x)$		$P(y_0 = 1\|x)$		$P(y_1 = 1\|x) - P(y_0 = 1\|x)$	
Year	LB	UB	LB	UB	LB	UB
1980	5.9	98.1	59.9	67.8	−61.8	38.2
90% Confidence Interval	5.8	98.1	59.7	68.0	−61.6	38.4
1996 Mature EDR	4.2	98.3	59.6	65.4	−61.3	38.7
90% Confidence Interval	4.1	98.4	59.3	65.7	−61.0	39.0
1996 New EDR	2.9	98.6	60.6	64.9	−62.0	38.0
90% Confidence Interval	2.8	98.6	60.2	65.2	−61.7	38.3
2000 Mature EDR	4.5	98.5	62.8	68.8	−64.3	35.7
90% Confidence Interval	4.4	98.6	62.6	69.1	−64.0	36.0
2000 New EDR	3.0	98.6	63.9	68.3	−65.3	34.7
90% Confidence Interval	2.9	98.7	63.6	68.6	−64.9	35.1

Note: LB indicates the lower bound and UB indicates the upper bound.
Source: 1980, 1996, 2000 CPS.

TABLE F.2. *Ninety Percent Confidence Interval on Combined Ordered Outcomes and Capped Outcomes Bounds if All States Allowed EDR (corresponds to Table 3.4)*

Year	Probability of Voting if All States Allowed EDR $P(y_1 = 1 \mid x)$		Classical Treatment Effect $P(y_1 = 1 \mid x) - P(y_0 = 1 \mid x)$	
	LB	UB	LB	UB
1980	65.8	75.6	0	15.7
90% Confidence Interval	65.6	76.4	NA	16.4
1996 Mature EDR	63.8	71.1	0	11.6
90% Confidence Interval	63.5	72.3	NA	12.7
1996 New EDR	63.4	66.9	0	6.3
90% Confidence Interval	63.2	68.5	NA	8.0
2000 Mature EDR	67.4	75.7	0	12.8
90% Confidence Interval	67.1	76.7	NA	14.0
2000 New EDR	66.9	68.7	0	4.7
90% Confidence Interval	66.6	70.3	NA	6.4

Notes: The ordered outcomes assumption tightens the lower bound; the capped outcomes assumption tightens the upper bound.
LB indicates the lower bound and UB indicates the upper bound.
Source: 1980, 1996, 2000 CPS.

Appendix G. Testing the Probit Assumptions

There are numerous potential estimators that might be brought to bear on policy questions such as the one studied in Chapter 6; but the proposal of new estimators is not a task to be taken lightly (Achen 2002). Probit and logit, though not perfect, have withstood the test of time. However, the distributional assumption implicit in these models might give us a false sense of where the effects are the largest. Although it is not useful in all circumstances, including some of those studied in Chapter 6, the bounds approach offers a simple, straightforward, and transparent means by which the probit assumptions can be tested. As reported in Chapter 6, the evidence from the results presented subsequently is insufficient to reject the assumptions maintained in the probit models.

In this appendix, I revert back to the exogenous selection assumption. As was shown in Chapter 3, the magnitude of the effects is influenced by whether one runs probit using the traditional or the difference in difference set up. However, my interest here is in comparing the relative size of the effects across levels of educational attainment. As will be demonstrated, the pattern of results across levels of education is the same whether probit is run on the difference in difference model or the traditional model; under each approach, by assumption, the effect will be the largest for those with an initial probability of voting $= 0.5$. Additionally, when estimating effects conditional on individual characteristics, the bounds approach requires that the sample be split accordingly, with the procedure run separately for each subgroup. To obtain reliable estimates, the sample size of each subgroup must be relatively large. Using the full CPS data set, rather than a selection of states, results in more precise estimates. Because the bounds approach is a method used on cross-sectional data and controls for previous turnout rates are not present, like the estimates from the traditional model, the overall sizes of the effects will be larger than the difference in difference estimates reported in Chapter 6. But again, my interest here is in how the effect varies as education varies.

In the next section I review the bounds approach, applying it to data from 1980, 1996, and 2000. To conclude, I compare the bounds estimates to those obtained from the traditional model run using probit.

EFFECTS OF EDR BY EDUCATION UNDER THE EXOGENOUS SELECTION ASSUMPTION[1]

As demonstrated in Chapter 3, although the ordered and capped outcomes assumptions are more plausible and reduce the width of the bounds considerably, in order to obtain point estimates that can be compared across categories, the exogenous selection assumption must be employed. If one is willing to accept the exogenous selection assumption, or if one thinks of this in terms of a best case scenario under the combined ordered and capped outcomes assumption, the bounds approach allows one to estimate who will be most sensitive to changes in registration laws without out the distributional and functional form assumptions implicit in logit and probit models. I employ the bounds approach assuming exogenous selection for the case of EDR, the effects of which, unlike the effect of motor voter, are more durable.

Equation 1 from Chapter 1 is reproduced here as a reminder to the reader how the bounds approach works:

$$P(y_1 = 1 \mid x) = P(y_1 = 1 \mid x, t = 1) * P(t = 1 \mid x)$$
$$+ P(y_1 = 1 \mid x, t = 0) * P(t = 0 \mid x) \qquad (1)$$

Under the exogenous selection assumption, it is assumed that the counterfactual probability, $P(y_1 = 1 \mid x, t = 0)$, is equal to the realized probability of voting under the treatment (here, living in a state that has EDR), $P(y_1 = 1 \mid x, t = 1)$. Thus, the overall probability of voting if all received the treatment in question is assumed to be equal to the probability of voting in the states that allow the treatment. That is, $P(y_1 = 1 \mid x) = P(y_1 = 1 \mid x, t = 1) = P(y_1 = 1 \mid x, t = 0)$. Following the

---

[1] Because the covariate values are discrete, cell means were used. Treating the covariate as continuous and estimating the bounds with the Gaussian kernel and Silverman's (1986) rule of thumb bandwidth did not alter the results. See Hardle (1990) for a discussion of nonparametric regression estimators.

procedures outlined in Chapter 3, I make full use of the data and report the estimated effects of EDR across three years and separately based on the maturity of the EDR systems.

Table G.1 presents estimates of the classical treatment effect under the exogenous selection assumption and 90 percent confidence intervals for each year and EDR treatment by education category. A number of patterns are noteworthy. In 1980, the largest effect was found among those with five to eight years of education. Overall, in the states that adopted EDR prior to 1980, the least educated tended to be the most sensitive to EDR, with estimated effects greater than ten percentage points. For the new EDR states, this pattern was not replicated. However, the confidence intervals around these estimates are relatively wide, impeding the ability to draw firm conclusions. Consistent with the direct estimates provided in Chapter 5, it appears that the least educated in the new EDR states did not take advantage of easier registration provisions; the effect of new EDR for the least educated was nonexistent.[2] In both 1996 and 2000, the effect of new EDR was the highest among those who had college degrees.

If one is willing to accept the exogenous selection assumption, then the results in Table G.1 reveal that the effect of EDR across education categories is not uniform across contexts. The bounds approach results for those in states that adopted EDR prior to 1980, like those from the difference in difference method, allow for substantive conclusions similar to those from Wolfinger and Rosenstone (1980), Mitchell and Wlezien (1995), Nagler (1994), and Highton (1997). However, for 1980, when separate estimates of the impact for those with zero to four years of education and those with five to eight years of education can be made, the results presented in Table G.1 suggest that the least educated group might not be the most sensitive to EDR. Rather, those with five to eight years of education followed by those with 9 to 11 years of education are estimated to be the most sensitive to EDR. The estimates for those with zero to four years of education and those with five to eight years of education fit within one another's confidence intervals, thus these estimates are not clearly distinguishable from one another. I now turn to a more detailed comparison between results from the bounds approach and the results from more traditional approaches.

---

[2] While the estimated effect is negative in several cases, the relatively wide 90-percent-confidence interval reveals that the estimates are not very precise.

TABLE G.1. *Bounds Estimates of the Effect of EDR by Education Category Assuming Exogenous Selection*

Category	1980	1996 Mature EDR	1996 New EDR	2000 Mature EDR	2000 New EDR
0–4 Years	8.0	NA	NA	NA	NA
90% Confidence Interval	−1 20				
5–8 Years	13.3	NA	NA	NA	NA
90% Confidence Interval	11 16				
0–8 Years	14.5	11.0	−4.9	18.7	−2.7
90% Confidence Interval	12 17	6 16	−13 3	12 25	−12 7
9–11 Years	12.1	10.3	4.7	13.5	−1.0
90% Confidence Interval	9 15	6 14	0 10	9 18	−6 6
High School Degree	10.3	7.2	2.2	7.7	0.8
90% Confidence Interval	9 12	5 9	0 4	6 10	−2 3
1–3 Years College	8.7	7.4	4.3	9.0	2.6
90% Confidence Interval	7 10	5 9	2 7	7 11	1 5
College Degree	7.8	7.6	7.3	6.1	3.6
90% Confidence Interval	6 10	5 10	4 10	4 8	1 6
College +	4.5	5.1	1.0	6.4	3.1
90% Confidence Interval	2 7	2 8	−3 5	4 8	−1 6

Source: 1980, 1996, 2000 CPS.

COMPARISON OF BOUNDS AND PROBIT RESULTS

In addition to providing greater clarity when applying assumptions, the bounds approach provides a useful tool to assess the validity of the distributional assumptions employed in probit models (Manski et al. 1992, Pepper 2000). That is, if the voting probabilities estimated using a probit model fall far outside the bounds made under weaker assumptions, there would be reason to reject the assumptions maintained in the probit model. Both the nonparametric bounds estimates and the probit estimates are run on the same cross-sectional data from the CPS.

Tables G.2 through G.6 present estimates of the probability of voting and the classical treatment effect (CTE) across education categories if all individuals were to have lived in states with EDR. The tables report the same underlying information, but each is based on a different set of data, defined by the maturity of EDR and the year. That is, there is a separate table for each of the following: EDR in 1980, Mature EDR in 1996, New EDR in 1996, Mature EDR in 2000, and New EDR in 2000.

Each of these tables is constructed as follows: The first four columns contain estimates of the probability of voting if all states had the EDR treatment, specifically: the first two columns contain the lower and upper bounds respectively under the combined ordered and capped outcomes assumption; the third column presents the nonparametric estimate assuming exogenous selection; and the fourth column presents the probit model estimates. The probit coefficients are reported in Tables G.7 through G.9 of this appendix.[3] The fifth column displays the estimates of the classical treatment effect under the exogenous selection assumption and the sixth column contains the corresponding estimates derived from the probit model.

The probit estimates will be assessed against the bounds approach estimates based on their closeness to the bounds approach estimates and the patterns of effects across education categories.[4] In addition, the plausibility of the combined ordered and capped outcomes assumption can be evaluated by examining the estimates of the upper bound compared with the lower bound.

In seventeen of the thirty-seven categories across Tables G.2 through G.6, the probit estimates fall outside the combined ordered outcomes and

---

[3] These probabilities were produced using the procedure described in Wolfinger and Rosenstone (1980) Appendix C, and summarized in Chapter 3.

[4] Given the size of the selection probability, all of the probit estimates lie within the worst case bounds.

TABLE G.2. *Comparison of Estimates of the Probability of Voting by Education if All States Allowed EDR in 1980*

Category	Ordered and Capped Outcomes		$P(y_i = 1|x)$		CTE	
	LB	UB	Nonparametric Model	Probit Model	Nonparametric Model	Probit Model
All	66	76	76	75	11	9
0–4 Years	40	48	48	51	8	12
5–8 Years	54	66	66	63	13	11
0–8 Years	52	65	65	61	14	11
9–11 Years	51	62	62	65	12	10
High School Degree	64	74	74	74	10	9
1–3 Years College	74	82	82	80	9	8
College Degree	85	92	92	89	8	6
College +	88	93	93	95	5	4

Notes: The ordered outcomes assumption tightens the lower bound; the capped outcomes assumption tightens the upper bound.
LB indicates the lower bound and UB indicates the upper bound.
CTE stands for classical treatment effect.
Source: 1980 CPS.

TABLE G.3. *Comparison of Estimates of the Probability of Voting by Education if All States Had Mature EDR in 1996 (Excludes New EDR States)*

Category	Ordered and Capped Outcomes		$P(y_i = 1|x)$		CTE	
	LB	UB	Nonparametric Model	Probit Model	Nonparametric Model	Probit Model
All	64	71	71	71	8	8
0–8 Years	46	56	56	50	11	9
9–11 Years	41	51	51	52	10	9
High School Degree	57	64	64	66	7	8
1–3 Years College	69	76	76	74	7	8
College Degree	80	87	87	85	8	6
College +	88	93	93	94	5	3

Notes: The ordered outcomes assumption tightens the lower bound; the capped outcomes assumption tightens the upper bound.
LB indicates the lower bound and UB indicates the upper bound.
CTE stands for classical treatment effect.
Source: 1996 CPS.

TABLE G.4. *Comparison of Estimates of the Probability of Voting by Education if All States Had New EDR in 1996 (Excludes Mature EDR States)*

Category	Ordered and Capped Outcomes		$P(y_i = 1 \mid x)$		CTE	
	LB	UB	Nonparametric Model	Probit Model	Nonparametric Model	Probit Model
All	63	67	67	68	4	5
0–8 Years	45	41	41	47	−5	6
9–11 Years	41	46	46	49	5	6
High School Degree	57	59	59	62	2	6
1–3 Years College	68	73	73	71	4	5
College Degree	79	86	86	83	7	4
College +	88	89	89	93	1	2

Notes: The ordered outcomes assumption tightens the lower bound, while the capped outcomes assumption tightens the upper bound.
LB indicates the lower bound and UB indicates the upper bound.
CTE stands for classical treatment effect.
Source: 1996 CPS.

TABLE G.5. *Comparison of Estimates of the Probability of Voting by Education if All States Had Mature EDR in 2000 (Excludes New EDR States)*

Category	Ordered and Capped Outcomes		$P(y_i = 1 \mid x)$		CTE	
	LB	UB	Nonparametric Model	Probit Model	Nonparametric Model	Probit Model
All	67	76	76	76	9	9
0–8 Years	45	62	62	53	19	12
9–11 Years	44	57	57	56	14	11
High School Degree	60	67	67	70	8	10
1–3 Years College	71	80	80	78	9	9
College Degree	84	90	90	89	6	6
College +	89	96	96	96	6	3

Notes: The ordered outcomes assumption tightens the lower bound; the capped outcomes assumption tightens the upper bound.
LB indicates the lower bound and UB indicates the upper bound.
CTE stands for classical treatment effect.
Source: 2000 CPS.

TABLE G.6. *Comparison of Estimates of the Probability of Voting by Education if All States Had New EDR in 2000 (Excludes Mature EDR States)*

| Category | Ordered and Capped Outcomes | | $P(y_i = 1 \mid x)$ | | CTE | |
	LB	UB	Nonparametric Model	Probit Model	Nonparametric Model	Probit Model
All	67	69	69	70	2	3
0–8 Years	43	41	41	45	−3	4
9–11 Years	44	43	43	48	−1	4
High School Degree	60	60	60	63	1	4
1–3 Years College	71	73	73	72	3	3
College Degree	84	87	87	84	4	2
College +	89	92	92	93	3	1

Notes: The ordered outcomes assumption tightens the lower bound; the capped outcomes assumption tightens the upper bound.
LB indicates the lower bound and UB indicates the upper bound.
CTE stands for classical treatment effect.
Source: 2000 CPS.

capped outcomes bound on the probability of voting if all states allowed EDR. However, for all but four of the seventeen categories, the probit estimates fall within the 90 percent confidence intervals of the bounds. It is noteworthy that the probit estimates violate the combined ordered and

TABLE G.7. *Probit Estimates of the Probability of Voting in the 1980 CPS*

	Coefficient	Standard Error	*p* Value
EDR	0.0897	0.0224	0.000
Closing Date	−0.0087	0.0006	0.000
Education	0.3131	0.0038	0.000
Age	0.0561	0.0013	0.000
Age Squared	−0.0004	0.00001	0.000
Black	0.0049	0.0148	0.740
South	−0.0768	0.0105	0.000
Mobility	0.1848	0.0042	0.000
Income Quartile	0.1229	0.0043	0.000
Constant	−3.2425	0.0380	0.000

$N = 104,725$.
Log likelihood = −57383.399.
EDR = election day registration.
Source: 1980 CPS.

TABLE G.8. *Probit Estimates of the Probability of Voting in the 1996 CPS*

	Coefficient	Standard Error	*p* Value
Mature EDR	0.1682	0.0326	0.000
New EDR	0.0793	0.0345	0.021
Closing Date	−0.0032	0.0009	0.000
Pre-NVRA Motor Voter	0.0108	0.0125	0.389
Education	0.3179	0.0049	0.000
Age	0.0389	0.0016	0.000
Age Squared	−0.0002	0.00002	0.000
Black	0.2250	0.0181	0.000
South	−0.0442	0.0126	0.000
Mobility	0.1610	0.0051	0.000
Income Quartile	0.1454	0.0053	0.000
Constant	−3.3743	0.0485	0.000

$N = 71,025$.
Log likelihood $= -39701.317$.
EDR = election day registration; NVRA = National Voter Registration Act of 1993.
Source: 1996 CPS.

capped outcomes bounds more so in the new EDR treatment than in the mature EDR treatment.

Evidence against the ordered and capped outcomes assumption is found in three cases. For those with fewer than eight years of education

TABLE G.9. *Probit Estimates of the Probability of Voting in the 2000 CPS*

	Coefficient	Standard Error	*p* Value
Mature EDR	0.2624	0.0359	0.000
New EDR	0.0524	0.0481	0.276
Closing Date	−0.0020	0.0009	0.023
Mature Motor Voter	−0.0312	0.0367	0.396
Education	0.3357	0.0053	0.000
Age	0.0349	0.0017	0.000
Age Squared	−0.0002	0.00002	0.000
Black	0.2797	0.0191	0.000
South	−0.0068	0.0138	0.621
Mobility	0.1548	0.0056	0.000
Income Quartile	0.1658	0.0058	0.000
Constant	−3.3236	0.0610	0.000

$N = 63,826$.
Log likelihood $= -34234.333$.
EDR = election day registration.
Source: 2000 CPS.

in new EDR states in 1996 (Table G.4) and for those with either zero to eight years or nine to eleven years of education in new EDR states in 2000 (Table G.6), the lower bound exceeds the upper bound under the combined ordered and capped outcomes assumption.[5] This translates into a negative estimate of the treatment effect (see column 5). This result makes little sense; if newly implemented EDR were available to all eligible citizens across the United States, one would not expect those who voted in its absence to abstain in its presence. However, zero is contained within the respective confidence intervals, indicating that the effect is statistically insignificant.

The upper bound under the combined ordered and capped outcomes assumption is equivalent to the estimate under exogenous selection. Thus, the closeness of the probit estimates of the probability of voting if all had EDR and the bounds approach estimates under exogenous selection has already been covered. For the most part, the estimates are similar. In addition to the seventeen cases just discussed, one case stands out. The probit estimate for those with zero to eight years of education under the mature EDR treatment in Table G.5 falls almost four points lower than the 0.05 quantile of the bootstrapped distribution of the bounds approach estimate. Although there is some reason for concern, the evidence presented thus far is not sufficiently strong to allow one to reject the probit models.

An examination of the estimated effects of the CTE across education categories casts some doubt on the probit models. For each year and EDR category, the probit model estimates suggest that the effect of EDR decreases as education increases. That is, the least educated are estimated to be the most sensitive to a change to EDR. This is consistent with the conclusions drawn by Wolfinger and Rosenstone (1980), Mitchell and Wlezien (1995), and Highton (1997). As noted earlier, the estimates from the bounds approach occasionally paint a different picture. For those in states that adopted EDR prior to 1980, the patterns match those from the probit models with only a few exceptions. Yet, in new EDR states, the least educated do not seem to gain at all from EDR. If one accepts the exogenous selection assumption, then, at least for new EDR states, there is reason to call into question the functional form and/or distributional assumptions maintained by the probit model. However, given that EDR

---

[5] The lower bound under the combined assumption is equivalent to the lower bound under the ordered outcomes assumption alone while the upper bound under the combined assumption is equivalent to the upper bound under the capped outcomes assumption alone.

in these states did not lead to an increase in turnout, there is little reason for concern.

In sum, the bounds approach did not produce patterns of results drastically different from those obtained with probit models. In the case of new EDR, additional research to study the occasional lack of correspondence between the bounds and probit results is called for. Doing so is beyond the scope of the present endeavor.

Appendix H. State Party Leader and State Election Official Survey Instruments

State Political Party Survey Instrument
Name, State, Position, Party: _____

Read to respondent:
This interview is completely voluntary. If we come to any questions you do not want to answer, just let me know and we'll go on to the next question.

1. What methods did you use to mobilize those who are registered to vote in the November 2002 election?
   1a. Which, if any, of these methods were used for the first time?
   1b. Which methods do you usually rely on the most?
2. In the November 2002 election, did you target specific populations?
   2a. If so, which populations did you target?
   2b. If so, what methods did you use to identify people as part of those populations?
3. What methods did you use to mobilize those who are not registered to register on election day for the November 2002 election?
   3a. Which, if any, of these methods were used for the first time?
   3b. Which methods do you usually rely on most?
4. In the November 2002 election, did you target specific populations?
   4a. If so, which populations did you target?
   4b. If so, what methods did you use to identify people as part of those populations?
5. How, if at all, do the ways your party mobilizes those who are registered to vote differ from what you would do if election day registration were not allowed in your state?
6. [*For new EDR states*] When election day registration went into effect in your state, did you change the way you mobilize those who are registered to vote?
   6a. What did you change?

6b. [*For new EDR states*] When determining your methodology, did you contact the [*insert appropriate party name*] party in states that already had election day registration?

6c. If so, how did this impact your efforts? [*Probe, ask which state(s) after each mention*]

7. How, if at all, do the ways your party mobilizes those who are not registered to vote differ from what you would do if election day registration were not allowed in your state?

8. [*For new EDR states*] When election day registration went into effect in your state, did you change the way you mobilize those who are not registered to vote?

8a. What did you change?

8b. [*For new EDR states*] When determining your methodology, did you contact the [*insert appropriate party name*] party in states that already had election day registration?

8c. If so, how did this impact your efforts? [*Probe, ask which state(s) after each mention*]

9. How would you compare the resources devoted to mobilization of those who are registered with the resources devoted to mobilization of those who are not registered?

10. Overall, how do you feel about the election day registration system used in your state?

11. Is there anything you would like to add?

Now I have a few questions about your current position and job history.

12. How long have you been in your current position?

13. How long have you worked for the State _____[*fill in Democrat or Republican*] Party?

That concludes the first part of the questionnaire. Thank you for your participation. Now I would like to know if information of the following type is available.

1. The annual budget?
2. Expenditures for the mobilization of registered voters?
3. Expenditures for the mobilization of unregistered citizens?
4. Number of contacts with registered voters?
5. Number of contacts with unregistered citizens?
6. Training manuals?
7. Electronic vote history files?

Thank you for your participation.

Elections Director, Survey Instrument
Name, Position, State: _____

Read to respondent:
This interview is completely voluntary. If we come to any questions you do not want to answer, just let me know and we'll go on to the next question.

1. Please explain to me the process a person goes through when registering on election day in your state. Please include a list of the items used for identification that are necessary for proper completion of the registration form.
    1a. Are there any other ways that can be used to identify the individual?
        Yes [*Go to Q1a1*]   No
    1a1. [*If Yes*] What are the other ways that can be used to identify the individual?
        1b. [*If necessary*] At the polling places, are there separate lines for registering and voting?
        Yes   No
        1c. Have any of these procedures changed since the inception of the law?
        Yes [*Go to Q1c1*]   No [*Go to Q2*]
        1c1. If yes, What has changed? [*Probe: anything else?*]
        1c2. When did change _____ go into effect?
2. Do election day registrants become permanent registrants?
    Yes   No
    2a. Are they informed of this?
        Yes [*Go to Q2a1*]   No [*Go to Q3*]
    2a1. How are they informed?
3. What would you say are the most common administrative difficulties associated with election day registration? [*Probe: anything else?*]
    3a. Starting with the most problematic and continuing sequentially, please list the top 5 most common administrative difficulties associated with election day registration: [*if offered, note ties*]
    1. _____
    2. _____
    3. _____
    4. _____
    5. _____

4. What additional costs, if any, are associated with election day registration that were not associated with your previous system? [*Probe: anything else?*]

5. How many election workers on election day are assigned to deal specifically with election day registration transactions?
   5a. How is this decided?

6. What, if any, cost savings have you been able to achieve over your previous system? [*Probe: anything else?*]

7. What is the approximate length of time it takes an election day registrant to register?

8. Would you say challenges of election day registrants by election workers is Very frequent, Somewhat frequent, or Not at all frequent?
   Very frequent   Somewhat frequent   Not at all frequent

9. Would you say challenges of election day registrants by poll watchers is Very frequent, Somewhat frequent, or Not at all frequent?
   Very frequent   Somewhat frequent   Not at all frequent

10. What measures are taken to prevent election day registration fraud? [*Probe: anything else?*]

11. Who handles investigations of fraud?

12. What penalties apply to those convicted of fraud?

13. How common would you say election day registration fraud has been?

14. Are county elections officials required to report to your office the number of election day registrants?
    Yes [*Go to Q14a*]   No [*Go to Q14b*]
    14a. [*If Yes*] How far back do your records of this information go?
    14b. [*If No*] Are such reports made as a matter of practice?
       Yes   No

15. Are attempts made to differentiate new registrants from those who are registered and are registering at their new address?
    Yes [*Go to Q15a*]   No [*Go to Q16*]
    15a. [*If Yes*] What steps are taken to differentiate new registrants from those who are registered and are registering at their new address? [*Probe: anything else?*]

16. Are local elections officials asked by your office, either through legal requirement or an administrative process to report difficulties related to election day registration?
    Yes [*Go to Q17*]   No [*Go to Q16a*]
    16a. [*If No*] Are such reports made as a matter of practice?
       Yes   No

17. What methods does your office regularly use to notify the public that eligible citizens can register on election day? [*Probe: anything else?*]

18a–f. What methods were used by your office to notify the public that eligible citizens can register on election day for the November 2002 election? Did you use:

18a. TV ads?:	Yes	No
18b. Radio ads?:	Yes	No
18c. Newspaper ads?:	Yes	No
18d. Mailings?:	Yes	No
18e. Information on official web site?:	Yes	No
18f. Email?:	Yes	No

18g. Are there any others (please specify all others)?:

1. _____	Yes	No
2. _____	Yes	No
3. _____	Yes	No

19a–f. Have any of the following been used in the past? [*Probe: if don't know, are records of this kept?*]

19a. TV ads?:	Yes	No
19b. Radio ads?:	Yes	No
19c. Newspaper ads?:	Yes	No
19d. Mailings?:	Yes	No
19e. Information on official web site?:	Yes	No
19f. Email?:	Yes	No

19g. Are there any others (please specify all others)?:

1. _____	Yes	No
2. _____	Yes	No
3. _____	Yes	No

20a–f. When election day registration was introduced, what methods were used by your office to notify the public that eligible citizens can register on election day? Did you use: [*Probe: if don't know, are records of this kept?*]

20a. TV ads?:	Yes	No
20b. Radio ads?:	Yes	No
20c. Newspaper ads?:	Yes	No
20d. Mailings?:	Yes	No
20e. Information on official web site?:	Yes	No
20f. Email?:	Yes	No

20g. Are there any others (please specify all others)?:

    1. _____

    2. _____

    3. _____

21 What methods does your office regularly use to inform those who are registered about upcoming elections? [*Probe: anything else?*]

22a-f. What methods were used by your office to inform those who are registered about the November 2002 election? Did you use:

    22a. TV ads?:   Yes   No

    22b. Radio ads?:   Yes   No

    22c. Newspaper ads?:   Yes   No

    22d. Mailings?:   Yes   No

    22e. Information on official web site?:   Yes   No

    22f. Email?:   Yes   No

    22g. Are there any others (please specify all others)?:

        1. _____ Yes No

        2. _____ Yes No

        3. _____ Yes No

23a-f. Have any of the following been used in the past: [*Probe: if don't know, are records of this kept?*]

    23a. TV ads?:   Yes   No

    23b. Radio ads?:   Yes   No

    23c. Newspaper ads?:   Yes   No

    23d. Mailings?:   Yes   No

    23e. Information on official web site?:   Yes   No

    23f. Email?:   Yes   No

    23g. Are there any others (please specify all others)?:

        1. _____ Yes   No

        2. _____ Yes   No

        3. _____ Yes   No

Now I would like to ask you to rate the effect of election day registration (EDR) with regard to a number of outcomes:

24a. With regard to increasing registration, would you say EDR has had a Large impact, Some impact, or No impact?

    Large impact   Some impact   No impact

24b. With regard to increasing turnout, would you say EDR has had a Large impact, Some impact, or No impact?

Large impact   Some impact   No impact

24c. With regard to making the electorate more representative of the population as a whole would you say EDR has had a Large impact, Some impact, or No impact?

Large impact   Some impact   No impact

24d. With regard to costs, comparing EDR to your previous system, would you say EDR led to a Large increase in costs, a Small increase in costs, No increase in costs, a Small decrease in costs, or a Large decrease in costs?

Large increase   Small increase   No increase
Small decrease   Large decrease

24e. With regard to vulnerability to EDR fraud, would you say that the system you have in place is Highly vulnerable to fraud, Somewhat vulnerable to fraud, or Not at all vulnerable to fraud?

Highly vulnerable   Somewhat vulnerable   Not at all vulnerable

25. Overall, how do you feel about the election day registration system used in your state? [*Probe: anything else?*]

26. If you could change the way election day registration is implemented in your state, would you make any changes?

Yes [*Go to Q26a*]   No [*Go to Q27*]

26a. [If yes] What changes would you make? [*Probe: anything else?*]

27. Would you recommend to officials in other states that they adopt election day registration?

Yes   No

27a. What are the primary reasons for your answer? [*Probe: anything else?*]

28. What advice would you give to officials in other states who are thinking about adopting election day registration? [*Probe: anything else?*]

29. Is there anything you would like to add?

Now I have a few questions about your current position and job history.

30. Is this an appointed position? Yes   No

31. How long have you been in your current position? _____

32. How long have you worked in the elections division? _____

That concludes the first part of the questionnaire. Thank you for your participation! Now I have a checklist of information that, if available

I would like to collect. I'll simply read off the list and you can tell me whether or not the information is available.

1. Annual budget of the elections division. Yes   No
2. Total expenditures for election day registration administration. Yes No
3. Expenditures to notify the public that eligible citizens can register on election day. Yes   No
4. Expenditures for information for local election officials regarding election day registration. Yes   No
5. Expenditures to inform those who are registered about upcoming elections. Yes   No
6. Expenditures for information for local election officials regarding upcoming elections, excluding costs related to election day registration. Yes   No
7. The number of challenges by election workers recorded? Yes No
8. The number of challenges by poll watchers recorded? Yes   No
9. [*If verification cards are used as a follow-up measure*] The number of verification cards returned by the postal service? Yes   No
10. The number of investigations of fraud. Yes   No
11. The number of fraud prosecutions. Yes   No
12. The number of fraud convictions. Yes   No
13. Records of the administrative difficulties with election day registration reported by local elections officials. Yes   No
14. Records of the problems with election day registration reported by the public?
    Yes   No
15. Reports (internal and external) on election day registration in your state. Yes   No

Thank you for your participation!

References

Achen, Christopher H. 1986. *The Statistical Analysis of Quasi-Experiments*. Berkeley: University of California Press.

———. 2002. "Toward a New Political Methodology: Microfoundations and ART." *Annual Review of Political Science*, 5:423–450.

———. 2006. "Expressive Bayesian Voters, their Turnout Decisions, and Double Probit: Empirical Implications of a Theoretical Model." Paper prepared for the Annual Meeting of the Society for Political Methodology, UC-Davis, July 20–22.

———. 2008. "Registration and Voting Under Rational Expectations: The Econometric Implications." Paper presented at the Twenty Fifth Annual Meeting of the Society for Political Methodology, Ann Arbor, Michigan July 9–12.

Aldrich, John H. 1993. "Rational Choice and Turnout." *American Journal of Political Science*, 37:246–78.

Alvarez, R. Michael and Stephen Ansolabehere. 2002. "California Votes: The Promise of Election Day Registration." DEMOS: A Network for Ideas and Action. http://archive.demos.org/pubs/california_votes.pdf, last visited 4/13/09.

Alvarez, R. Michael and Thad E. Hall. 2008. *Electronic Elections: The Perils and Promises of Digital Democracy*. Princeton, NJ: Princeton University Press.

Alvarez, R. Michael, Jonathan Nagler, and Catherine Wilson. 2004. "Making Voting Easier: Election Day Registration in New York State." DEMOS: A Network for Ideas and Action. http://www.demos.org/pubs/EDR%20-%20NY%20report%20b&w%20-%20Aug%202004.pdf, visited 6/01/06.

Ansolabehere, Stephen, and David M. Konisky. 2006. "The Introduction of Voter Registration and Its Effect on Turnout." *Political Analysis*, 14:83–100.

Bartels, Larry M. 1991. "Instrumental and 'Quasi-Instrumental' Variables." *American Journal of Political Science*, 35:777–800.

Bendor, Jonathan, Daniel Diermeier, and Michael Ting. 2003. "A Behavioral Model of Turnout." *American Political Science Review*, 97:261–280.

Bennett, Stephen E. 1990a. "The Uses and Abuses of Registration and Turnout Data: An Analysis of Piven and Cloward's Studies of Nonvoting in America." *PS: Political Science and Politics*, 23:166–171.

———. 1990b. "Rejoinder to Piven and Cloward." *PS: Political Science and Politics*, 23:173–175.

———. 2007. "Another Look at Nonvoting's Implications for Democracy in America." Paper presented at the Annual Meeting of the American Political Science Association, August 30–September 2, 2007.

Berelson, Bernard, Paul Lazarsfeld, and William McPhee. 1954. *Voting: A Study of Opinion Formation in a Presidential Campaign*. Chicago, IL: University of Chicago Press.

Berinsky, Adam J. 2005. "The Perverse Consequences of Electoral Reform in the United States." *American Politics Research*, 33:471–491.

Berinsky, Adam J., Nancy Burns, and Michael W. Traugott. 2001. "Who Votes by Mail? A Dynamic Model of the Individual-level Consequences of Voting-by-Mail Systems," *Public Opinion Quarterly*, 65:178–197.

Besley, Timothy and Anne Case. 2000. "Unnatural Experiments? Estimating the Incidence of Endogenous Policies. *The Economic Journal*, 110:F672-F694.

Blais, André. 2000. *To Vote or Not to Vote: The Merits and Limits of Rational Choice Theory*. Pittsburgh, PA: University of Pittsburgh Press.

Bowler, Shaun, Todd Donovan, and David Brockington. 2003. *Electoral Reform and Minority Representation: Local Experiments with Alternative Elections*. Columbus: Ohio State University Press.

Brennan, Geoffrey and James Buchanan. 1984. "Voter Choice: Evaluating Political Alternatives." *American Behavioral Scientist*, 28:185–201.

Brennan, Geoffrey and Loren Lomasky. 1993. *Democracy and Decision: The Pure Theory of Electoral Preference*. New York: Cambridge University Press.

Brians, Craig L. and Bernard Grofman. 1999. "When Registration Barriers Fall, Who Votes? An Empirical Test of a Rational Choice Model." *Public Choice*, 99:161–176.

———. 2001. "Election Day Registration's Effect on U.S. Voter Turnout." *Social Science Quarterly*, 82:170–183.

Brown, Robert D., and Justin Wedeking. 2006. "People Who Have Their Tickets But Do Not Use Them: 'Motor Voter,' Registration, and Turnout Revisited." *American Politics Research*, 34:479–504.

Burnham, Walter Dean. 1980. "The Appearance and Disappearance of the American Voter." In Richard Rose (ed.), *Electoral Participation: A Comparative Analysis*. Beverly Hills, CA: Sage Publications.

Cain, Bruce E., Todd Donovan, and Caroline J. Tolbert (eds.), 2008. *Democracy in the States: Experiments in Election Reform*. Washington, DC: Brookings Institution Press.

Caltech/MIT Voting Technology Project. 2001. *Voting: What Is, What Could Be*, at http://www.vote.caltech.edu/media/documents/july01/July01_VTP_Voting_Report_Entire.pdf.

Caltech/MIT Voting Technology Project. 2003. *Understanding Boston: Voting in Massachusetts*. The Massachusetts Institute of Technology, with funds from The Boston Foundation. http://www.tbf.org/uploadedFiles/VotinginMass.pdf

Calvert, Jerry W., and Jack Gilchrist. 1993. "Suppose They Held an Election and Almost Everyone Came!" *PS: Political Science and Politics*, 26:695–700.

Campbell, Angus. 1966. "Surge and Decline: A Study of Electoral Change." In Campbell, Angus, Philip E. Converse, Warren E. Miller, and Donald E. Stokes (eds.), *Elections and the Political Order*. New York: Wiley.

Campbell, Angus, Philip E. Converse, Warren E. Miller, and Donald E. Stokes. 1960. *The American Voter*. Chicago, IL: University of Chicago Press.

Campbell, David E. 2006. *Why We Vote: How Schools and Communities Shape our Civic Life*. Princeton, NJ: Princeton University Press.

Caplan, Bryan. 2007. *The Myth of the Rational Voter: Why Democracies Choose Bad Policies*. Princeton, NJ: Princeton University Press.

Card, David. 1992. "Do Minimum Wages Reduce Employment? A Case Study of California, 1987–89." *Industrial and Labor Relations Review*, 46:38–54.

Carter, Lewis F. 1990. *Charisma and Control in Rajneeshpuram: The Role of Shared Values in the Creation of a Community*. New York: Cambridge University Press.

Council of State Governments. *The Book of the States*. Lexington, KY.

DeNardo, James. 1980. "Turnout and the Vote: The Joke's on the Democrats." *American Political Science Review*, 74:406–420.

Dixit, Avinash, and John Londregan. 1996. "The Determinants of Success of Special Interests in Redistributive Politics." *Journal of Politics*, 58:1132–1155.

Donovan, Todd and Shaun Bowler. 2004. *Reforming the Republic: Democratic Institutions for the New America*. Upper Saddle River, NJ: Pearson Prentice Hall.

Downs, Anthony. 1957. *An Economic Theory of Democracy*. New York: Harper and Row.

Duff, Brian, Michael J. Hanmer, Won-ho Park, and Ismail K. White. 2007. "Good Excuses: Understanding Who Votes with an Improved Turnout Question." *Public Opinion Quarterly* 71:67–90.

Elazar, Daniel J. 1966. *American Federalism: A View from the States*, 1st ed. New York: Crowell.

Erikson, Robert S. 1981. "Why Do People Vote? Because They Are Registered." *American Politics Quarterly*, 9:259–276.

Federal Election Commission. 1997. "The Impact of the National Voter Registration Act of 1993 on the Administration of Elections for Federal Office 1995–1996." Washington, DC: Federal Election Commission.

———. 2001. "The Impact of the National Voter Registration Act of 1993 on the Administration of Elections for Federal Office 1999–2000." Washington, DC: Federal Election Commission.

Fenster, Mark J. 1994. "The Impact of Allowing Day of Registration Voting on Turnout in U.S. Presidential Elections From 1960 to 1992, A Research Note." *American Politics Quarterly*, 22:74–87.

Fitzgerald, Mary. 2005. "Greater Convenience but Not Greater Turnout: The Impact of Alternative Voting Methods on Electoral Participation in the United States." *American Politics Research*, 33:842–867.

Fortier, John C. 2006. *Absentee and Early Voting*. Washington, DC: American Enterprise Institute Press.

Franklin, Daniel P., and Eric E. Grier. 1997. "Effects of Motor Voter Legislation: Voter Turnout, Registration, and Partisan Advantage in the 1992 Presidential Election." *American Politics Quarterly*, 25:104–117.

Franklin, Mark N. 2004. *Voter Turnout and the Dynamics of Electoral Competition in Established Democracies Since 1945*. New York: Cambridge University Press.

Gans, Curtis B. 1990. "A Rejoinder to Piven and Cloward." *PS: Political Science and Politics*, 23:175–178.

Gerber, Alan S., Donald P. Green, and Ron Shachar. 2003. "Voting May Be Habit Forming: Evidence from a Randomized Field Experiment." *American Journal of Political Science*, 47:540–550.

Glass, David P., Peverill Squire, and Raymond E. Wolfinger. 1984. "Voter Turnout: An International Comparison." *Public Opinion*, 6:49–55.

Gosnell, Harold F. 1927. *Getting Out the Vote: An Experiment in the Stimulation of Voting*. Chicago, IL: University of Chicago Press.

Green, Donald P. and Alan S. Gerber. 2004. *Get Out the Vote!: How to Increase Voter Turnout*. Washington, DC: Brookings Institution Press.

Green, Donald P. and Ron Shachar. 2000. "Habit Formation and Political Behaviour: Evidence of Consuetude in Voter Turnout." *British Journal of Political Science*, 30:561–573.

Griffin, John D. and Michael Keane. 2006. "Descriptive Representation and the Composition of African American Turnout." *American Journal of Political Science*, 50:998–1012.

Griffin, John D. and Brian Newman. 2005. "Are Voters Better Represented?" *Journal of Politics*, 67:1206–1227.

Gronke, Paul, Eva Galanes-Rosenbaum, and Peter A. Miller. 2007. "Early Voting and Turnout." *PS: Political Science and Politics*, 40:639–645.

———. 2008. "Early Voting and Turnout." In Cain, Bruce E., Todd Donovan, and Caroline J. Tolbert (eds.), *Democracy in the States: Experiments in Election Reform*. Washington DC: Brookings Institution Press.

Gronke, Paul, Eva Galanes-Rosenbaum, Peter A. Miller, and Daniel Toffey. 2008. "Convenience Voting." *Annual Review of Political Science*, 11:437–455.

Gruber, Jonathan. 1994. "The Incidence of Mandated Maternity Benefits." *The American Economic Review*, 84:622–641.

Hanmer, Michael J. 2000. "Alternative Estimates of the Effects of Election Day Registration and Motor Voter Laws." Paper presented at the Annual Meeting of the American Political Science Association, August 31–September 3, 2000, Washington, DC.

———. 2002. "A Monte Carlo Simulation and Empirical Investigation of Scobit." Paper presented at the Annual Meeting of the American Political Science Association, August 29–September 1, 2002, Boston, MA.

———. 2006. "A Monte Carlo Simulation Investigation of Scobit." Working paper, University of Maryland at College Park.

———. 2007. "An Alternative Approach to Estimating Who is Most Likely to Respond to Changes in Registration Laws." *Political Behavior*, 29:1–30.

————. 2008. "The Dynamics of Turnout and Attitudes." Paper presented at the Annual Meeting of the Midwest Political Science Association, April 3–6, 2008, Chicago, IL.

Hanmer, Michael J. and Kerem Ozan Kalkan. 2008. "Behind the Curve: Calculating Predicted Probabilities from Limited Dependent Variable Models." Presented at the Annual Meeting of the Political Methodology Section of the American Political Science Association, July 9–12, 2008. University of Michigan, Ann Arbor, MI.

Hanmer, Michael J., Won-ho Park, Michael W. Traugott, Richard G. Niemi, Paul S. Herrnson, Benjamin B. Bederson, and Frederick G. Conrad. "Losing Fewer Votes: The Impact of Changing Voting Systems on Residual Votes." Forthcoming, *Political Research Quarterly*.

Hanmer, Michael J. and Michael W. Traugott. 2004. "The Impact of Voting By Mail on Voter Behavior." *American Politics Research*, 32:375–405.

Hanushek, Eric A. and John E. Jackson. 1977. *Statistical Methods for Social Scientists*. New York, NY: Academic Press.

Hardle, Wolfgang. 1990. *Applied Nonparametric Regression*. New York: Cambridge University Press.

Heckman, James J. 1979. "Sample Selection Bias as a Specification Error." *Econometrica*, 47:153–161.

Hero, Rodney E. 1998. *Faces of Inequality: Social Diversity in American Politcs*. New York: Oxford University Press.

Herrnson, Paul S., Richard G. Niemi, Michael J. Hanmer, Benjamin B. Bederson, Frederick G. Conrad, and Michael W. Traugott. 2008. *Voting Technology: The Not-So-Simple Act of Casting a Ballot*. Washington, DC: Brookings Institution Press.

Highton, Benjamin. 1997. "Easy Registration and Voter Turnout." *Journal of Politics*, 59:565–575.

————. 2004. "Voter Registration and Turnout in the United States." *Perspectives on Politics*, 2:507–515.

————. 2005. "Who Reports? Self-Reported Versus Proxy-Reported Voter Turnout in the Current Population Survey." *Public Opinion Quarterly*, 69:113–123.

Highton, Benjamin and Raymond E. Wolfinger. 1998. "Estimating the Effects of the National Voter Registration Act of 1993." *Political Behavior*, 20:79–104.

————. 2000. "The Political Implications of Higher Turnout." *British Journal of Political Science*, 30:1–16.

Hill, Kim Quaile and Leighley, Jan E. 1992. "The Policy Consequences of Class Bias in State Electorates." *American Journal of Political Science*, 36:351–365.

————. 1999. "Racial Diversity, Voter Turnout, and Mobilizing Institutions in the United States." *American Politics Quarterly*, 27:275–295.

Huang, Chi and Todd G. Shields. 2000. "Interpretation of Interaction Effects in Logit and Probit Analyses: Reconsidering the Relationship Between Registration Laws, Education and Voter Turnout." *American Politics Quarterly*, 28:80–95.

Huckfeldt, Robert and John Sprague. 1995. *Citizens, Politics, and Social Communication: Information and Influence in an Election Campaign.* New York: Cambridge University Press.

Jackson, Robert A., Robert D. Brown, and Gerald C. Wright. 1998. "Registration, Turnout, and the Electoral Representativeness of U.S. State Electorates." *American Politics Quarterly*, 26:259–287.

James, Deborah. 1987. "Voter Registration: A Restriction on the Fundamental Right to Vote." *Yale Law Journal*, 96:1615–1640.

Jennings, Jerry T. 1990. "Estimating Voter Turnout in the Current Population Survey." *Studies in the Measurement of Voter Turnout.* Washington, DC: U.S. Bureau of the Census. *Current Population Reports, Series P-23, No.* 168:21–29.

Karp, Jeffrey A., and Susan A. Banducci. 2000. "Going Postal: How All-Mail Elections Influence Turnout." *Political Behavior*, 22:223–239.

Key, V.O. 1949. *Southern Politics in State and Nation.* New York: Alfred A. Knopf.

Kim, Jae-on, John R. Petrocik, and Stephen E. Enokson. 1975. "Voter Turnout Among the American States: Systematic and Individual Components." *American Political Science Review*, 69:107–123.

Kimball, David C., and Martha Kropf. 2005. "Ballot Design and Unrecorded Votes on Paper-Based Ballots." *Public Opinion Quarterly* 69:508–529.

Knack, Stephen. 1995. "Does 'Motor Voter' Work? Evidence from State-Level Data." *Journal of Politics*, 57:796–811.

———. 1999. "Drivers Wanted: Motor Voter and the Election of 1996." *PS: Political Science and Politics*, 32:237–243.

———. 2001. "Election Day Registration: The Second Wave." *American Politics Research*, 29:65–78.

Knack, Stephen, and James White. 1998. "Did Motor Voter Programs Help the Democrats?" *American Politics Quarterly*, 26:344–365.

———. 2000. "Election-Day Registration and Turnout Inequality." *Political Behavior*, 22:29–44.

Knight, Brian G. 2000. "Supermajority Voting Requirements for Tax Increases: Evidence from the States." *Journal of Public Economics*, 76:41–67.

Kozol, Jonathan. 1991. *Savage Inequalities: Children in America's Schools.* New York: Crown Publishers.

Kraut, Robert E. and John B. McConahay. 1973. "How Being Interviewed Affects Voting: An Experiment." *Public Opinion Quarterly*, 37:398–406.

Leighley, Jan E. and Jonathan Nagler. 2007. "Unions, Voter Turnout, and Class Bias in the U.S. Electorate, 1964–2004." *Journal of Politics*, 69:430–441.

Lentz, Jacob. 2002. *Electing Jesse Ventura: A Third-Party Success Story.* Boulder, CO: Lynne Rienner Publishers.

Lijphart, Arend. 1997. "Unequal Participation: Democracy's Unresolved Dilemma." Presidential Address, American Political Science Association, 1996. *American Political Science Review*, 91:1–14.

Manski, Charles F. 1989. "Anatomy of the Selection Problem." *Journal of Human Resources*, 24:343–360.

———. 1990. "Nonparametric Bounds on Treatment Effects." *American Economic Review Papers and Proceedings*, 80:319–323.

———. 1994. "The Selection Problem." In C. Sims (ed.), *Advances in Econometrics, Sixth World Congress*. Cambridge, UK: Cambridge University Press.

———. 1995. *Identification Problems in the Social Sciences*. Cambridge, MA: Harvard University Press.

———. 1997. "Monotone Treatment Response." *Econometrica*, 65:1311–1334.

Manski, Charles F. and Daniel S. Nagin. 1998. "Bounding Disagreements About Treatment Effects: A Case Study of Sentencing and Recidivism." *Sociological Methodology*, 28:99–137.

Manski, Charles F., Gary D.. Sandefur, Sara McLanahan and Daniel Powers. 1992. "Alternative Estimates of the Effect of Family Structure during Adolescence on High School Graduation." *Journal of the American Statistical Association*, 87:25–37.

March, James G. and Johan P. Olsen. 1984. "The New Institutionalism: Organizational Factors in Political Life." *American Political Science Review*, 78:734–749.

Martinez, Michael D., and David Hill. 1999. "Did Motor Voter Work?" *American Politics Quarterly*, 27:296–315.

Matsusaka, John. G. 2006. "Direct Democracy and Electoral Reform." In Michael P. McDonald and John Samples (eds.), *The Marketplace of Democracy: Electoral Competition and American Politics*. Washington, DC: Brookings Institution and Cato Institute.

McDonald, Michael P. 2008. "Super Tuesday Turned Into A Super Flop." *Roll Call*, February 11.

McDonald, Michael P. and Samuel L. Popkin. 2001. "The Myth of the Vanishing Voter." *American Political Science Review*, 95:953–962.

McDonald, Michael P. and John Samples. 2006. "The Perfect Electoral Marketplace: 'If Men Were Angels…'" In Michael P. McDonald and John Samples (eds.), *The Marketplace of Democracy: Electoral Competition and American Politics*. Washington, DC: Brookings Institution and Cato Institute.

McKean, Dayton David. 1940. *The Boss: The Hague Machine in Action*. Boston, MA: Houghton Mifflin Company.

Meirick, Patrick C., and Daniel B. Wackman. 2004 "Kids Voting and Poltical Knowledge: Narrowing Gaps, Informing Votes." *Social Science Quarterly*, 85:1161–1177.

Mitchell, Glen E. and Christopher Wlezien. 1995. "The Impact of Legal Constraints on Voter Registration, Turnout, and the Composition of the American Electorate." *Political Behavior*, 17:179–202.

Nagler, Jonathan. 1991. "The Effect of Registration Laws and Education on U.S. Voter Turnout." *American Political Science Review*, 85:1393–1405.

———. 1994. "Scobit: An Alternative Estimator to Logit and Probit." *American Journal of Political Science*, 38:230–255.

National Commission on Federal Election Reform. 2001. *To Assure Pride and Confidence in the Electoral Process: Report of the National Commission on Federal Election Reform*. http://www.reformelections.org/publications.asp?pubid=246.

Nickerson, David W., Ryan D. Friedrichs, and David C. King. 2006 "Partisan Mobilization Campaigns in the Field: Results from a Statewide Turnout Experiment in Michigan." *Political Research Quarterly*, 59:85–97.

Niemi, Richard G., and Michael J. Hanmer. 2008. "Voter Turnout Among College Students: New Data and a Rethinking of Traditional Theories." Working paper, University of Rochester.

Niemi, Richard G., and Jane Junn. 1998. *Civic Education: What Makes Students Learn.* New Haven, CT: Yale University Press.

Niemi, Richard G., Michael J. Hanmer, and Thomas H. Jackson. 2008. "Where Can and Should College Students Vote? A Legal, and Empirical Perspective." Presented at the Annual Meeting of the State Politics and Policy Conference, Philadelphia, PA, May 30–31, 2008.

Oliver, J. Eric. 1996. "Effects of Eligibility Restrictions and Party Activity on Absentee Voting and Overall Turnout." *American Journal of Political Science*, 40:498–513.

Ornstein, Norman. 2004. "The Wealthy Have a Bigger Role in Politics. They Don't Need to." *Roll Call*, June 16.

Parry, Janine A., and Todd G. Shields. 2001. "Sex, Age, and the Implementation of the Motor Voter Act: The 1996 Presidential Election." *Social Science Quarterly*, 83:506–523.

Pateman, Carole. 1970. *Participation and Democratic Theory.* New York: Cambridge University Press.

Patterson, Samuel C. and Gregory Caldeira. 1985. "Mailing in the Vote: Correlates and Consequences of Absentee Voting." *American Journal of Political Science*, 29:766–788.

Patterson, Thomas E. 2003. *The Vanishing Voter.* New York: Vintage Books.

Pepper, John V. 2000. "The Intergenerational Transmission of Welfare Receipt: A Nonparametric Bounds Analysis." *The Review of Economics and Statistics*, 82:472–88.

Piven, Francis Fox, and Richard A. Cloward. 1988. *Why Americans Don't Vote.* New York: Pantheon Books.

———. 1989. "Government Statistics and Conflicting Explanations of Nonvoting." *PS: Political Science and Politics*, 22:580–588.

———. 1990. "A Reply to Bennett." *PS: Political Science and Politics*, 23:172–173.

———. 1994. "On the Motor Voter." *PS Political Science and Politics*, 27:7–8.

———. 2000. *Why Americans Still Don't Vote: And Why Politicians Want it That Way.* Boston, MA: Beacon Press.

Plutzer, Eric. 2002. "Becoming a Habitual Voter: Inertia, Resources, and Growth in Young Adulthood." *American Political Science Review*, 96:41–56.

Powell, G. Bingham Jr. 1986. "American Voter Turnout in Comparative Perspective." *American Political Science Review*, 80:17–43.

Primo, David M., Matthew L. Jacobsmeier, and Jeffrey Milyo. 2007. "Estimating the Impact of State Policies and Institutions with Mixed-Level Data. *State Politics and Policy Quarterly*, 7:446–459.

Rhine, Staci L. 1995. "Registration Reform and Turnout Change in the American States." *American Politics Quarterly*, 23:409–426.

———. 1996. "An Analysis of the Impact of Registration Factors on Turnout in 1992." _Political Behavior_, 18:171–185.

Richardson, Lilliard E. and Grant W. Neely. 1996. "Implementation of Early Voting." _Spectrum_, 69:16–23.

Riker, William H. 1982. _Liberalism Against Populism_. San Francisco, CA: W.H. Freeman and Company.

Rosenstone, Steven J., and John Mark Hansen. 1993. _Mobilization, Participation, and Democracy in America_. New York: Macmillan.

Rosenstone, Steven J. and Raymond E. Wolfinger. 1978. "The Effect of Registration Laws on Voter Turnout." _American Political Science Review_, 72:22–45.

Ruhm, Christopher J. "The Economic Consequences of Parental Leave Mandates: Lessons from Europe." _The Quarterly Journal of Economics_, 113:285–317.

Saltman, Roy G. 2006. _The History and Politics of Voting Technology: In Quest of Integrity and Public Confidence_. New York: Palgrave Macmillan.

Schuessler, Alexander A. 2000. _A Logic of Expressive Choice_. Princeton, NJ: Princeton University Press.

Silverman, B. 1986. _Density Estimation for Statistics and Data Analysis_. London: Chapman & Hall.

Smith, Daniel A. 2008. "Direct Democracy and Election and Ethics Laws." In Cain, Bruce E., Todd Donovan, and Caroline J. Tolbert (eds), _Democracy in the States: Experiments in Election Reform_. Washington, DC: Brookings Institution Press.

Smith, Daniel A., and Dustin Fridkin. 2008. "Delegating Direct Democracy: Interparty Legislative Competition and the Adoption of the Initiative in the American States." _American Political Science Review_, 102:333–350.

Smith, Daniel A., and Caroline J. Tolbert. 2004. _Educated by Initiative: The Effects of Direct Democracy on Citizens and Political Organizations in the American States_. Ann Arbor: University of Michigan Press.

Smolka, Richard G. 1977. _Election Day Registration: the Minnesota and Wisconsin Experience in 1976_. Washington, DC: American Enterprise Institute for Public Policy Research.

Southwell, Priscilla L., and Justin I. Burchett. 2000a. "The Effect of All-Mail Elections on Voter Turnout." _American Politics Quarterly_, 28:72–79.

———. 2000b. "Does Changing the Rules Change the Players? The Effect of All-Mail Elections on the Composition of the Electorate." _Social Science Quarterly_, 81:837–845.

Squire, Peverill, Raymond E. Wolfinger, and David P. Glass. 1987. "Residential Mobility and Voter Turnout." _American Political Science Review_, 81:45–65.

Stein, Robert M. 1998. "Early Voting." _Public Opinion Quarterly_, 62:57–69.

Stein, Robert M. and Patricia A. Garcia-Monet. 1997. "Voting Early, but Not Often." _Social Science Quarterly_, 78:657–671.

Teixeira, Ruy A. 1992. _The Disappearing American Voter_. Washington, DC: Brookings Institution Press.

Timpone, Richard J. 1998. "Structure, Behavior and Voter Turnout in the United States." _American Political Science Review_, 92:145–158.

_____. 2002. "Estimating Aggregate Policy Reform Effects: New Baselines for Registration, Participation, and Representation." *Political Analysis*, 10:154–177.

Tolbert, Caroline J., and Daniel A. Smith. 2005. "The Educative Effects of Ballot Initiatives on Voter Turnout." *American Politics Research*, 33:283–309.

Tolbert, Caroline J., Todd Donovan, and Bruce E. Cain. 2008. "The Promise of Election Reform." In Cain, Bruce E., Todd Donovan, and Caroline J. Tolbert. (eds), *Democracy in the States: Experiments in Election Reform*. Washington, DC: Brookings Institution Press.

Tolbert, Caroline J., Todd Donovan, Bridget King, and Shaun Bowler. 2008. "Election Day Registration, Competition, and Voter Turnout." In Cain, Bruce E., Todd Donovan, and Caroline J. Tolbert (eds), *Democracy in the States: Experiments in Election Reform*. Washington, DC: Brookings Institution Press.

Tolbert, Caroline J., John A. Grummel, and Daniel A. Smith. 2001. "The Effects of Ballot Initiatives on Voter Turnout in the United States." *American Politics Research*, 29:625–648.

Traugott, Michael W. 2004. "Why Electoral Reform Has Failed: If You Build It, Will They Come?" In Crigler, Ann N., Marion R. Just, and Edward J. McCaffery (eds.), *Rethinking the Vote: The Politics and Prospects of American Electoral Reform*. New York: Oxford University Press.

U.S. Dept. of Commerce, Bureau of the Census. CURRENT POPULATION SURVEY: VOTER SUPPLEMENT FILE, 1972 [Computer file]. ICPSR edition. Ann Arbor, MI: Inter-university Consortium for Political and Social Research [producer and distributor], 1973.

U.S. Dept. of Commerce, Bureau of the Census. CURRENT POPULATION SURVEY: VOTER SUPPLEMENT FILE, 1980 [Computer file]. ICPSR version. Washington, DC: U.S. Dept. of Commerce, Bureau of the Census [producer], 1981. Ann Arbor, MI: Inter-university Consortium for Political and Social Research [distributor], 1999.

U.S. Dept. of Commerce, Bureau of the Census. CURRENT POPULATION SURVEY: VOTER SUPPLEMENT FILE, 1984 [Computer file]. ICPSR version. Washington, DC: U.S. Dept. of Commerce, Bureau of the Census [producer]. Ann Arbor, MI: Inter-university Consortium for Political and Social Research [distributor], 1985.

U.S. Dept. of Commerce, Bureau of the Census. CURRENT POPULATION SURVEY: VOTER SUPPLEMENT FILE, 1988 [Computer file]. ICPSR version. Washington, DC: U.S. Dept. of Commerce, Bureau of the Census [producer], 1989. Ann Arbor, MI: Inter-university Consortium for Political and Social Research [distributor], 1990.

U.S. Dept. of Commerce, Bureau of the Census. CURRENT POPULATION SURVEY: VOTER SUPPLEMENT FILE, 1992 [Computer file]. ICPSR version. Washington, DC: U.S. Dept. of Commerce, Bureau of the Census [producer], 1992. Ann Arbor, MI: Inter-university Consortium for Political and Social Research [distributor], 1997.

U.S. Dept. of Commerce, Bureau of the Census. CURRENT POPULATION SURVEY: VOTER SUPPLEMENT FILE, 1996 [Computer file]. ICPSR version. Washington, DC: U.S. Dept. of Commerce, Bureau of the Census [producer],

1997. Ann Arbor, MI: Inter-university Consortium for Political and Social Research [distributor], 1997.

U.S. Dept. of Commerce, Bureau of the Census. CURRENT POPULATION SUR-VEY: VOTER SUPPLEMENT FILE, 2000 [Computer file]. ICPSR version. Washington, DC: U.S. Dept. of Commerce, Bureau of the Census [producer], 2001. Ann Arbor, MI: Inter-university Consortium for Political and Social Research [distributor], 2001.

Verba, Sidney, Kay Lehman Scholzman and Henry E. Brady. 1995. *Voice and Equality: Civic Voluntarism in American Politics.* Cambridge, MA: Harvard University Press.

Verba, Sidney, Kay L. Schlozman, Henry Brady, and Norman H. Nie. 1993. "Citizen Activity: Who Participates? What Do They Say?" *American Political Science Review*, 87:303–318.

Wand, Jonathan N., Kenneth W. Shotts, Jasjeet S. Sekhon, Walter R. Mebane, Michael C. Herron, and Henry E. *Brady.* 2001. "The Butterfly Did It: The Aberrant Vote for Buchanan in Palm Beach County, Florida." *American Political Science Review*, 95:793–810.

Wattenberg, Martin P. 2002. *Where Have All the Voters Gone?* Cambridge, MA: Harvard University Press.

———. 2007. *Is Voting for Young People?* New York: Pearson Longman.

Wolfinger, Raymond E., and Jonathan Hoffman. 2000. "Barriers to Turnout After Motor Voter." Paper Presented at the Annual Meeting of the American Political Science Association, August 31–September 3, 2000, Washington, DC.

———. 2001. "Registering and Voting with Motor Voter." *PS: Political Science and Politics*, 34:85–92.

Wolfinger, Raymond E. and Steven J. Rosenstone. 1980. *Who Votes?* New Haven: Yale University Press.

Index

absentee voting, 13, 22, 27, 47, 116, 145, 186
Achen, Christopher H., 26, 28, 30, 42, 45, 147
Aldrich, John H., 25
Alvarez, R. Michael, 4, 13, 187
Ansolabehere, Stephen, 4, 187
Arizona
  in comparison to NV, 116–117
Associated Press, 60

ballot initiatives, 13, 33, 186
Banducci, Susan A., 12
Bartels, Larry M., 80
Bederson, Benjamin B., 13
Bendor, Jonathan, 186
Bennett, Stephen E., 20
Berelson, Bernard, 11
Berinsky, Adam J., 12, 145, 186
Besley, Timothy, 45, 80, 81, 87, 116
Blais, André, 25, 26, 189
Bounds approach, 46, 80, 81, 93, 94, 96, 98, 99, 100, 102, 103, 104, 146, 157
  worst case bounds, 95, 97, 98, 100
Bowler, Shaun, 10, 189
Brady, Henry E., 22, 31
Brennan Center for Justice, 2
Brennan, Geoffrey, 26
Brians, Craig L., 18, 27, 29, 90, 149, 150, 151, 154, 155, 156
Brockington, David, 10, 189
Brown, Robert D., 25, 27, 29, 109, 148
Buchanan, James, 26

Burchett, Justin I., 12
Burnham, Walter Dean, 5
Burns v. Forston, 13
Burns, Nancy, 12, 186
Bush, George H. W., 84, 92, 118

Cabana, Deborah, 163
Cain, Bruce E., 3
Caldeira, Gregory, 12, 27, 47
Caltech/MIT Voting Technology Project, 4, 13, 187
Calvert, Jerry W., 29, 148, 164
campaigns
  more competitive, 191
  shorter, 190
  volunteer driven, 191
Campbell, Angus, 4, 148
Campbell, David E., 190
Canada
  mobilization stragegies, 10
Caplan, Bryan, 11
capped outcomes assumption, 98, 99, 100, 103
Card, David, 45
Carter, Lewis F., 14
Case, Anne, 45, 80, 81, 87, 116
CBC Television, 10
Chasnow, Jo-Anne, 109, 110
civic education, 10, 191–195
Clinton, William J. "Bill", 14, 84, 92, 118
closing date, 13, 22, 28, 32, 33, 34, 56, 61, 63, 68, 69, 74, 79, 80, 82, 89, 90, 116, 117, 148, 149, 155, 159

Cloward, Richard A., 11, 15, 18, 20, 23, 24, 35, 42, 46, 84, 104, 109, 110, 114, 127, 134, 150, 162, 164, 165, 184, 185, 187, 189, 195
Colorado
  adoption of motor voter, 27, 109, 110
compulsory voting, 187, 188, 194
Conrad, Frederick G., 13
Converse, Philip E., 4, 148
costs of voting, 4, 7, 12, 31, 32, 33, 35, 44, 46, 99, 181, 182
Current Population Survey (CPS), 16, 17, 81, 82, 88, 89, 90, 92, 94, 108, 112, 114, 121, 125, 126, 127, 128, 130, 134, 147, 148, 149, 151, 156, 170, 184, 185

DeNardo, James, 34
Diermeier, Daniel, 186
difference in difference approach, 45, 80, 81, 82, 86, 88, 89, 90, 91, 92, 93, 102, 103, 104, 106, 107, 108, 112, 114, 116, 117, 119, 146, 152, 154, 159
Dixit, Avinash, 25
Dole, Robert J., 84
Donovan, Todd, 3, 10, 189
Downs, Anthony, 12, 25, 31, 99
driver's license, 4, 14, 21, 32, 34, 35, 48, 106, 108, 109, 110, 114, 118, 120, 121, 124, 132, 134, 136, 137, 139, 186
Duff, Brian, 129
Dunn v. Blumstein, 13

early voting, 2, 4, 12, 22, 27, 145, 150, 186
educational attainment, 18, 29, 30–42, 43, 139, 150, 151, 152, 159
election day a holiday, 9, 184, 187
election day registration
  definition of, 2
endogeneity, 27, 28, 43, 45, 46, 48, 80, 81, 87, 89, 90, 103, 106, 107, 112, 122, 152
Enokson, Stephen E., 148
equality, 8, 11–12, 24, 47, 145
Erikson, Robert S., 24, 127
exogenous selection, 6, 28, 36, 40, 41, 48, 52, 53, 54, 56, 79, 80, 99, 101, 102, 103, 147
experimental design, 5–6, 27

expressive voting, 26, 27, 48
extrapolation, 4, 26, 108, 125

Federal Election Commission, 83, 121, 184, 185
Fergus Falls Daily Journal, 60
Fitzgerald, Mary, 27
fixed effects, 46, 80, 108, 122, 146, 155, 159
Flynn, Julie, 163
Ford, Wendell H., 66
Fortier, John C., 12
Franklin, Daniel P., 27, 109
Franklin, Mark N., 3, 124
fraud, 23, 58, 59, 62, 64, 65, 70, 72, 77, 172, 173, 174, 175, 176, 178, 180
Fridkin, Dustin, 13
Friedrichs, Ryan, 33

Galanes-Rosenbaum, Eva, 12, 27, 47, 150
Gans, Curtis B., 20, 184
Garcia-Monet, Patricia A., 12, 27
Gardner, William, 6, 69, 163
Gerber, Alan S., 33, 34, 124, 125, 130, 173
Gilchrist, Jack, 29, 148, 164
Glass, David P., 24, 127
Gosnell, Harold, 4
government
  federal mandate, 9, 12, 17, 42, 43, 71, 77, 93, 99, 103, 104, 107, 117, 124, 188
  responsibility, 10, 13, 14, 18, 24, 35–36, 59, 70, 183, 186, 194
Green, Donald P., 33, 34, 124, 125, 130, 173
Gregg, Judd A., 66, 74
Grier, Eric E., 27, 109, 137
Griffin, John D., 11
Grofman, Bernard, 18, 27, 29, 90, 149, 150, 151, 154, 155, 156
Gronke, Paul, 12, 27, 47, 150
Gruber, Jonathan, 45
Grummel, John A., 13

Hague, Frank, 182
Hall, Thad E., 13
Hanmer, Michael J., 3, 12, 13, 25, 30, 46, 128, 129, 147, 152, 155, 157, 160, 170, 179, 186, 188
Hansen, John Mark, 9, 18, 22, 34, 118, 163, 164, 165, 166, 170, 173, 181

Hanushek, Eric A., 27, 30
Hardle, Wolfgang, 217
HAVA. *See* Help America Vote Act of 2002
Heckman, James J., 45
Help America Vote Act of 2002, 3, 12, 21, 63, 105, 175, 176, 178, 182
Herbert, Bob, 1
Hero, Rodney E., 3, 82
Herrnson, Paul S., 13
Herron, Michael C., 22
Highton, Benjamin, 17, 18, 25, 27, 29, 31, 36, 106, 109, 110, 148, 150, 151, 157
Hill, David, 27, 109, 148
Hill, Kim Quaile, 28, 29, 145
Hoffman, Jonathan, 128, 132
Huang, Chi, 18, 27, 29, 149, 150, 151, 155
Huckfeldt, Robert, 3
Human SERVE, 109, 110, 164

Idaho
    adoption of EDR, 16, 56, 74–77
    effect of EDR on turnout, 74, 85, 90–92, 93
    effect of EDR on turnout by demographics, 152–157
    exemption from NVRA, 15
    implementation of EDR, 174–180
    new registrants. *See* new registrants
identification problem, 31, 37, 38, 39, 40, 41–54, 101
Institute for Public Accuracy, 2
Iowa
    adoption of EDR, 4, 14
    in comparison to MN and WI, 82, 83–84, 87–90, 152–157

Jackson, John E., 27, 30
Jackson, Robert A., 29, 148
Jackson, Thomas H., 179
Jacobsmeier, Matthew L., 45
James, Deborah, 23, 104, 187
Jennings, Jerry T., 17
Junn, Jane, 191, 193, 194

Kalkan, K. Ozan, 156, 157
Karp, Jeffrey A., 12
Keane, Michael, 11
Kennedy, Kevin, 6, 163, 176, 179

Key, V.O., 3
Kids Voting USA, 192, 194
Kim, Jae-on, 148
Kimball, David C., 13
King, David C., 33
Klassen, Lori, 163
Knack, Stephen, 27, 29, 44, 109, 137, 148, 149
Knight, Brian G., 80
Konisky, David M., 4
Kozol, Jonathan, 195
Kropf, Martha, 13

L.A. Times, 2
League of Women Voters, 57, 71, 73, 74
Leighley, Jan E., 28, 147
Lentz, Jacob, 168
Lijphart, Arend, 11, 24, 145, 187, 188
literacy tests, 24, 42
logit, 29, 46, 79, 93, 128, 147, 149, 151
Lomasky, Loren, 26
Londregan, John, 25

mail registration, 15, 32, 121, 136
Maine
    adoption of EDR, 14, 16, 56, 60–63
    adoption of motor voter, 109
    difficulty finding control state, 82
    effect of EDR on turnout, 8
    effect of EDR on turnout using Bounds, introduced, 94
    implementation of EDR, 174–180
    new registrants. *See* new registrants
    non-exemption from NVRA, 15, 66
    turnout and EDR, 7
Manski, Charles F., 36, 37, 39, 40, 46, 51, 52, 80, 93, 96, 98, 101
March, James G., 43, 48
Marston v. Lewis, 13
Martinez, Michael D., 27, 29, 109, 148
Matsusaka, John G., 13
McCarthy, Michael, 6, 163, 176
McDonald, Michael P., 10, 11, 83, 190
McKean, Dayton David, 182
McNulty, Michele, 6, 163, 176
Mebane, Walter R., 22
media
    better practices, 191
    change in practices, 191
Meirick, Patrick C., 192

Michigan
adoption of motor voter, 14, 106, 108,
109, 110
decentralization of election
administration, 21
effect of motor voter on turnout,
111–112, 120, 124
effect of motor voter on turnout by
demographics, 157–160
effect of NVRA on turnout, 123
Secretary of State, 108
Miller, Peter A., 12, 27, 47, 150
Miller, Warren E., 4, 148
Milyo, Jeffrey, 45
Minneapolis Tribune, 59
Minnesota
adoption of EDR, 7, 14, 16, 56–60
adoption of motor voter, 6, 14, 106,
109, 110
EDR in society, 6, 53
effect of EDR on turnout, 7, 8, 83–84,
87–90, 93
effect of EDR on turnout by
demographics, 152–157
effect of EDR on turnout using Bounds,
introduced, 94
effect of motor voter on turnout,
113–116, 120
exemption from NVRA, 15
implementation of EDR, 174–180
new registrants. *See* new registrants
Secretary of State, 60
Mississippi
in comparison to MN, 53, 182
Mitchell, Glen E., 27, 29, 149, 151, 154,
157
mobilization, 2, 33–34, 47, 104, 107, 125,
162, 163, 164, 166, 167, 169, 170,
173, 174, 181, 182, 189, 191
Montana
adoption of EDR, 4, 14
adoption of motor voter, 92, 109
in comparison to ID and WY, 82, 84–85,
90, 152–157
effect of motor voter on turnout, 92
motivation, 9, 34, 35, 44, 48, 93, 150,
181, 183, 186, 189
motor voter
definition of, 4

Nagin, Daniel S., 96, 101

Nagler, Jonathan, 4, 29, 147, 148, 149,
151, 157
National Commission on Federal Election
Reform, 187
National Election Study, 37, 162
National Voter Registration Act of 1993,
4, 6, 13, 14, 15, 17, 21, 22, 23, 36,
46, 65, 67, 68, 69, 70, 71, 72, 73, 74,
75, 76, 77, 78, 82, 92, 93, 99, 102,
103, 106, 107, 108, 109, 110, 111,
112, 117, 121, 122, 123, 125, 126,
127, 128, 130, 131, 132, 134, 136,
137, 139, 140, 141, 146, 148, 158,
159, 160, 162, 164, 165, 172, 173,
174, 180, 184, 185, 186, 195
effect on turnout, 122–124
effect on turnout by demographics,
157–160
lawsuits, 15
new registrants. *See* new registrants
registration rates, 122
Neely, Grant W., 12
Nevada
adoption of motor voter, 14, 106, 109,
110
effect of motor voter on turnout,
116–117, 120
effect of NVRA on turnout, 123
New Hampshire
adoption of EDR, 7, 16, 56, 69–74, 77
as possible control for ME, 82
effect of EDR on turnout, 85, 92–93
effect of EDR on turnout by
demographics, 152–157
exemption from NVRA, 15
implementation of EDR, 174–180
motor voter views, 6–7
new registrants. *See* new registrants
New Hampshire Secretary of State. *See*
Gardner, William
new registrants
by method and demographics, 138–141
by registration method, 130–137
Newman, Brian, 11
Nickerson, David W., 33
Nie, Norman H., 22
Niemi, Richard G., 13, 170, 179, 191, 193,
194
Nighswonger, Peggy, 163, 180
nonapplicability clause, 65, 66, 68, 69, 74
nonparametric, 46, 80, 93

North Carolina
  adoption of motor voter, 14, 106, 109, 110
  dormant motor voter, 110, 118
  early voting, 2
  effect of motor voter on turnout, 118–120, 124, 125
  effect of motor voter on turnout by demographics, 157–160
  effect of NVRA on turnout, 124
North Dakota
  effect of EDR on turnout using Bounds, introduced, 94
  exemption from NVRA, 15
  registration system, lackthereof, 2, 12, 13, 30, 47, 66, 82, 129, 148
NVRA. *See* National Voter Registration Act

Obama, Barack, 1
Ohio
  adoption of motor voter, 14
  in comparison to MI, 112, 157–160
Oliver, Eric J., 12, 186
Olsen, Johan P., 43
Olsen, Jonah P., 48
ordered outcomes assumption, 98, 99, 100
Oregon
  adoption of motor voter, 109
  EDR, 14
  effect of EDR on turnout using Bounds, introduced, 94
  rolloff, 186
  vote by mail, 12, 186
Ornstein, Norman, 187

paradox of voting, 25
Park, Won-ho, 129
Parry, Janine A., 109
Pateman, Carole, 188
Patterson, Samuel C., 12, 47
Patterson, Thomas E., 4, 11, 27, 189, 190, 191
Pepper, John V., 46, 98, 101
Perot, Ross, 84, 85, 92, 118
Petrocik, John R., 148
Piven, Francis Fox, 11, 15, 18, 20, 23, 24, 35, 42, 46, 84, 104, 109, 110, 114, 127, 134, 150, 162, 164, 165, 184, 185, 187, 189, 195

Plutzer, Eric, 34, 124, 125
political parties, 9, 10, 18, 26, 34, 47, 104, 107, 194
  response to EDR, 164–174
poll taxes, 42
Popkin, Samuel L., 11, 83
Powell, G. Bingham Jr., 12
presidential nomination process, 190
Primo, David M., 45
probit, 29, 46, 79, 86, 88, 93, 99, 102, 147, 148, 149, 151, 152, 157, 160
proportional representation, 10, 189, 194
public agency registration, 15, 32, 121, 128, 136

Radio Free Europe, 10
random assignment, 6, 27, 28, 31, 40, 41, 45, 48, 79
rational choice, 25, 26
Rhine, Staci L., 27, 109
Richardson, Lilliard E., 12
Riker, William H., 10
Rodacker, Lisa Kramer, 6, 163
Roll Call, 187
Rosenstone, Steven J., 4, 9, 18, 22, 27, 29, 30, 34, 80, 87, 89, 118, 148, 149, 150, 151, 152, 154, 155, 157, 163, 164, 165, 166, 170, 173, 181
Ruhm, Christopher J., 45
Russia
  mobilization strategies, 10

Saltman, Roy G., 13
Samples, John, 10
Schlozman, Kay Lehman, 22, 31
Schuessler, Alexander A., 26
scobit, 29, 147, 149
Sekhon, Jasjeet S., 22
selection of election laws, 6, 7, 27, 44, 45, 46, 47, 181
Shachar, Ron, 34, 124, 125, 130
Shields, Todd G., 18, 27, 29, 109, 149, 150, 151, 155
Shotts, Kenneth W., 22
Silverman, B., 217
Simpson, Alan K., 66
Smith, Daniel A., 13, 33
Smolka, Richard G., 145
social and political context, 3, 40, 41, 44, 48, 53, 126, 157, 181
socialization, 9

South
  Jim Crow, 7, 9, 22, 185
South Carolina
  in comparison to Minnesota, 6
  in comparison to NC, 118, 119
South Dakota
  in comparison to MN and WI, 82,
    83–84, 87–90, 152–157
Southwell, Priscilla L., 12
Sprague, John, 3
Squire, Peverill, 24, 127
St. Paul Pioneer Press, 59
Stein, Robert M., 12, 27, 47, 186
Stokes, Donald E., 4, 148
Switzerland
  low turnout, 11

Teixeira, Ruy A., 11, 27, 29, 31, 36, 46,
    106, 149, 151, 154, 189, 190, 191,
    192
Tennessee
  in comparison to NC, 118–120,
    157–160
Texas
  adoption of motor voter, 109
Timpone, Richard J., 27, 45
Ting, Michael, 186
Toffey, Daniel, 47, 150
Tolbert, Caroline J., 3, 13, 33, 118
Traugott, Michael W., 12, 13, 27, 186

universal registration, 2
Utah
  registration purge prior to NVRA, 82

Ventura, Jesse, 168
Verba, Sidney, 22, 31, 33, 43
Vermont
  adoption of motor voter, 15, 108
  in comparison to NH, 82, 85, 92–93,
    152–157
  new registrants. *See* new registrants
  as possible control for ME, 82
Virginia
  in comparison to NC, 118, 119
vote by mail, 12, 13, 145, 186, 188
voter identification requirements, 19
Voting Rights Act, 9, 13, 24, 42, 87, 119
voting technology, 2, 13, 21

Wackman, Daniel B., 192

Wand, Jonathan N., 22
Washington
  adoption of motor voter, 109
Wattenberg, Martin P., 11, 28, 151, 184,
    185, 187, 188, 190, 195
Wedeking, Justin, 25, 27, 109
weekend voting, 187
Wesbury v. Sanders, 23
White, Ismail K., 129
White, James, 29, 148, 149
Williams v. Rhodes, 23
Wilson, Catherine, 4
Wisconsin
  adoption of EDR, 7, 14, 16, 56, 63
  in comparison to MN, 113
  EDR in society, 6
  effect of EDR on turnout, 7, 8, 83–84,
    87–90, 93
  effect of EDR on turnout by
    demographics, 152–157
  effect of EDR on turnout using Bounds,
    introduced, 94
  exemption from NVRA, 15
  Governor, 63–65
  implementation of EDR, 174–180
  new registrants. *See* new registrants
  registration in small municipalities, 12
Wisconsin State Elections Board. *See*
    Kennedy, Kevin
Wlezein, Christopher, 27, 29, 157
Wlezien, Christopher, 149, 154
Wolfinger, Raymond E., 4, 18, 24, 27, 29,
    30, 31, 36, 80, 87, 89, 106, 109, 110,
    127, 128, 132, 134, 136, 148, 149,
    150, 151, 152, 154, 155, 157
Wright, Gerald C., 29, 148
Wyoming
  adoption of EDR, 14, 16, 56, 65–68, 77
  effect of EDR on turnout, 84–85, 90–92,
    93
  effect of EDR on turnout by
    demographics, 152–157
  exemption from NVRA, 15
  implementation of EDR, 174–180
  new registrants. *See* new registrants
  primary elections, 14
  Secretary of State, 68
Wyoming Eagle, 68

Yick Wo v. Hopkins, 23
Ysursa, Penny, 163, 177, 179, 180

CPSIA information can be obtained at www.ICGtesting.com
Printed in the USA
BVOW021639021012

301935BV00001B/67/P